Nacim Pak-Shiraz is the Head of Islamic and Middle Eastern Studies and Senior Lecturer in Film and Persian Studies at the University of Edinburgh. She holds a PhD from the University of London's School of Oriental and African Studies (SOAS) and has published widely on Iranian cinema, examining subjects ranging from genre and comedy to religious epics and constructions of masculinities. In 2017, she edited *Visualizing Iran: From Antiquity to Present*, a special issue of the *Iranian Studies* journal.

Nacim directed and produced *The Dream of Flight*, a documentary film about Iranian asylum seekers in Turkey. She has also curated film festivals for the Edinburgh Iranian Festival as well as organised and led workshops and panels at various international film festivals including the Edinburgh International Film Festival and the Fajr International Film Festival (Tehran).

She serves on several editorial and advisory boards, including Brill's *Studies on Performing Arts and Literature of the Islamicate World*, and *Iranian Studies*. She is a member of the Academic Council of the Iran Heritage Foundation, London.

'The topic of this book is interesting and unusual, the approach well justified and argued, and many of the film analyses eye-opening, original, and convincing.'
— Richard Tapper, Emeritus Professor, School of Oriental and African Studies (SOAS), University of London

'What is so impressive is that Shiraz has written a piece of film academia that is a story: that moves with the drive and pace of a great novel and will continue to raise heated debate in film schools and university bars for years to come. There is no higher form of praise than that.'
— Andrew Campbell, *Subtitled Online*

'This book is written in a sophisticated style, revealing a great depth of knowledge as well as innovative research. The result of extensive fieldwork and imaginative intellectual juxtapositions, Dr Pak-Shiraz successfully highlights the broad scope of religion as manifested in contemporary Iran."
— Lloyd Ridgeon, Lecturer in Islamic Studies, Department of Theology and Religious Studies, University of Glasgow

'... an informed and accurate exploration of both a complex and sensitive topic.'
— Nathalie Matti, *Journal of Shi'a Islamic Studies*

SHI'I ISLAM IN IRANIAN CINEMA

Religion and Spirituality in Film

Nacim Pak-Shiraz

Paperback edition published in 2018 by
I.B.Tauris & Co. Ltd
London • New York
www.ibtauris.com

Hardback edition first published in 2011 by
I.B.Tauris & Co. Ltd

Copyright © 2011 Nacim Pak-Shiraz

The right of Nacim Pak-Shiraz to be identified as the author of this work has been asserted by the author in accordance with the Copyright, Designs and Patents Act 1988.

All rights reserved. Except for brief quotations in a review, this book, or any part thereof, may not be reproduced, stored in or introduced into a retrieval system, or transmitted, in any form or by any means, electronic, mechanical, photocopying, recording or otherwise, without the prior written permission of the publisher.

Every attempt has been made to gain permission for the use of the images in this book. Any omissions will be rectified in future editions.

References to websites were correct at the time of writing.

ISBN: 978 1 78453 945 0
eISBN: 978 1 78672 964 4
ePDF: 978 0 85772 050 4

A full CIP record for this book is available from the British Library
A full CIP record is available from the Library of Congress

Library of Congress Catalog Card Number: available

To Fayaz
For the burnt notes and those long nights in November...

CONTENTS

List of Illustrations	ix
Note on Transliteration	xiii
Acknowledgements	xv
Introduction	1
Approaches to the Study of Religion and Spirituality in Western Cinema	4
Shi'i Islam in Iranian Cinema	10
1 Shi'ism in Iran: An Historical Overview	15
The Appeal of Shi'ism in Iran and the Foundations of Twelver Shi'ism	17
The Twelver Shi'i State of Iran and the Shi'i Ulama	23
Conclusions	32
2 Contemporary Iranian Discourses on Religion and Spirituality in Cinema	35
Cinema's Introduction into a Muslim Society	40
Cinema's Place within Islamic Jurisprudence	43
The Paradox of Cinema as a 'Technological Art'	46
Cinema as a Domain for Religious and Spiritual Discourse	53
Conclusions	64
3 Filmic Discourses on the Role of the Clergy in Iran	67
Resistance to Monopolising Islam	71
Parables on the World of the Clergy	75

	Morals and Values	85
	Conclusions	91
4	**Sight, Sound and Sufism: Mystical Islam in Majidi's Films**	93
	The Mystical Approach	96
	Pain and Suffering	101
	Self-Sacrifice and the Alchemy of Love	110
	Conclusions	119
5	**Cinema as a Reservoir for Cultural Memory**	123
	The Figure of Husayn and Iranian Shi'i Identity	129
	Ta'ziyeh: the only Islamic Drama	136
	Beyzaie: a Film-maker Rooted in 'Historical Genealogy'	144
	Ta'ziyeh and its Spectators	159
	Conclusions	163
6	**Thinking Films: Kiarostami, A Poetic Philosopher**	167
	Philosophy in Film	170
	Kiarostami, a 'Poetic Philosopher'	172
	Reading Life and Death in Kiarostami's Films	180
	Conclusions	191

Conclusion   193

Notes   199

Select Bibliography   215

Filmography   227

Index   231

LIST OF ILLUSTRATIONS

1 A caricature in the first issue of *Jashnvareh*, the official newsletter of the Fajr International Film Festival listing the six different cinematic symbols that would make a film 'spiritual'. *Jashnvareh*, 31 January 2005, p. 9   38
2 Parviz Parastooyi, the lead actor, in *Leyli is with Me* (Kamal Tabrizi, 1995)   69
3 *The Lizard* (*Marmulak*, Kamal Tabrizi, 2004). Obliged to lead the communal prayers en route to the village, Reza Marmulak fidgets   80
4 *The Lizard* (*Marmulak*, Kamal Tabrizi, 2004). As Reza Marmulak undresses in the public bath, he hurriedly tries to cover up his lizard tattoo from the sight of his ardent followers   81
5 *The Lizard* (*Marmulak*, Kamal Tabrizi, 2004). Reza Marmulak forgets to remove his turban as he changes from his clerical robes in the public toilets   82
6 *Colour of Paradise* (Majid Majidi, 1999). Mohammad Reza running through the village fields with his sisters   103
7 *Baran* (Majid Majidi, 2001). The moment when the wind blows the curtain, revealing Baran's reflection and, therefore, true identity, to Latif   113
8 *Baran* (Majid Majidi, 2001). Baran opening the door to Latif when he goes to deliver to her father, Najaf, the money he has raised from selling his ID card   117
9 *Baran* (Majid Majidi, 2001). A footprint, the only remaining trace of Baran, steadily filling with rain   119

10 A *ta'ziyeh* troupe in the roles of (left to right) Malek-e Ashtar's father, the teacher of Hasan and Husayn, Fatemeh, an extra, Malek-e Ashtar, Hasan, Husayn, and the Prophet Muhammad. The re-enactment of *ta'ziyeh* includes stories other than the martyrdom of Husayn. Here, the story of Malek-e Ashtar's conversion to Islam is performed. Photo: Pejman Pak. Tehran, August 2010   134
11 A *pardeh-khani* in Tehran, August 2010. Photo: Pejman Pak   135
12 The famous Ostad Torabi performing *naqqali* (storytelling) of the *Shahnameh*. Photo: Pejman Pak. Tehran, August 2010   137
13 Musicians playing for *ta'ziyeh* as well as *naqqali*. Among other things, the music cues the passage of time, sets the battle scenes and is an important component of the drama. Photo: Pejman Pak. Tehran, August 2010   138
14 A *mokhalef-khan* in the role of Qanbar's uncle, an idolator, who promises his daughter's hand in marriage to Qanbar on the condition that the latter kills 'Ali. Photo: Pejman Pak. Tehran, August 2010   139
15 A *mokhalef-khan* in the role of Malek-e Ashtar before his conversion to Islam. *Mazlum-khan*s and *mokhalef-khan*s are not allowed to move across their respective groups and usually remain confined to these roles for life. For example, the actor playing the imam(s) will continue to play a *mazlum-khan*. Similarly, the above actor could only act as a *mokhalef-khan*, even if his character converted into a friend of the Prophet or the imam(s) by the end of the play. As such, on the first day of the three-day performance, he was a *mokhalef-khan* acting the role of Qanbar, who converts by the end of the performance and only briefly plays the role of a *mazlum-khan*. The next day, the role of Qanbar is played not by him but by another actor who is a *mazlum-khan*. The above actor then continued in the role of another *mokhalef-khan*, this time as Malek-e Ashtar, before his conversion to Islam. Photo: Pejman Pak. Tehran, August 2010   140
16 *Mazlum-khan* Qanbar. Photo: Pejman Pak. Tehran, August 2010   141

LIST OF ILLUSTRATIONS   xi

17   A *mazlum-khan* in the role of Fatemeh, the daughter
     of the Prophet, singing his lines. Traditionally, the role
     of women is played by men as women are not permitted
     to perform in *ta'ziyeh*. Photo: Pejman Pak. Tehran,
     August 2010   142
18   *The Day of Incident* (*Ruz-e vaqe'eh*, Shahram Asadi, 1994).
     Rahila and 'Abd Allah   149
19   'Abd Allah wanders in the desert in *The Day of Incident*
     (*Ruz-e vaqe'eh*, Shahram Asadi, 1994)   151
20   A battle scene in a *ta'ziyeh* between Qanbar (left) before
     his conversion to Islam and Imam 'Ali (in green).
     *Mazlum-khan*s usually incorporate the colour green in
     their costumes. Photo: Pejman Pak. Tehran, August 2010   154
21   *Ta'ziyeh* performance. Having kidnapped Hasan and
     Husayn, Malek-e Ashtar prepares to kill them Photo:
     Pejman Pak. Tehran, August 2010   154
22   *Where is the Friend's House?* (*Khane-ye dust kojast?*, Abbas
     Kiarostami, 1987)   179

NOTE ON TRANSLITERATION

The system of transliteration used in this book generally follows that of the *International Journal of Middle East Studies* (*IJMES*), with minor modifications. For Persian vowels, the short 'o' is used in preference to 'u', and 'e' is used in preference to 'i'. The silent 'h' at the end of Persian words is rendered '-eh' as in *'ta'ziyeh'*. Diacritical marks have been dispensed with. Arabic and Persian terms appearing in a standard English dictionary (e.g. jihad, hadith, etc.) have not been transliterated or italicised. The transliteration of proper names of contemporary individuals follows either the most common spelling as it appears in English-language publications and official sources, or as used by the individuals themselves.

ACKNOWLEDGEMENTS

The research for this book was made possible through the generosity and unstinting support of The Institute of Ismaili Studies, for which I am deeply grateful. I am indebted to Professor Azim Nanji, former Director of the IIS and his successor, Dr Farhad Daftary, who never failed to inspire me by their quiet passion and example.

I received invaluable feedback from Professor Richard Tapper, who not only reviewed earlier drafts of this work, but who continued to read and comment on it even after his retirement from the School of Oriental and African Studies, University of London, absolved him of doing so. I would like to express my sincere thanks both to him and to Dr Ziba Mir-Hosseini for their support and friendship. I would also like to thank Professor Annabelle Sreberny who next supervised my studies and also read my work. Dr Reza Shah Kazemi read Chapter 4 of this book and provided helpful observations on *Baran*. Maria Marsh at I.B.Tauris has been wonderful – I could not have asked for a more supportive editor. The Farabi Cinema Foundation generously provided me access to the Fajr International Film Festival for three years between 2004–2006 when I undertook my research in Iran. I am grateful to all those at the Foundation who facilitated this access for me.

To my parents, Tahereh Radi and Gholam Hassan Pak: I know the many silent sacrifices you made so that I could pursue my dreams. Thank you for always being there for me. I would also like to acknowledge my brothers Ebrahim and Pejman Pak for their love and support. Pejman also took some stunning images for me, a number of which are published in this book.

My elder daughter, Pegah, has literally grown up with this and other projects. Her tender love and encouraging gestures in the form of drawings, charts, tailored achievement certificates and coffee treats for every chapter that I completed helped me soldier on. Her patience beyond years eased the pain of deferring all the little and great things we wanted to do together. My younger daughter, Anahita, who very quickly learnt to share my attention with the laptop, has been an incredible source of hope and inspiration. Finally, I would like to express my deepest gratitude to my companion and best friend, my husband, Fayaz Shiraz Alibhai, to whom this book is dedicated. Without him, this work would have never been possible.

INTRODUCTION

The Hollywood production of *Not Without My Daughter* (Gilbert, 1991) became a box office success in the West, grossing around $15 million just in US ticket sales. Sally Field played the American wife trapped in Iran, whose cruel and fanatic Iranian husband, Mahmoudy, would not allow her to leave the country with their daughter. It was the sensationalist storyline and Field's presence more than anything else that made it a hit amongst Western audiences. Not surprisingly, the film was never screened in Iran. The Iranian media, nonetheless, criticised it for demonising Iranian people and culture, referring to it as yet another Western weapon aimed at weakening the Islamic Republic. Mahmoudy, the real-life 'cruel husband', appeared on Iranian television to refute the claims alleged in both the film and the book. The Mahmoudy represented on Iranian screens differed significantly from his Hollywood version, snippets of which were shown on Iranian television. On the Iranian screens, the victim was Mahmoudy and not his wife.

The national attention the film received within Iran, however, was short-lived. In the larger socio-political context of 1990s Iran, *Not Without My Daughter* was insignificant. The country had just emerged from a long and bloody war with Iraq (1980–1988). Indeed, the Islamic Republic's social and political concerns ranged from the reconstruction of a war-ravaged country and people, to the repair of severed foreign relations, all of which far outstripped the concerns caused by the country's negative representation in a Hollywood film. Within the arena of Iranian cinema itself, far more exciting events were in the making. Mohammad Khatami resigned as the Minister of Culture and Islamic Guidance in 1991 for siding with Makhmalbaf's *A Time to Love* (*Nowbat-e 'asheqi*), a controversial film that year which upset the sensitivities of conservatives of the Islamic Republic for depicting amongst other things the story of an illicit love affair. By the end of the decade, many Iranian films were devoted to the plight of women suffering from the inequalities of living in a patriarchal society. Made from within the local context, and in many cases by women, these films had far greater relevance to the daily struggles of Iranian women than those depicted by Hollywood.

As I came to learn later, however, the image of *Not Without My Daughter* proved more enduring amongst many Westerners in the way that it shaped their view of Iran. In 2000, as part of my graduate programme in Islamic Studies in London, I travelled to Sanaa, Yemen, to attend an Arabic immersion programme. The majority of the students at the programme were Americans, many of whom repeatedly asked if it had been easy for me to leave Iran and if the situation of Iranian women was improving. Given the history of fraught relations between the two countries, I admired their interest in Iran and their concern for the social position of its women. But these conversations would inevitably lead to invocations of *Not without My Daughter* as though it were the only valid source available to understand the socio-political context of Iran and Iranian women.

I learned much from this encounter between cultures and it defined the direction I would later take in my studies. I was fascinated at the power of Western media and the way it continuously shapes the image of the 'Other'. Over time, however, I developed a greater interest in exploring the lesser-studied area of how these 'Others' construct images of themselves. Thus, instead of looking at Hollywood representations of Iran and Iranians or, in my case, Hollywood constructions of Iranian religiosity, I decided to study Iranian cinema. I was particularly interested in how this cinema, which emerges out of the only theocracy in the world, engages with religion and spirituality. To this end, I have focused on the post-Iran–Iraq war period. Although the 1979 Islamic Revolution and the eight-year war that followed shortly afterward strained much of the country's resources, Iran's post-war period has been referred to as the beginning of a period of recovery and qualitative growth as well as a time during which morality codes were relaxed.[1]

Academics, theologians, religious authorities and believers have defined religion and spirituality variously. A detailed study of what constitutes religion and spirituality is, however, outside the scope of this book. Religion is often approached either as a text with an emphasis on scripture and sacred texts, or as ritual with an emphasis on the legal norms. Indeed, many of the studies on Islam have approached it from one of these angles. However, focusing solely on sacred texts and rituals can limit our understanding of the experiences and engagements of believers with religion. Some scholars have, therefore, argued for a cultural approach to the study of religion, emphasising the importance of cultural construction in religious articulations and expressions. In my study of film's engagement with religion, the socio-historical as well as cultural context of Iran plays an important role in understanding Iranian Shi'i expressions of Islam. This book, therefore, lays great emphasis on the development of Shi'ism in Iran and in locating its religious expressions within that larger context.

Iranian Cinema is the one of the few cinemas to have emerged from a Muslim country and gained significant international acclaim. While this makes it an interesting and rich exploration for the engagement of film with religion and spirituality, it remains largely uncharted territory. Although there has been some research on film and religion in Iran from the post-war period[2] this has primarily taken the form of individual articles and chapters rather than full-length treatments of the subject. Furthermore, other than a few brief studies, religion and spirituality in Iranian films have been examined solely within the genres of propagandist films and Sacred Defence Cinema (*Sinama-ye defa'-e moqaddas*), a term coined by the Islamic Republic to refer to films that deal with the theme of the Iran–Iraq war.[3] As such, this book aims to contribute to filling in this gap by examining religion and spirituality, particularly its Shi'i expressions, in Iranian cinema outside of these two genres.

My research revolves around the following three themes:

1) Analysing diverse articulations of what constitutes 'religion' in film both in Western scholarship and inside Iran;
2) Exploring different modalities of Shi'i interpretations within Iran; and
3) Examining some of the ways in which Iranian films participate in and engage with Shi'i expressions of Islam.

Cinema in Iran is an industry monitored closely by the Ministry of Culture and Islamic Guidance to ensure its compliance with the Islamic Republic's aspirations. Amongst others, the following regulations ban all films and videos that:

1) Weaken the principle of monotheism and other Islamic principles, or insult them in any manner;

2) Insult, directly or indirectly, the Prophets, Imams, the guardianship of the Supreme Jurisprudent (*velayat faqih*), the ruling Council or the jurisprudents (*mojtaheds*); and
3) Blaspheme against the values and personalities held sacred by Islam and other religions mentioned in the Constitution.[4]

Considering the complex sensitivities outlined above, any approach to the depiction of religion that deviates from the official stance could result, at the very least, in the banning of the film or, indeed, even the arrest and imprisonment of the film-maker. Not surprisingly, most films that do directly refer to religion are those that exalt the Islamic regime and are, therefore, referred to as propagandist films. However, religious discourses in Iranian films are not limited to this category. Instead, many film-makers have creatively sought ways to engage in a different approach to religion, which may not necessarily be in line with officially endorsed Shi'i interpretations of Islam. What constitutes a serious engagement of film with religion, however, remains contentious. Before turning our attention to the Iranian example, let us first examine the various Western discourses on religion and film.

Approaches to the Study of Religion and Spirituality in Western Cinema

Long before its release, Mel Gibson's *The Passion of the Christ* (2004) had already caused a great stir in the media. The controversies included debates about the legitimacy of the long and gory scenes of torture, its anti-Semitism, and breaking Hollywood norms in rendering the entire dialogue in foreign languages (Latin and Aramaic), thus forcing audiences to read subtitles. These debates were not limited to the film alone and dragged Gibson himself into the picture, with his Catholic background becoming the subject of detailed discussions in the media. Indeed, the general furore culminated in television documentaries that examined his life and work against the backdrop of his religious beliefs and ideas.

The anticipation rapidly building up around the film became its greatest marketing tool, and contrary to initial predictions of a box-office failure, it succeeded in earning a record $125.2 million in its first five days in theatres across the United States. Many churches bought huge blocks of tickets, reserving theatres in advance, and news reports broadcast people emerging from the theatres in tears and comparing their film viewing to a religious experience.

The Passion of the Christ is a good example of the complexities surrounding the study of religion in film and the various criteria determining a film as addressing religion, or containing the religious. Would this film qualify as an appropriate example of religion in film for its depiction of a religious figure or is it, rather, a religious film because it parallels a certain theology, in this case Roman Catholic? Could it be studied as an attempt to shape a religious identity of one Self through demonising an Other (in this case the Jews and the Romans)? Alternatively, does it fit into the study of religion and film not so much because of its content, but because of its effect on audiences who considered it a religious experience? Equally, could it be studied as religious propaganda that attempts to impose one sect's reading onto others? Some Evangelicals condemned the film as idolatrous, and accused the Catholic Church of using this film 'as an excellent way to convey the Catholic Christ'.[5] Furthermore, is the religious background of the director as important as the film itself in determining the possibility of exploring religious themes in film? As mentioned above, many analysed and reviewed *The Passion* by situating it within the context of Gibson's own beliefs, ideas and biography. These are just some of the various approaches by which religion may be studied in this particular film, but without entering into a discussion on another problematic area – that of defining religion itself.

Within Western academia, various scholars have adopted different frameworks within which to situate their arguments on the study of religion and film. Some have approached this study through films with explicit religious references such as depictions of Jesus and Christ-figures (Baugh, 1997 and Tatum, 1997). Others have emphasised the autonomy of film as an art form, which they argue is inherently open to a religious interpretation (May, 1982 and Deacy, 2001). Lyden (2003), on the other hand, suggests that the reception of film, independent of its content, turns it into a religious experience, and thus proposes audience studies to examine religion in film. Yet others such as Martin (1995), Estess (1995) and Ostwalt (1995) study the medium's engagement with religion by drawing parallels between film and the principles and creeds of a particular theology. Similarly, Gordon (1995) and Nathanson (2003) argue that parallels can be drawn between the functions of film and mythology. Still another approach (Miles, 1996 and Martin, 1995) has been to examine how films perpetuate social and political hegemonies. Bird (1982) studies film as hierophany, suggesting that film styles enable the explorations of the sacred. Finally, there are those who are interested in studying philosophy through film (Falzon, 2002 and Litch, 2002) and film itself as philosophy that thinks (Goodenough, 2005). Here I will refer only briefly to some of these approaches.

The study of Jesus and Christ-figures in films comprises the most explored topic within the literature on religion and film. This is perhaps the result of the surfeit of films produced with these themes. In 1897, just two years after the invention of the cinematograph, two cinematic presentations of the passion play were produced: *The Passion of Christ*, also known as *Léar Passion*, was produced by Société Léar and filmed in Paris, and the American production filmed in Bohemia entitled *The Hortiz Passion Play* (Freeman, 1897). Following the success of the American production, *The Original Oberammergau Passion Play* (Vincent, 1898) was produced in New York a year later. This film is 'considered important in film-history and in the history of the religious film because it was one the first examples of a recreated or refictionalized version of a historical event in film'.[6] Even the cinematic Christ-figure can be traced back to as early as 1916 in D.W. Griffith's *Intolerance* with cinematic metaphors of innocent victims of human cruelty. The story of Jesus and the Christ-figure continued to be produced over the years. In fact, it could be argued that these cinematic themes were born alongside cinema itself.

The theological approach is one of the main approaches in the study of religion in film and analyses films by drawing parallels with the arguments of a certain theology. This approach, which derives its tools of analysis from religious studies, typically explores traditional Judaeo-Christian theological concepts in film, such as good and evil, the nature of God, redemption, salvation and grace. In discussing the theological approach, Martin and Ostwalt state that the 'basic assumption behind theological criticism is that certain films are properly understood, or can be best understood, as an elaboration on or questioning of a particular religious tradition, text or theme'.[7] They further argue that theological criticism depends entirely on the notion that either the 'critic, director, screenplay writer, or some other creative force behind the film develops a certain theological agenda or concept, and the distinctive goal of the theological critic is to uncover that concept'.[8]

It is not necessarily films with outwardly religious themes, such as the stories of the Old and New Testaments, that attract theological criticism.

For example, Grimes employs this method to analyse Hitchcock's *Psycho* (1960). He examines the depiction of bodies, sin, debt and death in *Psycho* within the Christian tradition and, in comparing the long scenes of waiting in the film to the Christian Advent, concludes that Hitchcock has made an Advent film.[9]

The mythological approach analyses how some films function in the same way as myth. Myth is the means through which religion communicates with its participants. It consists of 'stories that provide human communities with grounding prototypes, models for life, reports of foundational realities, and dramatic presentations of fundamental values'.[10] The mythical approach, thus, broadens the scope of exploring religion to include not only those traditions that fall outside the monotheistic institutions, but also those aspects of monotheistic cultures that are, strictly speaking, not part of their theology. Gordon analyses the first *Star Wars* (Lucas, 1977), employing Joseph Campbell's (1949) definition of the 'monomyth' and its three main stages of departure, initiation and return, to reveal the film's mythical structure. He attributes the film's success to Lucas's construction of 'a coherent myth out of his pastiche of pop culture'.[11] By situating the film within the context of contemporary American society, which he refers to as a 'world that seems drained of spiritual values', he concludes that Lucas has created 'out of the usable past, out of bits of American pop culture, a new mythology that can satisfy the emotional needs of both children and adults'.[12]

One of the main features of mythological films is to take audiences to 'places beyond the boundaries of the unknown and require the viewer to negotiate an encounter with "a world elsewhere," with a world that is "wholly other" and, therefore, sacred or religiously significant'.[13] Science-fiction films, such as the various episodes of *Star Wars* or *Alien* (Scott, 1979), are one of the most discussed genres in this approach, precisely because of their fantastical imagery and plot, which are comparable to those of myths.

The mythical function is not explored solely in films with overtly fantastical stories. Nathanson, for example, suggests that Woody Allen's *Shadows and Fog* (1992) is 'a specifically and characteristically (but not exclusively) Jewish way of thinking' based on religious tradition rather than on ethnic psychology or sociology.[14] He maintains that the film functions as a myth, albeit a 'secular myth', for it 'does for an ostensibly modern and secular society what religious myths do for traditional and religious societies. In this case, it brings viewers face to face with a mystery that lies at the core of human existence at all times and in all places: death'.[15]

Some critics do not explore the religious in the content of the film itself, but consider its form and reception to perform a religious function.[16] Lyden, for example, does not maintain a difference between religion and culture, contending that the realms of these two areas overlap much more than scholars of religion or culture would like to admit. In this way, he suggests, the classical distinction between 'religion' and 'culture' is to be 'put aside for a more nuanced view that sees all features of culture as having religious aspects that cannot be separated from their nonreligious aspects'.[17] As such, film as a cultural phenomenon, normally perceived as not having an inherently religious aspect, is identified as religious for the function it plays. As Plate states, 'religion is imagistic, participatory, performative, and world-creating – and sometimes it is cinema that best provides these activities'.[18] Ostwalt argues that the movie theatre itself has acted 'like some secular religion complete with its sacred space and rituals that mediate an experience of otherness'.[19]

Another approach to the study of religion in film is the religious interpretation of film. This approach does not seek to find explicitly religious themes and images in the study of religion in film. Instead, it proposes that some films, including mainstream and popular films, which appear to have little to do with religious themes, are open to religious interpretation. May is amongst the earliest proponents of this method. He suggests that regardless of the film-maker's reputation concerning his religious belief, the autonomy of the film as an art form needs to be respected. Indeed, for a work to be considered religious, 'one need not demand that the language of religion or theology be present in a work'.[20] It is thus 'more precise to speak of a film's world view as being *open* to a religious or sectarian interpretation or to appropriation for the faith experience'.[21] Similarly, Deacy more recently proposes that the study of religious films should not be limited to those that contain specifically religious material. Instead, he suggests, it may be 'more appropriate to speak of the "religious interpretation of film" rather than of the interpretation of religious film'.[22]

Deacy argues that the power of film can be recognised in the film critic's encounter and examination of 'such perennial religious themes as grace, forgiveness, alienation, the apocalypse and redemption' in popular films.[23] He applies this method of study to his examination of the Christian notion of redemption in American *film noir* of the post-Second

World War period. Deacy asserts that even though film is a secular medium, it may ultimately be seen to perform 'a religious function in contemporary western culture by addressing and confronting fundamental issues and themes which are distinctively and quintessentially religious in form'.[24] In illustrating the relevance of Christian redemption to *film noir*, he compares the teachings of St. Paul, St. Augustine and Martin Luther about the world and human existence, with the world and human condition of *film noir*. In both cases, the world is corrupt and filled with sin, and the human condition is depicted as alienated and estranged. Deacy argues that despite this seemingly bleak picture, redemption runs through *film noir*. In fact, *film noir* is a 'fertile repository' for redemption: 'As in the case of Christianity, redemption thus proceeds not from an escape from reality but from a more resolute *confrontation* with the truth and the actuality concerning the human condition'.[25]

Another approach is film as hierophany. This approach proposes that film style enables the exploration of the sacred. Eliade first proposed the term 'hierophany' to refer to the study of the sacred through the profane. He maintained that the sacred is not limited to holy places or things, but rather it is possible for the entire cosmos to become a hierophany.[26] Bird applies Eliade's general analysis of culture and its ability to manifest the sacred, to the specific art of film. He argues that the manifestation of the sacred in film is possible not through grand religious dramas, but through the medium's ability for realistic depiction. Following film theorists such as Bazin, Agel and Ayfre, Bird (1982) invokes the idea of film as an art form, which enables the disclosure of reality. These theorists argue that while art-as-transformation applies to other art forms such as painting, the same does not apply to film. Thus, while painting is an art only if the painter creatively transforms or interprets the reality in front of him rather than produce a mechanical imitation of an object, film does not follow the same argumentation. Instead, film achieves its purpose not by adding anything to reality but by virtue of its style, enabling the disclosure of reality. Drawing from these film theories of realism in cinema and Eliade's notion of hierophany, Bird concludes that film's style enables the exploration of the sacred.[27]

Bird dismisses the ability of so-called religious films with their grand drama and technical beauty to convey the sacred to the audience. These films fail because they neglect the stylistic virtues of the medium.[28]

According to him, the sacred needs to be experienced whereas these films overwhelm the very factors by which this experience would have been possible. Creating supernatural episodes in these ostensibly religious films hinders the possibility of experiencing the sacred. Employing Ayfre's theory, Bird argues that 'genuinely religious films' are those 'in which the cinematographic recording of reality does not exhaust reality but rather evokes in the viewer the sense of its ineffable mystery'.[29] He identifies Robert Bresson as one of the film-makers to have discerned the power of realism in film. He examines *The Diary of a Country Priest* (1951), to illustrate how Bresson's film style has enabled the exploration of the sacred. Bresson directs his actors to minimise their acting, and 'they pose as transparent figures through or behind whom a spiritual significance is discerned'.[30]

As in the example of Gibson's *The Passion of the Christ* mentioned at the beginning of this section, it is clear that one could employ a number of these various approaches to study religion in film. This would perhaps depend on two main factors: the film under study and the academic discipline from within which a scholar studies the film. In fact, there is no one method that would do justice to the study of religion in film in all its depth and breadth. Each method, when employed on its own, studies only a particular aspect of film. Film, on the other hand, is a rich and multi-layered text and art form in its own right. It is possible, therefore, for a film to have multiple layers through which religion is depicted, explored, referred to or criticised. It is, therefore, vital to clarify the specific aspects that a scholar intends to study while acknowledging that it is by no means exhaustive or all-embracing. Moreover, many of these approaches overlap in certain aspects, making it almost impossible to have a distinct and independent methodology in the study of religion in film.

However, since Western scholarship has focused mainly on examining Judaeo-Christian elements in Western productions, this study hopes to contribute to the field by exploring religion and spirituality in the parallel context of Islam, specifically Iranian Shi'i Islam.

Shi'i Islam in Iranian Cinema

Clearly, the nature of this study demands an in-depth understanding of Shi'ism in Iran. It is additionally imperative to understand the specificity of Shi'ism within the larger Islamic tradition if we are to understand

Iran and Iranian film, and particularly their engagement with religion and spirituality. My general approach, therefore, is to provide a cultural and socio-historical background to some of the different modalities of Shi'ism, which will be further explored in their filmic narratives in later chapters. Chapter 1, therefore, surveys the formation and development of Shi'ism and its manifestations in Iran. Situating my study within this larger context allows me to locate contemporary Iranian discourses on religion and spirituality in film, the subject of Chapter 2, as well as the filmic discourses themselves (i.e. discourses through the medium of film), within a much longer-standing and continuing discourse on religion and spirituality in Iran.

Chapter 2 goes on to compare and contrast the various debates both within and outside Iran. These include an analysis of the religious discourses on the permissibility of cinema itself, the debates around the compatibility of the medium with religion and spirituality as well as the launch of the 'spiritual cinema' (*sinama-ye ma'nagara*) category in Iran in 2005 and the various attempts by film-makers, journalists, academics and the authorities to define it adequately.

Shi'ism encompasses modalities of interpretation that range from the communal and public to the highly personal and spiritual. These variant approaches to religion and spirituality clearly demonstrate the plurality and complexity of Iranian Shi'i identity. In any study of Shi'i expressions of religion and spirituality in Iran, therefore, it is important to attend to both the formal and legalistic as well as the more personal approach to religion, each of which plays a formative role in these expressions. Given the breadth of the topic and the numerous expressions of Shi'ism in Iran, I have selected three main areas within the religious discourses, namely the formalistic, the mystical and the popular, and I examine some of the films that have seriously engaged with these broad themes in Chapters 3, 4 and 5, respectively. In addition, in Chapter 6, I study the philosophical approach to these religious discourses.

Chapter 3 explores the formalistic approach to religion, represented by the ulama and their centres of learning. A brief examination of the history of clerical influence within the Iranian context reveals a very complex picture: even though Iran has been governed and led by the clerics for the last 30 years, one cannot point to a consensus amongst them about their own social role. Indeed, the diversity of their views is a source of some of the most dynamic and profound debates on the role of the clergy in the long history of this institution in Iran. The films I study here articulate a discourse that is a significant departure from previous representations of the clergy in Iran.

This formal and institutional approach, however, has never been the sole expression of the beliefs and practices of the Shi'i laity. Indeed, the Sufi and mystical approach has often existed in tandem, as an alternative to the legalistic approach to religion and spirituality in Iran. But those whose personal approach to religion diverged from the public and communal aspects propagated by the establishment and centres of authority, were usually regarded unfavourably and subsequently marginalised by the latter. However, their rich and varied reading of ways to arrive at spiritual maturity has influenced many aspects of Iranian culture and thought. In Chapter 4, therefore, I study the highly personal and Sufi approach to religion. Here, I analyse how Majid Majidi's films, specifically, are depictions of man's struggle to spiritual attainment, a discourse that stems from Sufism, a mystical dimension of Islam.

In Chapter 5, I explore how cinema has provided a new medium of expression for one of the most popular discourses within Shi'ism. Here, I examine film's engagement with one of the oldest Shi'i narratives, the death of the third Shi'i imam, Husayn, through *ta'ziyeh*. *Ta'ziyeh* is a re-enactment of the events on the plains of Karbala that culminated in the death of Husayn. Referred to as the only Islamic drama, *ta'ziyeh* originates from much older pre-Islamic forms of performance. Being a popular discourse within Shi'ism, it does not always draw its language or facts from the official discourses on Husayn. Rather, these expressions of the laity have provided a means for personal and direct engagement with the figure of the Imam. They have also led to the creation of religious rituals, many of which have historically met with the disapproval of the clergy and been condemned by them as unIslamic.

Finally, Chapter 6 is about the philosophical approach to religion. By this I mean the approach that reflects upon the various religious discourses, be they formalistic, mystical or even scientific. In this chapter I examine the films of Abbas Kiarostami within a philosophical framework and demonstrate how they may be read as 'poetic philosophies' that both resonate with modern Western philosophy in the form of Wittgenstein's thought, and simultaneously emphasise the lyrical language of Iranian poets.

As a medium, film has so far received little, if any, serious attention in the analysis and understanding of Shi'i religious expressions and articulations. This work aims to situate film as a valid and important tool in the understanding of many of the current debates within Iran, rooted as they are in much older historical and traditional discourses on religion, power and politics.

CHAPTER 1

SHI'ISM IN IRAN: AN HISTORICAL OVERVIEW

It was not until I came across a curious fifteenth-century Persian manuscript painting of the Prophet Muhammad's *mi'raj* (ascension) recently that I remembered one of my grandmother's stories. Like Scheherazade of *The 1001 Nights* she always has a story to tell. She was born to be a performer, her talent of doing excellent impressions of other people the source of much mirth in the family. She chooses, however, to spend most of her spare moments in prayer and rolling her *tasbih* (rosary) while murmuring the praises of God. In the midst of family discussions, we could always count upon her to invoke a story, a Qur'anic reference or hadith, a few verses of poetry or a proverb that would neatly summarise her perspective of the situation at hand. Like Scheherazade, it was sometimes difficult to assess whether she was just a narrator of these axioms or whether she played a more active role in their creation or embellishment.

One of these stories, which she repeated 'out of love' during my teenage years concerned my unveiled hair and her attempts at 'guiding' me to the straight path and securing my salvation. The story in brief was as follows:

> They say in Hell there is a well atop which women are hung from every strand of their hair that they have exposed to a *namahram* (unrelated man). The walls of the well are filled with gnawing mice; the bottom, covered with snakes. It is because I do not want

you to face that fate that I am asking you to veil yourself when a *namahram* comes to your house!

I would smile in disbelief. She would look displeased and return to her murmurs on the beads, this time probably praying for my soul. As she always started these anecdotes with 'They say...', it was difficult to ascertain the origins of her story. For all I knew, it might have been used to teach her the significance of the hijab when she was young or a more recent invention she had come across in some religious gathering to justify the mandatory veiling in Iran. Whatever its origins, to my Ithna 'Ashari grandmother, this was the absolute truth and literal account of the fate of unveiled women. It was thus, that my chance encounter with the fifteenth-century manuscript brought back her story.

Like most other manuscript paintings from within the Muslim tradition on *mi'raj*, this illustration depicted the Prophet Muhammad riding Buraq with the angel Gabriel by his side. It was the location and the presence of a particular figure that made it a strikingly different depiction from all other *mi'raj* illustrations that I had seen before. Muhammad was not in Jerusalem or the Heavens, but at Hell with Satan guarding its gates. Burning in the overwhelming flames of hellfire were women hanging from their hair. I could hear my grandmother's warnings ringing in my ears, as though they were a voiceover to the illustration. The caption to the manuscript read: 'During his Night Journey, Muhammad visits hell, where he views women being hung by their hair and tormented by a demon for the sin of showing their hair in public.[1] The details varied slightly, but the fundamental principles of my grandmother's (now clearly age-old) story remained unchanged: women were duty-bound to veil and severe punishment awaited those who disobeyed.

Any understanding of contemporary expressions of Shi'ism would be impossible without recourse to its historical development in Iran. The first part of this chapter, therefore, charts the beginnings and spread of Shi'ism within Iran. The significance of the Shi'a in Iran is conventionally traced back to the rise of the Safavids in the early sixteenth century. The role and influence of the Shi'a in the Iranian lands, however, stretches as far back as the formative period of Islam. The second part of the chapter then continues with a discussion of the historical importance and development of two of the main features of the formal and institutional facets of Shi'ism, namely the clergy and the madrasas, from the time of the establishment of the Safavid state down to the present day. The discussion of these features here will help contextualise the themes discussed in Chapter 3 on the role of the clergy.

The Appeal of Shi'ism in Iran and the Foundations of Twelver Shi'ism

Disagreements surrounding the Prophet Muhammad's succession upon his death in 632 in Medina marked the beginning of what came to be referred to as the Shi'a-Sunni split. A few of the Companions of the Prophet elected Abu Bakr as successor, who thus became the first of the four 'Rightly Guided' caliphs. It has been argued, however, that 'Abu Bakr's succession was realized neither through a free election in any sense of the term nor through a free choice of the community'.[2] Indeed, a small group of Muslims regarded 'Ali b. Abi Talib, the son-in-law and cousin of the Prophet, as the rightful successor to the Prophet. They believed that 'Ali was best qualified for the position and they thus 'became generally designated as the *Shi'at 'Ali*, "party of 'Ali" or simply as the Shi'a'.[3] The dispute between the upholders of 'Ali's right to the caliphate and the supporters of Abu Bakr 'centred on considerations of *what is necessary under the circumstances, and what ought to be*',[4] with the Shi'a being of the latter opinion.

The Development of Shi'ism in the Early Islamic Period

The Shi'a believe that the Prophet Muhammad himself 'had designated 'Ali as his successor, a designation or *nass* instituted through divine command and revealed by the Prophet at Ghadir Khumm shortly before his death'.[5] The Sunnis maintain that since the Qur'an refers to Prophet Muhammad as the 'Seal of the Prophets' (33: 40), this means that 'he was not to be succeeded by any of his family according to God's design', but that Muhammad had left his community to decide on this matter based on the Qur'anic notion of *ijma'* or consultation.[6] The Shi'a, however, defend the doctrine of the imamate and assert that since the Sunni caliphs succeeded the Prophet in every aspect other than his prophethood, this status was clearly befitting of his own family. As such, the Shi'a, too, refer to the Qur'an and the examples of the earlier prophets mentioned therein to support their arguments:

> In the Qur'an, the descendants and close kin to the prophets are their heirs also in respect to kingship (*mulk*), rule (*hukm*), wisdom

(*hikma*), the book and the imamate ... the Qur'an advises the faithful to settle some matters by consultation, but not the succession to the prophets. That, according to the Qur'an, is settled by divine election, and God usually chooses their successors, whether they become prophets or not, from their own kin.[7]

'Ali was passed over two more times upon the deaths of the first and second caliphs. He was finally appointed as the fourth caliph in 656 but his rule ended with his murder four years later. This marked the establishment of the Umayyads (661–750) and the beginning of the dynastic caliphate in Muslim history. For the Shi'a, however, 'Ali's role as imam, or spiritual leader, was divinely designated and began immediately upon the death of the Prophet, independent of his political role as caliph and quite aside from the issue of the three caliphs before him having unjustly 'usurped' this position. For the early Shi'a, it was the protest against the Muslim majority who ignored this designation that separated the partisans of 'Ali from the rest of the Muslim community.[8] The revolutionary aspect of the Shi'a is, therefore, sometimes traced to the very beginnings of Islam.

The expansion of the Muslim Empire began with the rule of the second caliph, 'Umar (r. 634–644). The Muslim armies conquered many of the Near Eastern lands including territories of the Persian Empire in 636–637. The Arab conquerors were not as keen on imposing their religion on their new subjects as they were on imposing the *jizya*, a poll tax on each non-Muslim adult male, for the revenues they brought in. As with other conquered territories, very soon most of the Persians had also converted to Islam. However, they remained the only occupied land at that time to have been Islamicised but nevertheless to have resisted Arabisation.

The dissatisfaction of the various factions within the Umayyad empire contributed greatly to its fall in 750. The people of Khurasan, in Eastern Iran, were one such group frustrated at their loss of status and the imposition of unjust taxes. As such, when the Abbasid propagandists launched their revolt against the Umayyads in the name of the *ahl al-bayt* (the family of the Prophet), this appealed greatly to the Shi'a and the Persian *mawali* (non-Arab Muslims).[9] Claiming familial legitimacy through their ancestor 'Abbas, the Prophet's uncle, they won the support of many Shi'as and their sympathisers, including the disgruntled population of Khurasan. The Shi'a supporters were nevertheless left bitterly betrayed when the Abbasids aborted their Shi'a position upon coming to power.

Instead, they established a Sunni caliphate and disavowed any support for Shi'a belief.

Relations between the Abbasid state and Shi'ism were problematic. For a brief period, there was hope of a reconciliation between the Sunni caliphate and what came to be known as Twelver Shi'ism (the majority group within the Shi'a who believe in a line of twelve imams) when the Abbasid caliph al-Ma'mun (r. 813–833), appointed the eighth imam, 'Ali al-Rida as his heir. However, when al-Rida accompanied al-Ma'mun from Marv to Baghdad, he died under peculiar circumstances, 'poisoned at the caliph's orders, say a number of sources'.[10] The situation became even harder for the later imams, with the tenth and eleventh living under house arrest in Samarra. The Abbasids 'cultivated rivalries within the family of the 'Alid imams as a way of weakening the potential influence of any one claimant' and even went as far as assigning midwives to monitor their wives for any potential pregnancies.[11]

Things took a different turn for this majority group of the Shi'a with the death of their eleventh imam, Hasan al-Askari, around 874 when he was only 29. Various theories arose around the succession to the imamate after him, particularly because there were doubts as to whether he had left any heirs or not. Ultimately, however, the community accepted that he had indeed left a five-year-old heir, Muhammad, who was the twelfth imam but that he had gone into occultation. His occultation has been divided into two main periods – *ghaybat al-soghra* and *ghaybat al-kobra*, the minor and the major occultations respectively. The minor occultation lasted until 940, during which time the imam is believed to have communicated with his followers through his *safir*s (intermediaries) also referred to as *wakil*s (trustees) or *bab*s (gates), each appointed by the previous *safir*. The imam's major occultation started with the death of the fourth *safir*, 'Ali al-Samarri in 940–941, and continues down to the present day. Unlike his predecessors, al-Samarri did not appoint a *safir* to succeed him, stating six days before his death that the imam himself had dictated a letter to him asking him not to designate a successor.[12] To this day, the Twelver Shi'a await their hidden imam, Muhammad b. Hasan al-Askari, the Mahdi, to manifest himself.

The Iranian Influence

From the very early days of the Islamic empire – both during the Umayyad and, later, the Abbasid caliphates – many Persian elements were employed in the court. During the reign of the Umayyad caliph, Hisham (724–743),

> Persian court procedures were adopted, and the first translations of Persian political documents were made. Under the 'Abbasids, Persian scribes, merchants, workers, and soldiers saw to the translation of Persian manuals of behaviour and protocol (*adab*) for scribes and administrators into Arabic. The manuals contained advice on how to conduct affairs of state, carry out duties of various offices, and behave in the presence of rulers, and described the qualities required for different positions.[13]

Arabic, however, became the dominant intellectual language of the Islamic lands, which included Iran, and it was thus that the Persian language went 'silent' for about 200 years. It was only in the tenth century that, in an attempt to revive the Persian language, Persian scholars once again began writing in the vernacular.[14] Ferdowsi's (d. 1020) masterpiece, the *Shahnameh*, a national epic that took him over 30 years to write, was a seminal work in this period. Similarly, other Persian authors chose to write their travelogues, works of philosophy, astronomy and theology in Persian. Ahmad Nasafi (d. 943), Abu Rayhan Biruni (d. 1048), Nasir-e Khusraw (d. after 1072), and Khwaja 'Abd Allah Ansari (d. 1088) are just a few pertinent examples of this trend, which continued in the works of later scholars such as the philosopher, poet and astronomer, Nasir al-Din Tusi (d. 1274). This phenomenon has been seen as Persian resistance movement that began as a response to the Arabisation of Islam – a movement that was concerned with the preservation and protection of Persian culture and identity.

It was also around the tenth century that Shi'i revivals are witnessed in Iran. By then, the Abbasid empire was fragmented and had lost much of its direct control over the peripheral areas of its extensive territories. This resulted in the emergence of various dynasties in these regions. The Shi'i Buyids from the Caspian province of Daylam in Northern Iran are but one example. They rose to power and ruled much of the central provinces of the Abbasid empire during the tenth and eleventh centuries. In 945, they entered Baghdad, the seat of the Abbasid caliphate, but decided against overthrowing it. The Buyid ruler, Mu'izz al-Dawla,

> was aware that the Shi'is were in the minority, and that, had he destroyed the Caliphate in Baghdad, the institution would have

reappeared elsewhere. It was better to keep it under his thumb, both to legalise his authority over the Sunnis in his states and to strengthen his diplomatic relations with the world outside by the weight of the respected moral authority which the Sunni princes still enjoyed by right.[15]

The Buyids ruled until 1055 and it was under their patronage that Twelver Shi'ism 'began to take a more explicit doctrinal form'.[16]

The establishment of the Shi'a Ismaili Fatimids in North Africa in 909 had also attracted a small following in the Iranian lands. Following the crisis of the Fatimid leadership in 1094 the Ismailis split into two groups, the Musta'lis and the Nizaris. The insurgency of the Nizari Ismailis against the Sunni authorities appealed to many Iranians. The Nizari Ismailis, under the leadership of Hasan-e Sabbah, based their headquarters in Iran. The impregnable castle of Alamut, south of the Caspian Sea, which was captured by Hasan-e Sabbah in 1090, became the centre of their religio-political activities. Under Hasan,

> the Ismailis of Iran launched a scattered but vigorous revolt against the Saljuq regimes that dominated the Iranian world in the late eleventh and early twelfth centuries... The 'Ismaili revolt' was dramatic and, for a time, posed a serious challenge to the Sunni political order, and especially to the various Saljuq regimes.[17]

There are various reasons for the appeal of Shi'ism to the Iranian populace, not least the congruence between them in their concepts of leadership and authority. Indeed, the divinely designated leadership of the Shi'i imams was similar to the familiar kingship model of the pre-Islamic Sasanid Empire, itself also based on the idea of a divinely ordained ruler. The imperial ideology of the Sasanids espoused the idea of a God-King, in which the kings were not only supported by Ahura Mazda, the Good God, but also claimed divinity for themselves.[18] The kingship was restricted to a single lineage and the king's right to rule was sacral and divinely ordained.[19] Thus, the Shi'a idea of a divinely guided and divinely appointed leader was probably quite amenable to the Iranians, who were familiar with this leadership paradigm. Indeed, Aslan traces the early attraction of Iranians to Shi'ism to the time of the death of 'Ali, the first imam, in 661. He states that even though the *Shi'at 'Ali* were few, they were 'still an influential faction, particularly among the Iranians of the former Sasanian Empire, who saw in the ahl al-bayt an alternative to the ethnic Arab domination of the Umayyads'.[20]

Many scholars have also attributed the early Shi'i revolts popular in Iran more to national rather than religious sentiments. Thus, the Shi'i supporters of the Abbasids are seen to be motivated by nationalist reactions to the ruling Arabs. The Abbasid dynasty, in turn, adopted an imperial ideology by not only claiming familial relations with the Prophet but also promulgating the view that it was

> the successor of the ancient imperial dynasties in 'Iraq and Iran, from the Babylonians through the Sasanians, their immediate predecessors. In this way they were able to incorporate Sasanian culture, which was still the dominant culture of large masses of the population east of 'Iraq, into mainstream 'Abbasid culture.[21]

The Nizari Ismaili movement is seen as a similar reaction against the ruling Saljuq Turks: 'Less conspicuously, Hasan's revolt was an expression of Persian "national" sentiment – a factor that accounts for its early popular appeal and widespread success in Persia'.[22]

With the continuing persecution, particularly during the Abbasid caliphate, of the imams of what came to be known as Twelver Shi'ism, followed by the occultation of their twelfth imam, the Shi'a settled for a quietist policy. In the thirteenth century, the Mongol invasion of the Islamic lands was followed by large-scale murder and plunder. The Nizari Ismaili state in Persia came to an end in 1256 with the fall of Alamut to the Mongols. Two years later, in 1258, the Mongols conquered Baghdad and abolished the Abbasid caliphate. As Berkey notes, 'When they arrived, the Mongols practiced a religion ... commonly labelled "shamanism", which is to say they did not embrace any of the universalist, and generally monotheistic faiths which had emerged from the ancient Near East'.[23] They did, however, pursue a policy of religious diversity and one of its 'major and far-reaching consequences ... was the gradual erosion of some of the tensions that had previously divided various religions and sects under the Saljuqs'.[24]

As a result, following a long period of persecution and quietism, Twelver Shi'ism finally found respite, even if inadvertently, under the Mongols. Two of their main rivals – the Sunni Abbasids and the Nizari Ismaili Shi'as – were eliminated or driven underground and the policy of relative religious tolerance gave them a new-found scope of activity. The famous Twelver Shi'i scholar, Allama Hilli, moved to Persia in 1305 and even converted the Mongol ruler Oljeytu who had previously converted from Shamanism to Christianity and later to Sunni Islam before becoming a Shi'a. Subsequently, even though

> Sunnis remained the majority in Persia and continued to dominate its major urban centres for several centuries, there was a gradual resurgence of Twelver Shi'ism which was allowed, for the first time, to organise and express itself openly without the fear of persecution ... At the same time, there is evidence of a general movement away from Sunnism to Shi'ism during the Mongol period. According to Bausani, these people sought refuge in Shi'ism because they were disgusted with the squabbles among the different Sunni schools, and especially as regards Iran, between the Shafi'ites and the Hanafites.[25]

Even though the Shi'a had generally adopted a quietist approach, there were, however, periods when they challenged Sunni hegemony as in the case of the Fatimids in North Africa, the Buyids in Baghdad and the Nizaris in Iran. As we have seen, Shi'a sympathies within the Iranian lands posed a significant challenge to the status quo at various times. The appeal of Shi'ism to Iranians was thus both a religious conduit for nationalist responses to Sunni Arab dominance as well as an authoritative form of governance bearing close affinity to the earlier pre-Islamic Iranian models of empire. Clearly, the significance of the Shi'a in Iran cannot be overlooked. Indeed, as shown above, their role and influence in these lands stretches back to the formative period of Islam, and not merely to the rise of the Safavids in the early sixteenth century as is conventional in most other historical accounts of the development of Shi'ism in Iran.

The Twelver Shi'i State of Iran and the Shi'i Ulama

The Mongol dynasty of the Ilkhanids in Iran and Iraq lasted until the death of Abu Sa'id, the last Ilkhanid ruler, in 1353. From then onwards, Iran witnessed a period of political upheaval with short-lived dynasties including the Sunni Turko-Mongol Timurids who entered from Transoxania. The fourteenth and fifteenth centuries witnessed a spread of Shi'ism and Sufism in Iran. It was during this time that the Safavi Sufi order found widespread support. The order took its name from its ancestor and founder, Shaykh Safi al-Din Ardabili (d. 1334). By 1488, the order obtained a markedly Shi'a characteristic: Shah Haydar, the Sufi leader of the time, dreamt that the Imam 'Ali instructed him to wear a distinctive headgear with twelve pleats to commemorate the twelve Shi'a imams.

The consolidation of Shi'ism in Iran came about with the political rise of the Safavids, for 'by the fifteenth century, Sheikh Safi's descendants had emerged as political rulers in northwestern Iran, the border area between Iran and Azerbaijan'.[26] In 1501 Shah Ismail I established what became the Safavid dynasty (1501–1736). From very early on, the Safavids patronised and established numerous religious schools, or madrasas, on a grand scale. This attracted a steady stream of learned Shi'i men from other parts of the Islamic world, mainly southern Iraq and Lebanon, and very soon Iran turned into an important Shi'i centre.

On becoming Shah, Ismail Safavi declared Twelver Shi'ism to be the official religion of Iran. It was during this time that its clerics developed a hierarchical role which evolved to demand obedience from the believers and, ultimately, the right to rule over them (I will discuss this further in Chapter 3). Over the centuries, various events contributed to the growth of power amongst the Iranian Shi'i clergy, culminating in the Iranian Revolution of 1979 and the subsequent establishment of the Islamic Republic, which brought about the rule of the clergy. The claims to power of the Iranian Shi'i clergy take a unique expression, rooted as they are in the historical and political development of the country. In this section I will briefly examine these historical developments so as to situate current debates amongst the intellectuals and, consequently, draw parallels with contemporary filmic discourses in the subsequent chapters.

Superiority of the Clergy over Laity

It was during the Safavid period that the Shi'i ulama arrogated to themselves an elevatory role over the laity. Ordinary people, they argued, 'are incapable of recognising and thus unable to choose on their own the most learned and pious from among the 'ulama'.[27] Thus, the Shi'i clergy not only enjoyed political support from the state, but also came to be seen as necessary in the lives of the believers. The hierarchical organisation of the Shi'i clergy is not a feature of the Sunni ulama. Indeed, it was a new development, one that did not exist in either the early Shi'i doctrines or organisations.[28] Thus, even though we have examples of Shi'i ulama previously holding key roles within the ruling elite, such as Allama Hilli in the Mongol court or the Shi'i viziers of the Abbasid caliphate, they were usually individuals who out of their personal quality or merit had succeeded in attaining high positions. It was only from the time of the Safavids that the Shi'i ulama as an institution found great significance. It is in this regard, Keddie continues, that hierarchical organisation became a characteristically Iranian Shi'i development.[29] Indeed, similar developments amongst the Shi'a outside Iran are due to more recent Iranian influences.

Another factor that contributed to the growth of clerical power was the victory of the Usuli or Mujtahidi school of ulama over the Akhbari school by the early nineteenth century. The Akhbari school was established during the Safavid period under Shaykh Muhammad Sharif Astarabadi (d. 1624), but 'its greatest influence was when the ulama were excluded from participation in the affairs of a Shi'i state, namely the interregnum between Safavid and Qajar rule.[30] It was mainly Aqa Muhammad Baqir Behbahani (1705–1803) who led the doctrinal reassertion of the Usulis. He

> ...asserted the legitimacy of the functions of mujtahid, as the dominant one in Shi'i Islam, attempted to repress Sufism, taught and inspired a large number of mujtahids who attained great influence in Iran in the reign of Fath 'Ali Shah (1797–1834), and in his own person vigorously asserted the functions of mujtahids claiming 'enjoining good and prohibiting evil' to be his peculiar duty.[31]

The main difference of interpretation between these two schools lay in the understanding of the role and necessity of the clergy as intermediaries between man and God. The Akhbaris maintained that 'individual believers could understand the Qur'an and the Traditions (*akhbar*) of the Prophet and the Imams and did not need to follow the guidance of *mujtahid*s, who claimed the right of *ijtihad* ('effort to ascertain correct doctrine')'.[32] The Akhbaris argued that *ijtihad* was an innovation in Shi'ism, dating from the time of Kulayni (d. 941), author of *Kitab usul min al-kafi*, a collection of traditions of the imams, a guide to authoritative Twelver doctrine in theology and *fiqh*. Indeed, they accused the Usuli *mujtahid*s of adopting Sunni positions of Hanafi rationalism. The Akhbaris gave total precedence to *naql* (transmitted doctrine) over '*aql* (exertion of reason) and argued that all believers should be *muqallid*s (emulators) only of the imams and not the *mujtahid*s.³³

The Usulis, however, had succeeded in asserting the necessity of the *mujtahid*s and maintained that 'every believer was required to follow the rulings of a living *mujtahid*, and whenever there was a single chief *mujtahid*, his rulings took precedence over all others'.³⁴ These *mujtahid*s were referred to as *marja'-e taqlid* or models for emulation. The Usulis, therefore, soon established a clerical power that positioned themselves as intermediaries between believers and God, and this has been the dominant Shi'i theology to this date. Accordingly, any Shi'a who has not attained the same level of authoritative judgement in interpreting the law from the sources 'must choose a *mujtahid* to be their own spiritual guide (*marja' al-taqlid*, 'model for/source of emulation'), whose opinions in matters of religious law are binding on those who follow him'.³⁵

By the early nineteenth century, in addition to establishing clerical superiority to the laity, 'the Shii clergy were able to get their right to direct collection of religious taxes'.³⁶ The religious dues of *khums* and *zakat* were thus paid directly to them. This economic independence further strengthened their position and consequently gave them political freedom from the ruling state.

The clergy's organised ties with the merchants or *bazaari*s was another empowering factor. As Keddie states, the ties between these two groups have been very close and very often both were from the same families through intermarriage. In fact, 'ulama' was not an occupational term but rather a reference to men with certain religious learning.³⁷ Thus, many of the clerics were occupied in various professions; indeed, some of them were *bazaari*s, while others were craftsmen, shopkeepers and even landlords. The ulama and *bazaari*s 'worked together in a variety of ways and influenced each other, so that any picture of merchants as a discrete group getting ulama as a divergent group to do something is belied by the interconnected history of the two'.³⁸

Even though the first records of the ulama's claims to rule go back to the late seventeeth century,³⁹ these did not materialise until the victory of the Islamic Republic in 1979 under Ayatollah Ruhollah Khomeini (1902–1989). Soon after the 1979 Revolution, the doctrine of *velayat-e faqih*, or guardianship of the jurist, was introduced. This gave the leader the final say in the running of country. Named as 'Leader for Life' in the constitution, 'Ayatollah Khomeini now combined supreme temporal and religious authority'.⁴⁰ This transition from charismatic leader of the

Revolution to head of state seemed natural. Khomeini, however, was initially irresolute when it came to entrusting the reins of the country to the clerics. Indeed, he was concerned that the earthly desires of politics would corrupt the clergy and subsequently jeopardise their credibility with the public.[41]

Khomeini's rapid change of position in entrusting the running of the state to the clergy may be traced to a few key events soon after he came to power. The death of some 70 of his supporters in the June 1981 bombings of the headquarters of the Islamic Republican Party (IRP) is one such crucial factor. This was followed two months later by the death of two of his other allies, the newly-elected president, Mohammad Ali Raja'i, and Prime Minister Mohammad Javad Bahonar. These and other political assassinations were blamed on the Islamic-Socialist party of Mojahedin-e Khalq (MK). The final straw was when President Abolhassan Bani-Sadr (b. 1933), an Islamic modernist opposed to clerical rule, and the leaders of IRP were unable to resolve their differences.[42] Khomeini then had 'little choice but to exercise his "revolutionary duties" by siding with the clerics whose actions deeply worried him'.[43]

With all rival parties defeated and Khomeini's stamp of approval on clerical rule, the clergy stabilised their power in the ensuing years. Khomeini, for his part, attempted to articulate this new responsibility within his theological discourse. Giving it a mystical dimension, he asserted that it was not rational knowledge nor the need to determine interests that entrusted the clergy with the duty to rule. Rather, this duty 'could only ensue from a form of mystical revelation that anyone could strive for, but only a few among the clerics would attain'.[44] He also delegated the rulings of secondary ordinances – a narrow range of contractual issues that were not directly addressed in the Qur'an – to the clergy. As Brumberg states, these had traditionally fallen within the government's remit. Khomeini, however, declared that he could not 'imagine that God would not have looked at every aspect of any problem' and thus by 'implying that secondary rulings were also mandated by God, Khomeini virtually equated the clerical power to issue such rulings with the authority of God himself!'[45]

The Shi'a Madrasas

In recounting his studies, Ibn Sina (Avicenna), the eminent tenth/eleventh-century Persian philosopher and scholar provides us an insight into the methods of learning in the mediaeval muslim world. These included 'the wandering from teacher to teacher, the informal discussion circle, the debates of learned men thrust into each other's presence by a bored and curious monarch'.[46] These encounters were the norm before the appearance of the madrasas proper.

> *Madrasa*, in the modern usage, [is] the name of an institution of learning where the Islamic sciences are taught, i.e. a college for higher studies, as opposed to an elementary school of traditional type (*kuttab*); in mediaeval usage, [it is] essentially a college of law in which the other Islamic sciences, including literary and philosophical ones, were ancillary subjects only.[47]

The madrasas originally began as private endowments of scholars teaching their students but gradually developed into institutions that were supported by rulers and other men of power.[48] In fact, it was no longer solely a matter of scholarly interest and patronage that led their founders to establish these schools. Rather, the

> establishment of madrasas served the political interests of those who founded them, both individually and collectively, but the institutions themselves, and the academic activities they supported, were not subjected to systematic governmental regulation and control, and did not undergird any particular political program.[49]

Many of these patrons would usually found madrasas of their own denomination and some were closely involved with the actual running of the school. For instance, the endowment acts of the Nizamiyya of Baghdad, established by and named after Nizam al-Mulk, the eleventh-century Persian Shafi'i vizier to the Saljuq sultans, stated that teachers had to be either Shafi'i or Ash'ari. Indeed, he himself was directly involved in the selection of the teachers.[50]

It has been argued that the madrasa is the result of a three-stage development of the college in Islam. The first was the period during which teaching took place within the confines of the mosques, especially in their designation as non-congregational mosques. The second stage was that of the *masjid-khan* complex, where the mosque (*masjid*) was also used as a hostelry (*khan*) for out-of-town students. Finally, the madrasa proper appeared when the functions of both mosque and hostelry were combined in an institution based on a single endowment deed.⁵¹ Madrasas were, therefore, a development born from the spaces and activities within the mosques.

The first madrasa appeared in the tenth century in north-east Iran and was later 'spread by the Seljuqs over the whole of Iran to Iraq, Syria and Asia Minor'.⁵² In Cairo, the Shi'i Fatimids founded the Azhar mosque complex in 970. Al-Azhar 'developed into a center for higher learning and was richly endowed to support students, teachers, and one of the largest libraries of the time in the Muslim world'.⁵³ Later, in 1005, the Fatimid Imam-Caliph al-Hakim, founded the *dar al-'ilm,* also known as the *dar al-hikma,* which was devoted to Ismaili Shi'i teachings. It is, therefore, important to note that even though 'madrasa' became the dominant term, in their initial stages of development there were different centres of learning in the Muslim world, referred to by different names.

In fact, it has been argued that the sudden surge of the Sunni Saljuq madrasas was a reaction to these centres as 'a counter to the propaganda efforts of militant Ismaili Shi'ism organised by the Fatimids from Al-Azhar'.⁵⁴ This in turn had the ripple effect that other Shi'i centres surfaced around the same time as the Saljuq madrasas in many Iranian cities, including Rayy, Qom, Kashan, Varamin, Sabzevar and elsewhere. However, 'to judge by the later consonance between the Sunni and Shi'i *madrasas* in the Iranian world, there was probably no formal distinction between them'.⁵⁵ In any case, it was not until the end of the eleventh century, but 'at least a hundred years before their Western counterparts, the European universities',⁵⁶ that the madrasas made their definitive appearance.

As discussed earlier, with the coming to power of the Safavids, numerous Shi'i madrasas were built to help propagate and establish Twelver Shi'ism as the new state faith. Shi'ism was in fact an instrument to gain legitimacy for the new state based on religious authority. Traditionally, the Shi'i madrasas have been 'located mainly in religious centres which tended to be shrine cities: Najaf, Kerbala and Samarra in Iraq as well as the Iranian cities of Mashhad and Qum'.⁵⁷ In Iran, the significance of the madrasas grew so much that even with the advent of modern sciences into the country and the training of lawyers and physicians, these members of the upper class elite were still likely to have undergone at least some aspects of this traditional education. As Mottahedeh observes,

> With their huge endowments and their wide acceptance as the citadels of true knowledge and correct belief, *madresehs* usually

dominated and often monopolised the world of Iranian education. In the Shiah Islamic world they had surprisingly uniform curricula and methods – something unthinkable in the time of Avicenna – and they therefore dominated the content and methods of education as well.[58]

Zubaida mentions three cycles, each lasting four years, in the Iranian Shi'i madrasa curriculum. The first cycle concentrates on the study of the Qur'an, Arabic language and grammar. Upon completion of this first level, the graduates may perform minor religious functions in mosques as well as read and recite the stories of Karbala during the mourning ceremonies of the month of Muharram. During the second cycle, students study *fiqh* (jurisprudence) and are introduced to the intricacies of sharia through appropriate texts, commentaries and methods of deduction. This allows them to lead mosques and congregations and, in some cases, act as judges. At the final stage they are trained in *ijtihad* (arriving at independent opinion on matters of law and interpretation) by further exploring texts, traditions and commentaries. When students feel that they have arrived at that stage of independent judgement, they submit a written piece of work to their teacher. If accepted, the student is given a licence to practice *ijtihad*, at which point he becomes a *mujtahid*.[59]

The traditional education system in Iran was significantly affected by its encounter with Western secular education. In 1851, the Iranian government established the Polytechnic College, with the aim of educating Iranians in the European sciences. Thus, for the first time, an educational system modelled on a Western system was introduced in Iran. This had its own varying effects in Iranian society, including the formation of a new elite and intellectuals who wanted a change in the country's entire system of law. 'By the end of the century some of these intellectuals demanded a "fundamental law" for the state, a constitution that described the limits of the government's power'.[60] These demands voiced against the government gradually extended beyond the intellectuals to include, at least initially, some of the ulama as well. However, after the Constitutional Revolution of 1906, the first such revolution in the Middle East, the ulama slowly parted company with the intellectuals, paving their own way to lead society.

The success of the Constitutional Revolution resulted in honour and fame for the supporters of the new educational system. However, this support did not extend nationwide or indeed seem to be evident among people from different walks of life. Some of the *bazaari*s, who, as discussed earlier, had always maintained a close relationship with the religious authorities, despised the new learning and regarded it as irreligious and hence unworthy. It is likely that they recognised the power of the new educational system, for by its very secularised nature it was largely independent from the religious authorities. This new rival power posed a threat to the religious authorities and, thereby, to the *bazaari*s too.

This threat became even more potent after Reza Shah (r. 1925–1941) came to power and embarked on his modernising project. Adopting a policy of secularising the educational system, he went as far as to shut down all the *maktab*s (religious schools for the teaching of Qur'an and hadith, equivalent to elementary schools in modern times) in Iran. However, that he spared madrasas the same fate is a testament to the power of the clergy and its institutions, and suggests that he realised that it would be folly to completely eliminate them. Reza Shah's strategy to enforce modernisation was frequently twinned with violence, particularly towards the religious establishment. After he was forced to abdicate in 1941 in favour of his young son, Mohammad Reza Pahlavi, the latter adopted a more conciliatory attitude towards the religious establishment. In fact, in 1946 Ayatollah Boroujerdi (1875–1962), who emerged as the 'undisputed chief *marja'* of the Shi'i world ... worked out a *modus vivendi* with the state, based on the clergy keeping out of politics and opposition, but being assigned their niche in the religious institutions and general respect and dignity'.[61] In this way, the 'shrine cities in Iran and their *madrasa* and religious culture continued to provide centres of autonomy for the *ulama* and a means of perpetuating their institutions and discourses'.[62]

Boroujerdi remained true to his word for the rest of his life, during which the religious establishment remained largely aloof from the political upheavals of the country. Indeed, when Ayatollah Kashani (1882–1962) and a few other clerics participated in the political turmoil of 1951, first siding with the Prime Minister, Mohammad Mosaddeq (1882–1967), on nationalising Iran's oil and later changing sides, they were sidelined by the religious establishment.[63] Khomeini, too, another disaffected cleric, did not openly oppose the ruling regime out of respect for his teacher, Ayatollah Boroujerdi. However, upon the latter's death, he felt himself relieved of this restriction and, building upon his earlier ideas, began a vociferous campaign against the Pahlavi regime. Thus, Qom turned into a political centre for Khomeini's opposition. On the day of 'Ashura 1963, he gave a defiant speech directly attacking, satirising and ridiculing the Shah.

> In a charged atmosphere of mounting confrontation between security forces and the religious students in Qum and elsewhere, retribution was swift: government forces laid siege to the city and to Khomeini's residence, and in the clashes that followed there was much violence and bloodshed.[64]

By the time of his release within the year, all the other senior *mujtahid*s had reconciled themselves with the government. Khomeini, however, once again took the opportunity to denounce the Shah's policies, this time regarding concessions of extra-territorial immunity to the US and Israeli personnel. He was arrested yet again and sent into exile.

Conclusions

The establishment of the Safavid state in Iran marks the beginning of the consolidation of the power of the Shi'i clergy. The hierarchical organisation of the clergy, the dependence of the laity on them in their relation with God, particularly after the victory of the Usulis, and their economic independence through direct collection of religious taxes, all contributed to strengthening their increasing influence. This growth culminated in the victory of the Islamic Republic and the clergy's acquisition of political power through the supreme leadership of *velayat-e faqih*. The madrasas became influential not just as religious institutions, but also as powerful political centres that were actively engaged with developments in state and society. Their roles in the Constitutional Revolution of 1906 and in the overthrow of the Pahlavi Shah in 1979 are illustrative of this point.

In the foregoing discussion I have explored the more formal and institutional facets of Shi'ism and its development in Iran. But these aspects were not and have not always been in line with the actual practices of the laity. Additionally, even a brief examination of the history of clerical influence in the Iranian context reveals a very complex picture: although as a theocracy Iran is currently governed and led by clerics, one cannot point to a consensus amongst the clerics themselves about their social role. On the contrary, there is a staggering diversity of views and understandings, turning current debates into one of the most profound and dynamic situations in Iran's history. I shall turn to these debates in Chapter 3.

CHAPTER 2

CONTEMPORARY IRANIAN DISCOURSES ON RELIGION AND SPIRITUALITY IN CINEMA

The 10-day Fajr International Film Festival (FIFF) is one of the most exciting times for film-makers and filmgoers in Iran. It takes its name from and coincides with the 10-day Fajr celebrations that mark the victory of the 1979 Islamic Revolution.[1] The festival not only showcases the most recent productions within the country but also recognises the achievements of those who have contributed significantly to the industry in various capacities.

The Farabi Foundation[2] had kindly issued me with a press pass for two of three consecutive years (2004–2006) that I attended the FIFF in Tehran. Every winter, in order to gain access to the Festival, I visited the Farabi Cinema Foundation located within the complex of the glass museum in the south of Tehran and presented them a certified letter from my university, which further bore the stamp of the Iranian consulate in London. I was then granted either a series of tickets or a press pass to attend the Festival. The press pass was by far the better one: each year, one of the participating cinemas in the Festival is allocated exclusively to film critics and journalists, and the press pass allowed me unlimited access to that particular cinema and its film screenings over the entirety of the Festival. Of all the cinemas participating in the Festival, this one becomes the most vibrant and exhilarating for the cinema world in Tehran.

The number of other events taking place in this designated cinema far exceeded the screenings, which usually began around 10:00 in the morning and continued until late at night. There was always a real buzz about the place, frequented as it was by stars of the Iranian silver screen who turned up to attend either the screenings of their own films or the evening panels. These daily panels provided an opportunity not only for journalists to interview film casts and crews but also for the latter to publicise their recent work. Outside the screen hall, the conversations in the lobby and upper-level café varied from the latest legislation out of the Ministry of Culture to gossip about spoilt B-rated actresses who still played with Barbie dolls. Iranian hospitality was displayed through the free tea, coffee and numerous trays of sweets and cakes that were laid on the café counter during the breaks. The round tables in the café would quickly fill up after each screening and the sweets in the trays would fly off at the same speed as the heated views that were being exchanged about the last screening. The fog would then begin to thicken. The no-smoking regulation that applied to all Iranian cinemas was constantly flouted during this 10-day period in this particular cinema or, to be more precise, it was very difficult to enforce.

Looking back now, I have to admit that despite suffering constant headaches, the heavy smoke in the old and unrenovated cinema actually gave the place a particular charm, as did the crowd of journalists frequenting it, sporting balmoral hats and long overcoats that had once again become fashionable in 2006 Tehran. Tehran's infamous air pollution outside the downtown cinema was not much of an alternative to my passive smoking inside during the breaks. In any case, I preferred to stay inside and mingle with all these people who seemed to be incredible sources of information. I conducted interviews with a number of directors as well as had many informal chats with journalists, critics and Farabi insiders, all of whom shared their knowledge and insights with me.

Films participating in the Fajr International Film Festival are entered into numerous competing and non-competing sections such as 'International Cinema', 'Asian Cinema', 'Iranian Cinema', 'Guest Films', and cinemas of a specific region or film-maker. The 2005 festival witnessed a new addition to its categories, namely 'Spiritual Cinema', rendered in Persian as *sinama-ye ma'nagara*.[3] This marked the beginning of heated debates amongst journalists, film critics, authorities and lay film fans as to what constituted *sinama-ye ma'nagara*. The title *ma'nagara* became the centre of these arguments both outside and inside the festival circle, including the festival's own 20–30 page newsletter, *Jashnvareh*.

Jashnvareh is published daily during the festival and rounds-up the latest news on its participating films, directors, actors and other film crew. The first issue of *Jashnvareh* for the 2005 festival carried an interview with Alireza Rezadad, director of the Farabi Cinema Foundation and the Fajr International Film Festival, which marked the beginning of many attempts at defining the controversial term '*sinama-ye ma'nagara*':

> *Interviewer*: There is also a new and notable section, which is Spiritual Cinema. This section is very disputable from many viewpoints. How do you describe Spiritual Cinema?
>
> *Rezadad*: We've described it many times. Spiritual cinema is a trend, not style nor genre or kind. It's actually a tendency. This kind of cinema consists of those movies, which concern ultra-material [extra-material] phenomenon. This possibility exists in the nature of cinema and recent changes in the film industry have afforded more potential for all filmmakers. Furthermore, human being's [sic] today need for [sic] spirituality, religious and natural tendencies make the world pay special attention to Spiritual Cinema.[4]

This was the only part of the interview to be translated and included in the short English section of the newsletter. The main discussion on Spiritual Cinema, however, continued in the long Persian report of the interview. The next question revolved around the word '*ma'nagara*' itself, which Rezadad explains by referring to the two different meanings of the root-word '*ma'na*' in Persian:

> In the [Persian] dictionary, *Dehkhoda*, one of the meanings of '*ma'na*', which has a philosophical aspect, is that it is the opposite of 'form'. '*Ma'na*' in the cinema of *ma'nagara* does not apply [to the other meaning of *ma'na*] as meaning. Instead, it is passing from form and appearance to the other side of the material world, [it is] a path that passes through the material world.[5]

This was one of the earliest attempts at defining *sinama-ye ma'nagara*. On a lighter note, the first issue also devoted its cartoon page to the

Figure 1 A caricature in the first issue of *Jashnvareh*, the official newsletter of the Fajr International Film Festival listing the six different cinematic symbols that would make a film 'spiritual'. *Jashnvareh*, 31 January 2005, p. 9.

Table 1 A translation of the caricature, *opposite*, appearing in *Jashnvareh*, 31 January 2005

A Discussion Regarding the Symbols of Spirituality-makers!	
First Symbol: Rain	Second Symbol: Wind
Creating Instruments: ewer (*aftabeh*), hose, watering can, anything that pours water ... !	*Creating Instruments*: shovel + shovel handle + heap of soil, anything that creates wind.
Emanating Meaning: pouring love ... love pouring, the rain of love, teardrops	*Emanating Meaning*: the wind of life, the wind will bring us, kite, you were in my wind, I've given myself to your wind.
Third Symbol: A Child	Fourth Symbol: Afghans
Creating Instruments: Bald child, snot-nosed child, bare-footed child, any other thing that evokes a child.	*Creating Instruments*: one Afghan, Afghan accent, Afghan clothes, anything that looks Afghan.
Emanating Meaning: childish pity, stupid-wise children, children are always wise and adults always stupid, the balder and more snot-nosed the child ... the wiser!	*Emanating Meaning*: misery with an accent, Afghan accent with a dressing of misery, the clothes of misery, violence against women, zombies, dirty-cleans.
Fifth Symbol: An Apple	Finally, the Sixth Symbol: A Camcorder
Creating Instruments: Apple tree, an apple itself, anything red that looks like an apple.	*Creating Instruments*: Second-hand camcorder, a broken camcorder, anything that has the capacity to film badly, a cameraman who hiccups (the consistent shaking of the camcorder makes it more *ma'nagara*!)
Emanating Meaning: love-y apple, round-red love, apple-y poetry, apple-y love, I would love to bite into your apple, a poem that can be bitten into, a round-red edible thing.	*Emanating Meaning*: Innovation in seeing, a new insight into seeing, another way of seeing simply, a new style of creation, transformation in seeing-recording.

new category of Spiritual Cinema, listing six different cinematic symbols that would make a film 'spiritual'. These included rain, wind, a child, Afghans, an apple and, finally, a camera (see Figure 1). A translation of these caricatures can be found in Table 1. Clearly, these are references to Majid Majidi's *Baran* (lit. rain), Abbas Kiarostami's *The Wind Will Carry Us*, the numerous Iranian films with children, or equally, Afghans, as their protagonists, Samira Makhmalbaf's *The Apple*, and the cinema vérité style of film-making.

These humorous snippets allude to the more serious problems and difficulties of defining 'Spiritual Cinema'. Whilst the term has been around in the English language and Western studies for a while, its rendition into Persian proved to be more of a conundrum than was perhaps anticipated. Despite the fact that Persian language and culture, which boasts centuries of history on the explication of the 'spiritual', whether in its written texts or its religious practices, the Farabi Cinema Foundation had run up against a problem. This difficulty was not only confined to the choice of the term but also extended to the definition of what exactly constituted Spiritual Cinema: one of the Persian equivalents of 'spiritual' is *'rowhani'*, which is also a term of respect for referring to the clergy, especially since 'mullah' or *'akhund'* are now largely considered derogatory terms, particularly amongst the clergy themselves. Rendering Spiritual Cinema, therefore, as *'Sinama-ye rowhani'* could equally – and perhaps unhappily for the industry – imply 'clerical cinema'. Even though the term *ma'nagara* as a replacement for 'spiritual' managed to deflect attention from the clergy, its manifold implications, which we shall come to presently, ironically served to make what was being referred to even more unclear. For the time being, however, the term appears to be here to stay, but the challenge still remains: what, precisely, is *sinama-ye ma'nagara*?

In this chapter, I will focus on how religion and spirituality in film are discussed in the Iranian context. I will first explore the various responses, particularly those of the clergy and traditionalists, to the introduction and integration of cinema in Iran. These include the harsh reactions of the clergy to the medium and their later change of heart. Next, I will analyse debates on the encounter of Iranian cinema with religion and spirituality, and the question of the medium's compatibility or incongruity with religion and spirituality. In the last section, I will study the discussions that followed the introduction of *ma'nagara* cinema in the 23rd FIFF in 2005. This opened up a whole new arena for the articulation of religious discourse in the Islamic Republic. I will then conclude by considering the relevance of these definitions to the study of religion and spirituality in Iranian cinema.

Cinema's Introduction into a Muslim Society

The debate over religion and film in Iran predates the introduction of Spiritual Cinema as a category in the 2005 Fajr Festival. In fact, it can be traced as far back as the early days of cinema's public introduction in Iran. In a tradition where sharia and *fiqh* (Islamic jurisprudence) played an important role, this new Western medium provoked many questions, reactions and heated debates. Some rejected it outright and others argued for its merits. Cinema's position and status in Iran has thus not been stable and the reactions to it have varied. At times it was religiously decreed as forbidden (*haram*) and at other times allowed (*halal*).[6] This section will briefly examine these responses to cinema in Iran before turning to how Islamic scholars in post-Revolutionary Iran have tried to articulate cinema's status within Islamic jurisprudence.

The Early and Later Responses to Cinema

The first public movie theatre opened in Cheragh-Gaz Avenue in Tehran in 1904. It was a 'long hall, its floors covered with cheap Persian rugs called *zilos*, upon which people sat as they did in the mosques or while attending rowzeh or ta'zieh'.[7] However, only a month after its opening, the cinema was forced to shut down because of 'religious opposition to cinema and political harassment of its founder'.[8] The clergy and traditionalists harshly opposed the introduction of this new medium, arguing that cinema was morally corrupting and against the Islamic doctrines that objected to any visual representation. On the other hand, 'Western-educated people welcomed it as a modernizing agent'.[9]

Cinema was there to stay, however, and it became an important medium in the negotiations of change that took place in Iran. By 1930, the number of theatres across Iran had grown to 33. Issari mentions two main developments between 1930 and 1936 which led cinema to become an important source of communication:[10] In 1932, as part of his modernising project, Reza Shah banned the performance of the *ta'ziyeh*, thus forcing the abandonment of major religious gatherings and encouraging instead secular activities and interests. The second development was the banning of the veil in 1936. Although women had attended cinemas before, they were no longer admitted if veiled. Additionally, unlike at public ritual gatherings such as *ta'ziyeh* and *rowzeh*, where men and women were segregated, in cinemas they were allowed to sit next to each other. It can be argued, therefore, that cinema was not only a new Western medium introduced into Iranian Muslim society, but also a social instrument that broke the old order. Equally, it was not merely that the content of the films and the inappropriate role-models offered through the characters posed a threat to the religious classes and their beliefs, but also that by creating a space for mixed-sex entertainment, cinema also created a dangerous new 'unIslamic' leisure ritual.

The positions on cinema, however, did not remain static, either amongst the clergy or indeed even amongst the educated elites, who had first welcomed it. By the 1960s, many Iranian intellectuals had already begun articulating their disenchantment with modernity and what it had to offer. For example, Jalal Al-e Ahmad (1962) proposed a return to the Self against what he defined as Westoxication (*gharbzadegi*, literally West-struckness). This disillusionment with the West and a need to 'return to roots' was also reflected amongst some of the elite film-makers. Their films departed from the mainstream, commercial *film farsi* genre, which comprised mainly tough-guy movies and low-quality melodramas, and instead tried to reflect this return to the Self through nativism.[11] This trend was referred to as the New Wave Movement. Afterwards, during the anti-Shah protests of the late 1970s, some Islamists who had condemned cinema as supportive of the Shah's westernisation project and US hegemony, burned or demolished 185 cinemas. Khomeini, on the other hand, who had earlier denounced cinema as a Western ideological tool detrimental to Islamic values and the development of the country's youth, now reversed his original position, seeing it as a powerful tool that could be put to the service of the Revolution. In his famous speech at the Behesht-e Zahra cemetery in 1979, he declared:

> Cinema is a modern invention that ought to be used for the sake of educating the people, but as you know, it was used instead to corrupt our youth. It is the misuse of cinema that we are opposed to, a misuse caused by the treacherous policies of our rulers.[12]

Thus, cinema got its stamp of approval within the first day of Khomeini's return to Iran after the Shah's downfall. However, it has arguably been one of the most contentious media in the Islamic Republic, strictly codified and closely monitored by the Ministry of Culture and Islamic Guidance (MCIG) to ensure its compliance with the Islamic Republic's aspirations. The MCIG codes, however, are not the sole factors that control which films make it to the screens. There are many cases of post-Revolutionary films that were banned after a short period despite obtaining screening approval from the authorities. To give a very recent example, even though *The Lizard* (*Marmulak*, Tabrizi, 2004), discussed in more detail in Chapter 3, was never officially banned, the clergy's protests resulted in it being removed from the cinemas only a month after its first screening.

Cinema's Place within Islamic Jurisprudence

Once cinema and religion were no longer opposed territories, some of the traditionalists felt the need to articulate this new relationship within an Islamic discourse. One such attempt was Ayatollah Moravveji's book, *Cinema in the Mirror of Fiqh* (1999).[13] The introduction to the book, by Mohammad Reza Jabbaran, a cleric based in Qom, provides an interesting overview on the necessity of discussing cinema in *fiqh*. Jabbaran states that since Islamic *fiqh*, and particularly the profound and fertile school of Shi'ism, has never been silent or indifferent towards any aspect of human life, it should, therefore, also have a stance about this important phenomenon.[14] The reason for the silence of *fiqh* towards cinema up until this point, he continues, was that this industry and the art of acting throughout the world, including in pre-Revolution Iran, was contaminated by 'forbidden acts'. Even though Jabbaran does not immediately elaborate on what exactly constitutes forbidden acts, it is obvious to the Iranian reader that he is referring to the *film farsi* genre of pre-Revolutionary films that depicted scantly-dressed women with scenes of singing, dancing and sometimes erotic images. Thus, the term 'cinema' suggests vulgar acts undertaken by indecent individuals called actors.[15] He concludes that, at present, even if one did not believe in the necessity of cinema and actors in society, the industry has already imposed itself upon people's lives. Post-Revolutionary Iran, however, he continues, has proved through the efforts of its artists and film-makers that cinema does not require the inclusion of forbidden acts.

Cinema in the Mirror of Fiqh is divided into various topics ranging from lying, backbiting and men and women mingling together, to playing the roles of the Prophet and the imams, and cross-dressing. Moravveji begins by stating that the book is about the position of the Muslim believers and Muslim artists regarding cinema.[16] His analysis, however, does not directly deal with cinema. Instead, it examines various, and occasionally contradictory, hadiths on each of the listed topics. If any of these are verified as prohibited or approved, then by extension the same applies to those topics within film and acting. Therefore, rather than being a discussion of cinema per se, the text is like any other treatise on Islamic jurisprudence.

One of the topics of Moravveji's discussion, for example, is the issue of the indirect gaze. An indirect gaze is defined as looking at a woman through her reflection in a mirror or in water, in a photograph or on the television screen. After examining different hadiths and viewpoints, he concludes that, like the direct gaze, the indirect gaze is forbidden, the only exceptions being photographs, television and film. Thus, if the images in the photographs, television or film are of unknown women, looking at any part of their body is permissible – but only if the gaze is without the intention of pleasure. Moravveji reasons that pictures of unknown women on screen or in photographs are similar to imaginary drawings of unknown women on paper and, therefore, are permitted.

Of course, whilst one Shi'i jurisprudent might decree one way on a topic, another might be of a completely contrary view on the same issue. Thus, Moravveji's statements do not necessarily represent the unanimous opinion of all the Shi'i ulama in Iran. For example, quoting from Ayatollah Azari-Qomi, Mir-Hosseini lists 'Watching bad films, even if the actors are unknown Muslim or even non-Muslim women' as one of the sources of *fisad* or corruption.[17] However, Azari-Qomi does not define what constitutes a bad film, basing his argument on the assumption that everyone knows what a bad film is. In the three kinds of 'looks' that should be avoided under any circumstances, Azari-Qomi mentions films as the third look, which 'leads to chaos (*fetneh*), resulting in a forbidden act, even if it does not involve the intention of pleasure or evil'.[18] By comparing the views of these two jurisprudents on the issue of the gaze in films, we note immediately that the legitimacy of looking at Muslim or non-Muslim women, whether known or unknown, with or without the intention of pleasure, differs according to each of these ulama. Whilst Moravveji deems that looking at images of unknown women on screen without the intention of pleasure is permitted, Azari-Qomi adjudges it as forbidden.

Interestingly, even though these discussions are rooted in *fiqh,* they are not too far removed from current Western theories, such as feminist film theory. According to psychoanalytic discourses in the study of film, for example, one of the pleasures offered by cinema is scopophilia (pleasure in looking): 'In a world ordered by sexual imbalance', this pleasure is 'split between active/male and passive/female' and the 'determining male gaze projects its fantasy onto the female figure, which is styled accordingly'.[19] Thus, in both feminist film theory and *fiqh*, one of the main criticisms against including the female body in film is the fact that it is usually constructed to satisfy the male gaze and pleasure.

Considering that Moravveji's treatise on cinema and *fiqh* was published two decades after the Revolution, it might strike us as surprising that Moravveji goes to such great lengths solely to approve an already permitted practice. Moreover, from very early on in his text, he makes it clear that he is addressing Iranian audiences. In any case, cinemas already operate throughout the country and Iranians know that film-making is an acceptable profession if practised within the set rules. Thus, Moravveji's assertion that 'Filmmaking and acting by themselves do not necessitate any forbidden act, and as long as they do not include any forbidden intentions and actions, they are unproblematic',[20] might appear a foregone conclusion stated only too obviously. However, his detailed examination of the Qur'anic verses and hadith can be read in a different light – as an exercise that goes beyond simply attempting to decree cinema as a permitted industry.

For many decades the clergy had strongly condemned cinema and decreed it *haram*. Treatises such as Moravveji's provide the space to employ the same religious vocabulary to justify the acceptance of a formerly forbidden activity. Thus, contrary to the common view, *fiqh* is not always a closed corpus. Rather, it can be a resource that allows for a flexible interpretation of the divine law in order to incorporate new circumstances within the life of the believer. Mir-Hosseini explains Ayatollah Azari-Qomi's contradictory views on gender issues by his wish to 'keep the old interpretations and yet have women participate in political life'.[21] Moravveji's writings can also similarly be seen as an attempt to marry the traditional theoretical positions to the laws of the state as well as to current social practices.

Cinema has been one of the most controversial media in Iran. As a Western product imported into a Muslim society, it aroused many a debate regarding its place within society and a Muslim's life. The Islamic Republic's acceptance of cinema did not end these debates. However, the subject of the discussion did diverge from the initial arguments of the acceptability of the medium to focusing on the content of the films. Cinema, therefore, did manage to obtain religious approval and sanction. Provided that it followed the rules set by the Islamic Republic's code of practice, it was an acceptable form of entertainment and/or an educational tool in society. However, cinema's ability to engage seriously with religion and to join in the debates within the country on religion and spirituality remained an important arena in which scholars, intellectuals and traditionalists continue to debate.

The Paradox of Cinema as a 'Technological Art'

Before the introduction of the Spiritual Cinema category at FIFF, scholarship on the treatment of religion and spirituality in Iranian cinema was scarce. Indeed, it consisted primarily of discussions about the early attempts of the Islamic Revolution to create an 'Islamic Cinema' and their subsequent failure, rather than the examination of this medium in its encounter with religion and spirituality. Of the few early studies of the treatment of religion and spirituality in film there are only two serious works, written by authors with diametrically opposed perspectives. Interestingly, however, they both employed the same analytical tools in their arguments. One is Mohammad Maddadpur, from the centre of Islamic Republic of Iran's Islamist ideology and the other is Hamid Dabashi, from an adamant secularist stance in opposition to the Islamic Republic. Both Maddadpur (1997) and Dabashi (2002) base their arguments on Heidegger's theory of technology. Among more recent works, authors such as Mir-Ehsan (2005) also employ Heidegger's philosophy in their analysis of the treatment of religion and spirituality in film. These authors' heavy reliance on Heidegger's framework in fact reflects the fascination of a generation of Iranian intellectuals with Heideggerian thought.

The influence of Heidegger amongst Iranian intellectuals goes back to Ahmad Fardid (1912–1994). Fardid introduced Heidegger to Iranian intellectuals throughout the 60s, 70s and even the 80s. These intellectuals, who comprised the country's leading philosophers, translators and social thinkers, 'used to deliberate on oriental and occidental philosophical questions'.[22] It was through Heidegger that they sought to understand and provide a philosophical understanding of their disenchantment with modernity and its rapid implementation through the Pahlavi Shahs' modernising projects. Fardid, it appeared, had taken upon himself 'the task of introducing Heidegger's antimodern philosophy into the intellectual circles in Iran'.[23] Boroujerdi elaborates that the Iranian intellectuals' appeal to Heidegger's ideas and his like 'should not be compared as counter intuitive'. Rather, it was 'through the eyes of this latter group that the Iranian intellectuals castigate[d] the West and the age of modernity'.[24] By drawing an analogy between nativism and 'orientalism proper', Boroujerdi states:

> The fondness of many Iranian intellectuals for Heideggerian thought emanated from this yearning for wholeness. These intellectuals could easily relate to Heidegger's redolent romanticism and daring antimodernism because they themselves were affronted by and contemptuous of the modern age.[25]

It is within this context that one can examine Dabashi, Maddadpur and Mir-Ehsan's fascination with Heidegger's philosophy in discussing the question of religion and spirituality in Iranian cinema.

Incongruity of Technology and Art

In *Seyr va suluk-e sinamayi (Cinematic Spiritual Journey*, 1997), Maddadpur attempts to locate cinema's position within the discourse of religion, spirituality and technology.[26] Maddadpur (1955–2005) held a doctorate in the Philosophy of Art from the University of Heidelberg and was a student in Fardid's circle. He held various academic positions in Iran, including Head of Religious Research of Islamic Arts and Culture of the Islamic Development Organisation. According to Maddadpur, cinema is an intrinsically Western art whose origins differentiate it from all other forms of art such as painting, music, architecture or poetry. Whilst the latter originated independently from within various civilisations and cultures, cinema was essentially a Western art imported into other countries; it is, in fact, a manifestation of the 'technique system'. As a technological product, cinema is rooted in modern Western thought and philosophy, inherent in which is a reductionist view of religion. Consequently, it would be impossible for cinema to depict any religious truth.[27]

Maddadpur examines the incongruities between cinema and religion from various angles. These may be summarised as follows: First, religious narrations and themes possess an otherworldly truth that is discordant with the technical and this-worldly aspect of cinema.[28] Cinema, therefore, can only address the worldly side of human beings, which is carnal, nervous and erotic. Thus, transforming religious narratives and themes into films erodes their divine, sacred and profound characteristics, leaving them as mere entertainment. Secondly, a film-maker with an impious soul preoccupied with this-worldly life cannot transcend to other-worldly status. In fact, individuals looking for perfection do not engage in cinematic representation and consequently become prisoners of the snare of imagination and illusion by giving to it their hearts and souls, and forgetting the truth about themselves.[29] Finally, it is impossible to have an Islamic Cinema, for cinema can be only as Islamic as a camera or machine can be Islamic.[30]

Indeed, Maddadpur employs Heidegger's ideas on technology to refute the notion of cinema as a true art. He parallels cinematic technique with Heidegger's definition of *techne*. According to Heidegger, the word 'technology'

> stems from the Greek. *Technikon* means that which belongs to *techne*. We must observe two things with respect to the meaning of this word. One is that *techne* is the name not only for the activities and skills of the craftsman but also for the arts of the mind and the fine arts. *Techne* belongs to bringing-forth, to *poiesis*, it is something poetic. The other thing that we should observe with regard to *techne* is even more important. From earliest times until Plato the word *techne* is linked with the word *episteme*. Both words are terms for knowing in the widest sense. They mean to be entirely at home in something to understand and be expert in it. Such knowing provides an opening up. As an opening up it is a revealing.[31]

According to Maddadpur, true art is a way of truth gained through the unveiling of the physical world. The 'unveiling' that Maddadpur refers to is in fact derived from Heidegger's definition of *techne*. Heidegger states that 'what is decisive in *techne* does not at all lie in making and manipulating, nor in the using of the means, but rather in the revealing, not manufacturing, that *techne* is bringing-forth'.[32] True art, Maddadpur argues, is achieved through the 'greater' or 'lesser' struggle (*jihad-e akbar* and *jihad-e asghar*), the inner struggle and outer struggle respectively.[33] In Islamic theology the *jihad-e akbar*, or 'greater struggle', is against one's ego, and the *jihad-e asghar*, or 'lesser struggle', is against unbelievers. Maddadpur asserts that if film-makers try to impose themselves on the cinematic technique, this will result in chaos ruling over the film.[34] Interestingly, he ranks Iranian film critics and film-makers much lower than their Western equivalents by stating that:

> The Western sciences and philosophy such as that of [Neil] Postman[35] and [Marshall] McLuhan have arrived at a kind of

self-awareness ... However, this experience even in its lower form is rarely seen amongst our intellectuals and their cinema is also suffering from this chaos.[36]

Having explored the incongruence between religion and cinema in general, Maddadpur turns to Iranian cinema in particular, which he refers to as a 'Westoxicated Eastern art',[37] and situates within the larger history of Iran. He draws parallels between Reza Shah's modernising projects and the pioneers of cinema in Iran. He asserts that the first two founders of cinema in Iran – Sepanta, a Zoroastrian, and Ohanians, a Christian – were pursuing the modernising project in the same way as Reza Shah. Indeed, their eagerness to do so far exceeded that of Reza Shah, evident in the fact that they anticipated him in introducing the unveiling of women.[38] This is most likely a reference to the first Iranian film *Abi and Rabi* (*Abi va Rabi*, Ohanian, 1930), which was made before Reza Shah's forced unveiling of women in 1936.

Post-Revolution cinema does not fare any better in Maddadpur's estimation. He argues that while cinema during the Pahlavi period was based mostly on 'erotic images', after the Revolution it drew from the heritage of so-called abstract art. Although he does not give any examples to support this claim, he goes on to assert that this was only an imitation of Western artists such as Gauguin or Kandinsky. For Maddadpur, trying to force religious forms onto Western art was a fruitless effort. When faced with egoistic art, Maddadpur continues, Iranian artists, who lack the real spiritual journey, feel compelled to imitate Western artists. Thus, they resort to poets such as Rumi, Hafez, 'Attar, and/or the Sufi paths in order to conceal this void, in the same fashion that Gauguin resorted to Eastern and African art without having attained real imagination or presence. Maddadpur then concludes that the present avant-garde Iranian cinema, with its semi-religious mysticism and complete lack of a spiritual journey, has in fact replaced the 'roguery' (*lutigari*) and eroticism of pre-Revolutionary cinema.[39]

Having refuted the notion of cinema as true art, rejected the possibility of exploring religion and spirituality in film, and repudiated the works of Iranian film-makers who attempt to do so, Maddadpur does, surprisingly, allow some hope for the future of Iranian cinema. He appears to accept one film-maker as having attained true art: Morteza Avini, the war-documentary film-maker who filmed the Iranian frontlines during the Iran-Iraq war. His programmes, according to Maddadpur, were the way of the Illuminationist (*shive-ye ishraqi*),[40] and of the proximity to the holy truth, for the veil of technique and technology were torn apart and the truth disclosed.[41] However, we are left to merely accept this view without further explanation of precisely how Avini's way was that of the Illuminationist or if, by proximity to the holy truth, he is referring to Avini's presence in the battlegrounds of the war. In fact, it is clear that he is borrowing Heidegger's terms to state the disclosure of truth. Heidegger asserts that *techne* is 'a dimension of truth (*aletheia*): unconcealment, unhiddeness, disclosedness. *Techne* reveals in advance what does not yet show itself and thus does not stand forth'.[42] Maddadpur ultimately concedes that, although so far no one other than Avini has managed to achieve true art, Iranian cinema today is somehow beginning the long road to finding a way out of its Westoxicated orbit.

Poetry through Technology

In a much shorter work, Dabashi, like Maddadpur, finds Heideggerian theories relevant to the discussion of arts and technology in Iran. Although, like Maddadpur, Dabashi (b. 1951) is also educated in the West (he received a dual Ph.D. in the Sociology of Culture and Islamic Studies from the University of Pennsylvania), he is, however, an emphatic opponent of the Islamic Republic and an anti-war activist. He has held various academic positions in the United States and authored numerous books and articles on a range of topics relating to Iran. In Dabashi's view, the state of art in Iran can be explained with a slight modification of the Eurocentric definition of the crisis of technological modernity.[43] Colonialism, he states, is the essence of technology and as Heidegger had mentioned, the confrontation with technology is only possible in the realm of art. Like all other colonised territories standing at the peripheries of technological modernity, for Iran too, technology is mysterious and doubly problematic. Not only are these territories at the mercy of the technological, but also, it is the colonisers riding these technologies.[44] However, in a colonial site such as Iran,[45] it is not the traditional that responds to technology but an ideological resistance, namely Islamism. Ironically, Islamism itself is a political and ideological resistance to colonialism and, therefore, a colonial product rooted in it.[46] Thus, 'Islamic art, the perturbed spirit of our moral resistance to colonial subjection, is nothing but a further Islamization of ideological resistance to colonialism as the extended arm of Technological Modernity'.[47]

Mohsen Makhmalbaf's films become Dabashi's field for exploring both the site of ideological resistance to colonialism and the artistic endeavour to find a saving power. Dabashi draws from Makhmalbaf's interesting and varied background as a Muslim ideologue turned artist, to draw parallels with Heideggerian thought and, therefore, demonstrate its relevance to Iranian cinema. In his view, Makhmalbaf's generation[48] was interested neither in the Islam conducive to Pahlavi rule, nor in the 'Orientalist production of subjectivity on behalf of colonialism'.[49] Instead, this generation resorted to Islamic art as a resistance against Capitalist Modernity. In a period lacking a theory on the nature of an Islamic art, Makhmalbaf sought to create one through which he could reflect the truth and philosophy of Islam. His early cinematic career, which began soon after the Revolution, was entirely committed to the ideas of the Islamic Revolution. However, 'when a post/colonial subject, the Muslim ideologue turns into an artist, initially he cannot do anything but further cultivate the site of resistance to colonialism in what he now considers to be "artistic" terms'.[50]

However, Makhmalbaf's films move from a 'quintessentially colonial nature' in resistance against colonialism to that of 'systematically exorcizing his ideological demons'.[51] Thus, according to Dabashi, from the films, and the danger in which Makhmalbaf and his nation were living, emerged the 'saving power' as a therapeutic antidote. Once again Dabashi employs Heidegger's view that 'The closer we come to the danger, the more brightly do the ways into the saving power begin to shine'.[52] Thus, according to Dabashi, the saving power in Makhmalbaf's work lies in the transformation of the site of resistance from the merely political to the poetic.[53] Whilst cinematic mysticism is a universal trap into which many accomplished film-makers such as Dariush Mehrjui or Stanley Kubrick have fallen, Makhmalbaf's achievement was to recover from it.[54] Dabashi concludes that 'Makhmalbaf is a spectacular example of relentless honesty, with the real literally pulling the artist out of the mystifying misery of casting a metaphysical gaze on an already brutalized world'.[55]

Both Maddadpur and Dabashi have employed the technological framework of Heidegger to discuss the treatment of religion and spirituality in cinema. Both have dismissed the efforts of most film-makers who have attempted to deal with religion and spirituality through film, leaving little room for films that qualify as engaging with religion and spirituality. However, putting Heideggerian thought in the service of discussions on religion and spirituality in film still continues. In the first series of the

Farabi Cinema Foundation's publications on Spiritual Cinema in 2005, the only Iranian work was Mir-Ehsan's *Padidar va ma'na dar sinama-ye Iran (Phenomenon and Meaning in Iranian Cinema)*.[56] Mir-Ehsan also sets out to discuss film and spirituality within a Heideggerian framework of modernity and the technological imagination that dominates the modern world. An academic, literary critic and documentary film-maker based in Iran, Mir-Ehsan is also familiar with Fardid's ideas – as evidenced by his writings – and it is, therefore, not surprising that he, too, employs Heideggerian ideas in his analysis and definition of Spiritual Cinema.

In doing so, Mir-Ehsan aims to demonstrate the possibility of overcoming the limits of technology within cinema. He argues that cinema is the most essential mirror of modern technology. Heidegger, he suggests, overcomes the separation of the physical and metaphysical worlds proposed throughout the history of Western philosophy. The idea of the disunion of these two worlds is rooted in Greek philosophy. However, when cinema as a technological art turns to a poetic understanding, it overcomes this disjunction. Thus, even though the image might appear harrowing and a serious impediment at first, in fact, it can call us from the Essence.[57]

The poetic approach is thus contrasted with the scientific approach. The scientific approach, Mir-Ehsan argues, begins with itself and ends within itself without extending beyond the senses. The Heideggerian method of the poetic approach will liberate cinema from the cul-de-sac created by the scientific approach. By employing the Heideggerian approach we can, he asserts, have a cinema that asks contemplative and fundamental questions about existence. Cinema as a technological art can therefore have a non-technological essence and remain faithful to the origins of the art. Through cinema, art can overcome technology and therefore lead us on a spiritual journey.[58] It is not just any film-maker, however, who attains this. Rather, it is only an artist who has experienced the Hidden with all his soul and follows the Sacred Command, who can establish the compound semiotics through the images. These images can then represent that desire of being called by the Hidden and asking questions from the Hidden.[59] Mir-Ehsan proceeds to clarify his position regarding cinema, modernity and spirituality in his later works, which I will discuss shortly. Here, however, it sufficed to examine only his employment of Heidegger in the question of religion and spirituality in film.

It is clear that all of the initial attempts of Iranian film critics and scholars to understand cinema as a vehicle for discussing religion and spirituality have relied heavily on Heidegger. More importantly, Heidegger's philosophy is employed in contradictory approaches, to refute (Maddadpur) as well as support (Dabashi, Mir-Ehsan) the notion that cinema is able to seriously engage with religion, spirituality, the metaphysical world or the Sacred. However, in all these cases, it is Heidegger's theory of the '*aletheia*: unconcealment, unhiddenness, disclosedness' that allows for the possibility of cinema's treatment of religion and spirituality. Where these scholars remain divided is on the process and the particular films or film-makers by which cinema is able to achieve this '*aletheia*'.

Limiting the study of religion and spirituality in film to the Heideggerian approach, however, does little justice to the multiple possibilities that the medium offers. Recently, the Farabi Cinema Foundation has attempted to articulate definitions and characteristics of spiritual and religious films through other approaches, which I will discuss next.

Cinema as a Domain for Religious and Spiritual Discourse[60]

In 2005, the Farabi Cinema Foundation set up the Spiritual Cinema Centre and introduced 'Spiritual Cinema' as a category in the Fajr International Film Festival. This represented a clear seal of approval on cinema's ability to deal with religion and spirituality. The festival's inclusion of this new category was also followed by a wave of discussions on the subject in the press, which variously debated, welcomed or rejected this new approach to films. The Spiritual Cinema Centre also published and translated many books on the topic in order to clarify and justify the relevance of this newly-introduced category, and by its second year it appeared to have a clearer idea of its aims and purposes. By then, the arguments were no longer as much about cinema's ability to engage with religion and spirituality; rather they focused on what constitutes a religious cinema, and more particularly, 'spiritual cinema'.

The Official Definitions

As mentioned early on in this chapter, Alireza Rezadad's attempts to define Spiritual Cinema in the first issue of the 2005 *Jashnvareh* daily newsletter did not end disputes among the critics. They continued to debate the appropriateness of the term *sinama-ye ma'nagara*, and pointed to its ambiguity. The publications of Farabi's Spiritual Cinema Centre were in turn an attempt to clarify these ambiguities. More importantly, these works forced Farabi to articulate, not only to the critics but also to themselves, a clearer definition of Spiritual Cinema and its characteristics. This was achieved mainly through Iranian works, some of which will be discussed below, rather than Western sources in translation. Although these translated works provided an interesting introduction to the field, they obviously focused largely on Western films, with references to Christianity and Judaism. More importantly, of course, these works did not originate in response to the creation of a category within a national film industry. Instead, they explored the religious or spiritual in films much more broadly. The Iranian case was different.

Before Farabi could even begin to explore the religious and spiritual in films, it had to define what it meant by *sinama-ye ma'nagara*. Clearly, this task could not be achieved by relying solely on external sources. Indeed, there was an indisputable need for an Iranian articulation that drew upon the complex social, cultural and religious system of the country.

The English section of the official website of the Farabi Cinema Foundation defines Spiritual Cinema as one that:

> considers the current realities of mankind life in reference to its esotericism. This means that this cinema tries to find its path from 'image to meaning', 'exterior to interior', 'substance to spirit' and 'presence to absence'. And as the meaning of existence tends to go towards completion, the Spiritual Cinema pays attention to the mysterious reality of existence through tending towards completion. Thus we can say the nature and essence of the stable values of mankind, accepted by worldwide civilizations, is the main subject of Spiritual Cinema... the satanic aspects and obstacles of human exaltation are reviewed in this cinema as well. ... Paying attention to the enigmas and mysteries of existence and mankind life in the Spiritual Cinema does not necessarily lead to solving the mysteries because the mysteries of existence cannot be solved easily and thus indicating and pointing out the current mysteries of mankind life and the daily realities of the world are actually attending to the inner and spiritual meaning of the world.[61]

This short introduction is followed by a list of the aims and activities of the Spiritual Cinema Centre. Farabi's publications, however, provide a more varied and detailed analysis of the topic. Numerous authors approach *ma'nagara* cinema from different angles, often offering opposing views and definitions. The remainder of this chapter presents these articulations of the authorities with regard to *ma'nagara* cinema. These discussions include the views of Abdollah Esfandiyari, head of the Spiritual Cinema Centre at the Farabi Cinema Foundation; Hasan Bolkhari,[62] Cultural Consultant to the Minister of Education who also headed the jury of the *ma'nagara* cinema entries at the 10th Tehran International Short Film Festival; as well as more recent writings of the film and literary critic Mir Ahmad Mir-Ehsan, whose first work on this topic was discussed earlier.

Sinama-ye ma'nagara was criticised as an inappropriate term immediately after the announcement of the new category. '*Ma'na*' in Persian means 'meaning' and so the term *ma'nagara* implied that films outside this category were meaningless. The authorities were, therefore, immediately faced with the need to justify the choice of the term. In his attempt to do so, Bolkhari compares *ma'nagara* films with other meaningful films. He states that 'some films have meaning but there are yet others which are seekers and, therefore, are possessors of meaning'.[63] Accordingly, it is this second group of films that are *ma'nagara*.

Esfandiyari states that it was Mohammad Mehdi Heydariyan, the Deputy Minister of Culture and Islamic Guidance, who first suggested the notion of *ma'nagara* cinema. Esfandiyari then explains the problems of finding a suitable term for this cinema and their concern that inappropriate and limiting terms such as 'religious' (*sinama-ye dini*), 'mystical' (*sinama-ye 'irfani*), or 'intellectual' (*sinama-ye andishe*) would be (and, indeed, still are) attributed to these films.[64] '*Rowhani*', another term for 'spiritual', which is also an honorific reference to the clergy, was another alternative. Esfandiyari admits that this was the closest term to the notion they had in mind, since it encompassed films that were about both this world and the other, body and soul, form and meaning as well as transcendence and harmony with religion and religious aims. However, it was not felt to be comprehensive enough and might have excluded parts of transcendental or intellectual cinema.[65]

Even though all of Farabi's English literature referred to 'Spiritual Cinema' as the equivalent for *sinama-ye ma'nagara*, it was not regarded as the best translation. According to Esfandiyari, although 'spiritual' is the closest translation of '*ma'nagara*', *ma'nagara* is more than just spiritual.[66] However, as evident from the discussions below, this objection is based on a very narrow definition of the English word 'spiritual'. Bolkhari states that 'spiritual' refers only to 'ghosts' and 'the afterworld', and is only used when the human soul leaves the body. It is, therefore, a term that refers to the time of death. However, in 'Iranian-Islamic thought', the term '*ma'na*' has a far deeper and wider meaning than soul, ghost or death. In this worldview, '*ma'na*' is not the equivalent of death, but rather its opposite – for '*ma'na*' is life itself, and the truth that human beings seek in their struggle for perfection during their lifetime. In this sense, the English translation 'Spiritual Cinema' reduces *ma'na* to death and is, therefore, inappropriate.[67] *Ma'na*, however, Bolkhari continues, is one of the key concepts of Islamic, Eastern and humanistic wisdom. Bolkhari then locates the term within the thought of Iranian philosophers: In the philosophy of the twelfth-century Sohravardi, founder of the School of Illumination – one of the most important schools in Islamic philosophy – *ma'na* is a degree of light. According to Mulla Sadra, the seventeenth-century philosopher, *ma'na* is one of the degrees of existence. In the works of the thirteenth-century philosopher and poet, Rumi, *ma'na* is the opposite of form and image. Bolkhari then concludes that *ma'na* is a profound term and that the term *sinama-ye ma'nagara* is one that invites its viewer to think.[68] Bolkhari's approach to the English term 'spiritual' remains narrow and while he provides a broad as well as in-depth analysis of the word '*ma'na*', when it comes to cinema he still appears to confuse it with the very specific popular concept of 'spiritual', with references to ghosts and the afterworld.

Bolkhari also argues that *ma'nagara* cinema is a production not solely of the film-maker but also of the audience. He states that it is the auteur film-makers and the *ma'na*–seeking audiences who make *ma'nagara* cinema. *Ma'nagara* cinema is, therefore, not a movement that can be produced or given a specific direction; rather, it is a cinema that only cinema itself creates, not the people in the industry nor the authorities of a state.[69]

According to Esfandiyari, *ma'nagara* cinema deals with the reality of the world and man, whilst referring to their esoteric aspects. *Ma'nagara* cinema seeks the secrets that exist behind these realities. It deals with the mysteries of the world without necessarily trying to resolve them, instead referring to these enigmas and the signs surrounding them. It, therefore, strives to advance from the attributes of a phenomenon to its essence, from form to meaning, from exoteric to esoteric, from outer to inner, from material to essence, from body to soul and from obvious to hidden. Consequently, *ma'nagara* cinema does not dissociate any of these binary sides of the real world from each other.[70]

The official definition broadens the domain of *ma'nagara* cinema to include popular films. Bolkhari refers to *Pinocchio* (Benigni, 2002) as an example of a *ma'nagara* film that demonstrates how seeking a life of pure pleasure leads to the life of an absolute ignoramus or donkey. The film, in fact, invites us to reflect upon the real meaning of life.[71] Esfandiyari states that *ma'nagara* cinema is not a 'genre' or 'type' of cinema, but a contextual phenomenon that can occur in any kind of cinema.[72] He lists twelve topics that provide the context for *ma'nagara* cinema, but without entering into an analysis of how they constitute *ma'nagara* cinema. It remains unclear, therefore, whether the inclusion of any one of these topics would be necessary and sufficient to interpret a film as *ma'nagara*. In some instances, Esfandiyari briefly compares their filmic references to Qur'anic verses and hadith. Here are the topics he lists, with just some of the examples he provides:[73]

1) The soul, such as *Ghost* (Zucker, 1990), *Flatliners* (Schumacher, 1990)
2) The hereafter, such as *What Dreams May Come* (Ward, 1998)
3) The mind and eyes, such as *The Sixth Sense* (Shyamalan, 1999), *A Beautiful Mind* (Howard, 2001)
4) Unusual human power, such as *Carrie* (Carson, 2002)
5) Healing powers, such as *Indigo* (Simon, 2003)
6) Discovery and grace (those with the powers of knowing and seeing), such as *Final Destination* (Wong, 2000)
7) Dreams and nightmares, such as *Leyli is with Me* (Tabrizi, 1996)
8) Miracles and divine grace, such as *O Brother, Where Art Thou?* (Coen brothers, 2000), *The Ten Commandments* (DeMille, 1956), *Ben-Hur* (Wyler, 1959) and *The Passion of the Christ* (Gibson, 2004)
9) Satan and angels, such as *Wings of Desire* (Wenders, 1987)
10) *Jinn*, such as *The Exorcist* (Friedkin, 1973)
11) Lyrical and intuitive, such as films by Tarkovsky and Kiarostami
12) Relationship with the dead, such as *Dragonfly* (Shadyac, 2002) and *White Noise* (Sax, 2006).

Similarly, Mir-Ehsan asserts that *ma'nagara* cinema can be found in both intellectual art films and popular films. More interestingly, he explores spirituality in the often-condemned *film farsi* genre of pre-Revolutionary Iranian cinema. According to him, the populist *film farsi*, despite erotic scenes and song and dance sequences, *did* support the traditional and ethical values of faithfulness, integrity and belief in *halal* and *haram* (the permissible and forbidden), all of which are rooted in religion.[74] As discussed earlier, Maddadpur condemned early Iranian film-makers, including Ohanian, as pioneers of the Westernisation and modernisation project in Iran. Mir-Ehsan, however, hails Ohanian's *Haji Aqa, the Cinema Actor* (*Haji Aqa, actor-e sinama*, 1932) as the best and most intelligent film on the opposition between tradition and modernity. He reads the film within the framework of the Heideggerian approach to modernity and spirituality, arguing that it demonstrates the coexistence of the two. Modernity has continuously defended its spiritual values and meanings, even as they differ from the traditional world. *Haji Aqa*, he argues, displays the new spirituality in modernity and shows that not everything that is new is unethical.[75]

As seen from the examples provided by Esfandiyari and Mir-Ehsan's inclusion of the ethical and traditional values in reading religion and spirituality in films, these discourses parallel a category within Western scholarship, discussed in the Introduction, namely the theological approach to the study of religion and spirituality in film.

The Film Critic's Approach

There were various responses to the *ma'nagara* category amongst film critics. Some endorsed the Farabi approach, others were less convinced. Let us first turn to the discussions which looked upon the *ma'nagara* category. Like Bolkhari, mentioned above, Abolfazl Horri and Chista Yathribi both emphasise the role of the audience in *ma'nagara* films. Horri, a Qur'anic researcher and film critic, states that it is the audience who reads a film as spiritual or religious.[76] The viewer's engagement with *ma'nagara* film can thus become a religious experience. Indeed, the film can act as a medium between the audience and the sacred. If this is achieved, it is as though the viewer has participated in a religious ritual.[77] Similarly, Yathribi, a film critic, editor and university lecturer, argues that *ma'nagara* films are dependent on the viewers; how they read a *ma'nagara* film depends on how their consciousness encounters it.[78] She also asserts that, like worship, the experience of watching a *ma'nagara* film should recreate the experience of inner wisdom and faith. Furthermore, Muslims believe that it is important to picture the infinite and immortal essence of God in a mortal framework. Thus, the outward form of the sacred is represented in ritual ceremonies, images and buildings. The inner form, however, is esoteric, and lives in every creature and should never be illustrated. Eastern religious cinema does not illustrate the essence of the Sacred, the prophets or the imams. Instead, it provides us with an illustration to imagine their glory in different affairs.[79] However, Yathribi fails to elaborate what exactly constitutes 'the outer form', 'the inner form', 'the essence of the Sacred' and 'imagining the glory' in cinema.

The distinction between spiritual (*ma'nagara*) and religious films remains uncertain. Whilst the authorities were adamant that *ma'nagara* films were not religious films,[80] some critics seem to have conflated the two into one category. Yathribi begins her discussion by using the terms *ma'nagara* and *dini* (religious) interchangeably, but finally settles on *dini*. She contrasts what she calls Eastern and Western religious films, and lists a series of differences between them. Western religious cinema, such as the works of Ingmar Bergman, attempt to find answers to man's despair and search for meaning. Eastern religious cinema, on the other hand, is not about man's quest for hope or faith, because he already possesses it. Rather, this cinema expresses his understanding of the world and his worshipful attitude. Western religious cinema, like the Existentialist philosophers, states Yathribi, expresses fear and anxiety. It approaches contemporary human circumstances with an apocalyptic gaze. The films are, therefore, a search for a glimmer of love, faith and the salvation of the soul. Eastern religious films she says, however, look at the world with love and without any Existentialist anxiety. Western religious films have a specific time and space whereas their Eastern counterparts do not belong to any real time or space and are, in fact, beyond both. Western film-makers, Yathribi continues, use everything in their films for practical reasons alone and not for aesthetics. Eastern film-makers, such as Iranian film-makers, Kobayashi (Japan), Satyajit Ray, Vijaya Mehta, Shaji N. Karun (India), Parajanov and Tarkovsky (Russia) turn every ordinary and living thing into religious signs and creations. In addition, Yathribi states, Western religious cinema separates art from life, thus the films have a direct missionary approach and are propagandist, such as *The Ten Commandments* (DeMille, 1956) and *Moses the Lawgiver* (de Bosio, 1974). Eastern religious cinema, by contrast, depicts the life and customs of ordinary people and their rituals. Yathribi states that this cinema does not necessarily have apparent religious symbols, figures or epics, but nonetheless, without referring to religious issues, reflects the primacy of the spiritual world over the material world. Thus, in the works of Tarkovsky and Bergman, she continues, there is a fresh approach to the depiction of faith, salvation and forgiveness. The subject of Western religious cinema is man's relationship with God and his creation from beginning to eternity. The subject of Eastern religious cinema, on the other hand, is people's relationships with each other in a world that is constantly observed by God.[81]

Yathribi's list of comparisons, however, does not provide a better understanding of *ma'nagara* cinema or, in fact, the differences between Eastern and Western religious films. Her arguments are instead sweeping generalisations about each of these categories, and her selection of examples of films or film-makers is often inconsistent. Ingmar Bergman, for instance, is initially categorised as a Western film-maker, only to move into the Eastern category a little later, where he fits better within the framework of that particular discussion. Moreover, she draws a narrower boundary around Western religious films, confining them to the depiction of explicitly religious themes, such as religious figures or events.[82] The boundaries for the Eastern category, however, are wider, more fluid and include all films that 'reflect the primacy of the spiritual world over the material world'. Moreover, drawing a crude distinction between 'Western' and 'Eastern' religious films does not achieve the complex task of deciding whether a cinema is 'religious' or 'spiritual'. Indeed, the determining factors of 'Western' and 'Eastern' cinema remain unclear in Yathribi's arguments. Is it the nationality of the film-maker, the setting of the film, or the philosophy and worldview that the film endorses, which classifies a film as 'Eastern' or 'Western'? For instance, Tarkovsky's films are consistently used as examples of 'Eastern' religious films. However, his notable works not only were made and set in Europe and in European languages, but also bore significant Christian themes and metaphors. Therefore, one can argue that there are far more 'Western' elements than 'Eastern' in his films.

Defining a certain category of films by dividing world cinema into two loose geographical zones is clearly unproductive. Putting films from India, Japan, Russia and Iran into one homogeneous group, and films from the 'West' into an opposite group, does little to tell us about their different approaches to the treatment of religion. Yet another problem with Yathribi's groupings is that her examples of Western religious cinema are confined to Hollywood films, overlooking cinema in Europe and America (e.g. the works of Lars von Trier and Robert Bresson). Moreover, even though she refers to Hollywood religious films as propagandist, she fails to acknowledge the many 'Eastern' films that follow the same Hollywood conventions, and are by the same token then also 'propagandist'.

However, Yathribi's approach could be loosely compared with Western discourses on film as hierophany, which was discussed in the Introduction.

As seen earlier, Yathribi dismisses the exploration of the spiritual only through explicit religious figures, symbols or epics. Like Bird,[83] she argues for the primacy of the spiritual over the material, and cinema's ability to bring this out without referring to the religious issues. However, Yathribi does not refer to these films as hierophany and her efforts at distinguishing between 'Eastern' and 'Western' films imply the possibility of hierophany only within 'Eastern' films.

Another approach in analysing films as *ma'nagara* is to contextualise them within the sacred texts of the Qur'an and hadith. The film director, scriptwriter and critic Farokh Ansari-Basir, for example, states that *ma'nagara'i* ('*ma'nagara*-ness') is recognising the symbols of the hidden world's effect on the material world.[84] He argues that the following Qur'anic verse will help us understand the roots of this kind of understanding:

> Behold! In the creation of the heavens and the earth; in the alternation of the night and the day; in the sailing of the ships through the ocean for the profit of mankind; in the rain which Allah sends down from the skies, and the life which He gives therewith to an earth that is dead; in the beasts of all kinds that He scatters through the earth; in the change of the winds, and the clouds which they trail like their slaves between the sky and the earth – (Here) indeed are Signs for a people that are wise.[85]

Thus, according to Ansari-Basir, film-makers who know their Qur'an attempt to base the semiotics of their films on the Qur'anic interpretation of the world, for example Tabrizi's *One Piece of Bread* (*Yek tekkeh nan*, 2005). The world of this film is a world with God's direct involvement. Ansari-Basir says that even though there are weaknesses in the selection of some of the symbols in *One Piece of Bread*, the overall result is impressive, for the film succeeds in depicting God's constant presence in the world and His miracles.[86] However, he does not limit the Qur'anic context to Iranian films. In his analysis of Stanley Kubrick's *2001: A Space Odyssey* (1968) and Alejandro Amenábar's *Others* (2001), he locates these Western films within the framework of the Qur'anic worldview. The life cycle of the astronaut in *2001: A Space Odyssey*, he says, does not end with old age and death. Rather, it continues after death into a foetus-like being. He then compares this continuation of life, albeit this time from a far more advanced terminus a quo, to Qur'an 84:19, which states: 'Ye shall surely travel from stage to stage'.[87]

Unlike Yathribi, Ansari-Basir does not divide films into Western or Eastern categories. Rather, he looks at themes in films that can be paralleled with the sacred Islamic texts, and thereby enables the categorisation of these films as *ma'nagara*. As with Esfandiyari and Mir-Ehsan in the previous section, this is similar to the theological approach discussed in the Introduction on Western discourses on religion and spirituality in film. The problem with this approach, however, is that it is almost impossible not to force a certain interpretation onto films that are highly unlikely to have been inspired by the Islamic texts. Ansari-Basir is aware of this and tries to justify his approach:

> I am not saying that these films are indebted to the Holy Books such as the Qur'an. Instead, I want to emphasise that if a film is truly *ma'nagara*, it can be compared to the teachings of the Sacred Books. These Sacred sources should be the yardstick to distinguish between real *ma'nagara* metaphors and those that feign spiritual meanings in the film.[88]

As we have seen, a number of Iranian discourses on religion and spirituality focus on popular Western films. Interestingly, however, the parallels between these foreign films are not drawn with their corresponding Judaeo-Christian tradition, as one might expect, but instead with Qur'anic verses and hadith. Indeed, these comparisons are sometimes even extended to include the ideas of Muslim figures as separated in time as Sohravardi, Rumi and Mulla Sadra. Thus, by reading into such films those concepts that are specific to Islam, the theological approach common within Western studies of religion in film is rendered with an Islamic twist.

The examples above highlight the parallels that can be drawn between the Iranian and Western discourses. Whether or not Iranian critics have consciously borrowed these Western approaches or arrived at them independently is difficult to gauge, particularly because bibliographic references are not often included in their works. By 2006, however, there were over five volumes of these Western studies on religion and spirituality in cinema that were translated into Persian, including titles such as *Finding God in the Movies: 33 Films of Reel Faith* (Barsotti and Johnston, 2004), and *Robert Bresson: A Spiritual Style in Film* (Cunneen, 2003), and sold at the Fajr International Film Festival desks and bookshops.[89] As suggested earlier, one of the main differences between the Iranian and Western discourses, however, was the concern of those Iranian critics whose primary focus was on the congruity and relevance of the medium of cinema with Muslim Iranian society; this concern did not arise in Western discourses. In any case, it is clear that one cannot easily dismiss these Western studies as irrelevant to the Iranian context. But what the Iranian approaches focus on is drawing out the relevance to their own context, mapping connections between the films they study and ideas that are Islamic, and particularly Shi'i.

Opponents of 'Ma'nagara'

Not all critics, however, endorsed the Farabi definitions of *ma'nagara* cinema and many remained unconvinced by the Foundation's reasoning. In an interview with *Mehr News* on 18 February 2006, Javad Shamaqdari, art advisor to the President, stated that 80 per cent of all the Iranian films that participated in the 24th FIFF did not conform to the political ideas of President Ahmadinejad's government. The fact that a significant number of them depicted the breakdown of family life and ethical values was, in his view, a conspiracy by outside (i.e. Western) forces, to destroy the local culture from within. Shamaqdari refers to some participating Iranian films as vulgar depictions, without specifying exactly what he means by this. In the same interview, he objects to *ma'nagara* cinema, stating:

> I am opposed to the title of *ma'nagara* proposed by the Farabi Cinema Foundation. Had Iranian cinema ever worked outside the realm of meaning that it intends to do so now? Had [post-Revolution] Iranian cinema ever gone towards vulgarity? Have we ever produced films that had anything but spiritual outlook and values? Overall, I feel that this grouping is not appropriate. Our Revolution was *ma'nagara* and our art and cultural products have also been in line with these values.[90]

He then goes on to argue that since Iran already had religious cinema, there was no need to replace it with *ma'nagara* cinema. When one hears the word 'religious cinema', he says, the audience undoubtedly expects films with divine and spiritual concepts. However, the introduction of the new category of *ma'nagara* has paved the way for various philosophies, ideas and even inappropriate concepts to easily be imported in the name of cinema. He continues that this is, in fact, extremely dangerous.[91]

Nasir Bakideh, the director of the Iranian Young Cinema Society, is another critic of the category of *ma'nagara* cinema. Like most others, he begins by criticising the term '*ma'nagara*' itself. He states that every cinematic work has a specific meaning and value and that these are indivisible. It is wrong to assume that *ma'nagara* films are religious films. For Bakideh, all Iranian films have a particular approach to Iranian and Islamic culture, rich as it is, and with this approach it is possible to create meaningful works. Thus, *ma'nagara* cinema as a separate entity does not really exist.[92]

In all, the creation and general acceptance of the new category of Spiritual Cinema proved far more complicated than the Farabi Cinema Foundation had initially anticipated. The need to articulate a definition of *ma'nagara* cinema opened up interesting debates and resulted in a gamut of theories that included vague classifications, contradictory views and debatable comparisons. Some proponents of the category laid emphasis on the film-maker, others on the audience and yet others on the medium of film itself. Opponents do not fare any better in their argumentations. Their articulations, too, are weak and at times contradictory. Nevertheless, there was a consensus, among both opponents as well as proponents of the *ma'nagara* category, that cinema was indeed a proper domain for religious and spiritual discourse.

Conclusions

The history of cinema in Iran is both colourful and eventful. It has always been entwined with both the religious authorities and the state (whether in its secular or its religious manifestation). Reza Shah, for example, used it as a tool in his modernising project. The clergy and traditionalists, on the other hand, strongly opposed it in the beginning, but ultimately, with Khomeini's blessing, it came to be regarded as an ideal educational tool for society. As such, the Islamic Republic, which merged religious and political powers, was no longer concerned as to whether cinema was acceptable or relevant to Muslim Iranian society. Indeed, Moravveji's treatise on Islamic jurisprudence and cinema was no more than an exercise in aligning the traditional theoretical positions with state laws and contemporary social practices. The question instead was cinema's ability to seriously engage with religion and spirituality. A few, such as Maddadpur, still lingered on what they saw as a contradiction between a Western medium and Islamic religious values. The compatibility of these two, however, was no longer an issue for most. Iranians had embraced the modern Western medium and succeeded in making it their own.

The launch of *sinama-ye ma'nagara* as a new category in the 2005 Fajr International Film Festival and the formal endorsement of 'spiritual' films resulted in heated debates. The various subsequent attempts at defining *ma'nagara* cinema by the Farabi Cinema Foundation, academics, journalists, film-makers and others have so widened its scope of interpretation that it is clear there is no one comprehensive definition and no one approach can do justice to the numerous possibilities of studying religion or spirituality in film. What is significant is the recognition of cinema's legitimate participation in discourses on religion and spirituality and, more importantly, cinema's ability to articulate its own religious or spiritual discourse. This has opened up a new arena that employs a completely modern medium to express religious and spiritual ideas, and an opportunity to retell in a new dimension both the truths of a fifteen-century-old religious tradition as well as the numerous facets of its expression and experiences.

In this regard, prescriptive approaches and checklists of characteristics that would constitute religious or spiritual films are far more limiting than illuminating. Thus, having pointed to the dilemmas facing those who have tried to articulate 'religious' and/or 'spiritual' films, I do not follow suit in an attempt to resolve these dilemmas. In the chapters that follow, I instead intend to explore the various ways in which the Iranian Shi'i discourse – in its various mystical, theological and ritual forms – emerges on the silver screen. These filmic discourses constitute, therefore, a new addition to the rich corpus of Shi'i religious expressions in literature, poetry, art and architecture.

CHAPTER 3

FILMIC DISCOURSES ON THE ROLE OF THE CLERGY IN IRAN*

In some Muslim traditions, a man who has divorced his wife three times can only remarry her after she has married and divorced another man. And only after this second marriage is consummated can the second husband divorce her so that it is permissible for her to remarry her original husband. This second husband is referred to as *muhallil*, literally meaning '"someone who makes a thing legal, legaliser, legitimator", the figure who, in classical Islamic law acts as something like a dummy or a "man of straw", in order to authenticate or make permissible some legal process otherwise of doubtful legality or in fact prohibited'.[1] The title of the *film farsi* comedy, *Mohallel* (*The Legaliser*, Karimi, 1971), is a telling reference to the story of the film, which surrounds the 'triple divorce' of a woman whose ex-husband, Haj Agha, wants to remarry her.

Haj Agha is a jealous husband who holds very strict views on women's modesty and chastity. When he mistakenly assumes that his wife is having an affair he consents, in his rage, to the mullah's suggestion of a triple divorce. However, after all is revealed he regrets his hurried decision and becomes desperate to remarry his now ex-wife. To his utter dismay he finds out the full consequences of a triple divorce and the attendant need of a *muhallil* if he wants his wife back. The ex-husband's efforts at finding a *muhallil* whom he can trust, and his obsession with watching over his wife when she is finally married to this *muhallil*, make for some truly comical scenes in the film.

The film contrasts the Shah's modernised legal system with the traditional one. In the former, the husband is not legally allowed to divorce his wife without first referring to the secular courts, and triple divorce is in any case forbidden by the law. Nonetheless, the cleric, representing the sharia law, pronounces the divorce decree. Consequently, even though the divorce has not been formally registered and Haj Agha is still legally married to his wife, the obligations of the sharia do not allow him to continue their marital relationship, and husband and wife become forbidden to each other. The film depicts the cleric, with his comic appearance and accent, as shortsighted and stubborn. He stresses that the 'the law of God is justice itself'. However, he is at the core of the problems that arise in the film, as he insists on a blind following of what he refers to as the Prophet's tradition, even as it ruins the lives of a happy family. As well as criticising some traditional attitudes such as patriarchy and the ideals of masculinity, the film is a satire on the clergy.

In fact, there have been very few satires on the clergy in the history of Iranian cinema. Until recently in post-Revolutionary Iran, there were only deferential references to the clergy in cinema. Other than leading ritual acts such as prayers, marriages, deaths and sermons, these men of God were removed from the quotidian concerns of ordinary people, and remained largely peripheral to the main characters of the films. This is unsurprising, considering the sensitivity of the topic and the strict codes set down by the Ministry of Culture and Islamic Guidance which, as we saw earlier, bans all films and videos that 'blaspheme against the values and personalities held sacred by Islam and other religions mentioned in the Constitution'.[2]

However, the new millennium saw a resurgence of films with the clergy as their protagonists. These included Mirkarimi's *Under the Moonlight* (*Zir-e nur-e mah,* 2001) and Tabrizi's *The Lizard* (*Marmulak,* 2004), both of which opened to general release in Iran. Reza Mirkarimi, a graduate of graphics from Tehran University, was born in 1966. His initial experiences of film-making were in short films and television series. *Under the Moonlight* was his second feature film, after his debut *The Boy and the Soldier* (*Kudak va sarbaz,* 2000). Most of his films carry a religious theme; his *So Far, So Close* (*Kheyli dur, Kheyli nazdik,* 2005), an entry in the 'Spiritual Cinema' category of the 23rd Fajr International Film Festival, won its Best Film award.

Kamal Tabrizi was born in 1959 and graduated from the Art University in Tehran. After a series of short films and working with the cultural sections of the Islamic Republic of Iran Broadcast Television, he made his first feature film, *The Passage* (*'Obur*), in 1989. Amongst his other works, before the making of *The Lizard,* the comedy *Leyli is with Me* (*Leyli ba man ast,*

FILMIC DISCOURSES ON THE CLERGY 69

Figure 2   Parviz Parastooyi, the lead actor, in *Leyli is with Me* (Kamal Tabrizi, 1995).

1995) was a notable success. A satire on the Iran-Iraq war, *Leyli is with Me* employs the same lead actor as in *The Lizard*, Parviz Parastooyi; he plays a television cameraman who, despite desperate efforts to stay well away from the war zone, finds himself in the frontline and then is inadvertently taken for a hero. Many of Tabrizi's films deal with religious themes, a reflection of his own religious background. His *One Piece of Bread* (*Yek tekkeh nan*, 2005), was a distinct departure from *The Lizard*, with references to the metaphysical world. The screenwriter of this film, Mohammad-Reza Gohari, is the co-screenwriter of Mirkarimi's *So Far, So Close*. *One Piece of Bread* was also entered into the 'Spiritual Cinema' category of the 23rd FIFF, but it was not received well. Some reviewers criticised it as a 'letter of repentance', a film made to appease those he had upset with his earlier film *The Lizard*.[3] During the 2005 presidential elections, Hashemi Rafsanjani, who ultimately lost to Mahmoud Ahmadinejad, employed Tabrizi as his campaign manager. Some Iranians, therefore, sarcastically referred to the campaign film he made for Rafsanjani as *Marmulak II* (*The Lizard II*). More recently, the 2010 Fajr International Film Festival banned the screening of Tabrizi's *Reward* (*Padash*, 2010) for 'not observing the ethical and value systems'. In this context, it is notable that during the

2009 elections, Tabrizi had clearly expressed his support for Mir-Hossein Mousavi, the main challenger to President Ahmadinejad.[4]

Each of the films, *Under the Moonlight* and *The Lizard*, articulates a discourse that differs from previous cinematic representations of the clergy. They not only propose a different engagement of the clergy with the public, but also critically examine the lofty positions they enjoy in society, which in turn serves only to further emphasise their hierarchical relationship with the laity.

This chapter examines the formalistic approach to religion through *Under the Moonlight* and *The Lizard*, and draws parallels with recent discourses on the Iranian clergy. I argue that these filmic narratives provide a space for the articulation of debates on the role of the clergy within society, including some of the more contentious issues that have otherwise been difficult to discuss publicly inside Iran. I also demonstrate how these film-makers have creatively employed the medium of film to actively engage in some of these debates. This chapter, therefore, argues that the films do not merely reflect these debates, but are themselves part of them and of a larger discourse within Iranian society. Whilst the published discourses of intellectuals such as Soroush are regarded as authoritative both within and outside of Iran, these parallel filmic discourses have not yet received such recognition.

This oversight does injustice to the potential of a medium that can often be more effective than its written or oral equivalents, particularly in the context of Iran. First, the metaphorical language of film provides a space for discourses that might otherwise face harsh censorship. Even when films are banned, the film-makers are not usually punished with the severity reserved for authors or lecturers propagating similar ideas through their own media. Moreover, a ban on an Iranian film usually turns it into a highly popular commodity, with considerable demand for pirated copies. Indeed, film-makers are sometimes accused of deliberately stirring up contentious debates around their films in order to ensure high sales upon final release. Secondly, the accessibility of the medium has enabled these films to engage very effectively with a wider audience, even if the level of engagement varies according to the background of each individual.

I begin with a brief review of debates that have questioned the legitimacy of the clergy's power over the laity. I will then critically examine the current role of the clergy through *Under the Moonlight* and *The Lizard* and locate these filmic discourses within the wider discussions propounded by Iranian intellectuals. Finally, I will demonstrate how these films subtly compare not only the institutionalised morals and ideals of society with the ethical values of individuals, but also the relevance of religious injunctions to people's everyday modern life.

Resistance to Monopolising Islam

The clergy's rise to power began with the establishment of the Shi'i Safavid state, which was discussed in Chapter 1. The subsequent history of Shi'i Iran witnessed many events that contributed to this power, reaching a pinnacle during the Islamic Revolution in 1979. By the seventeenth century, the right to the direct collection of religious taxes gave the clergy economic independence. The victory, in the nineteenth century, of the Usulis over the Akhbaris endowed the clergy with the power to act as intermediaries between man and God. The clergy, therefore, became a necessity in the lives of the believers for in the absence of the hidden imam, it was only from amongst the ulama that a source of emulation (*marja'-e taqlid*) could be sought. The believers were thus obliged to follow the religious opinions of their particular source of emulation and so the clergy were placed in a hierarchical position above the laity. When Ayatollah Khomeini introduced the concept of *velayat-e faqih*, or guardianship of the jurist, in 1979, the Constitution of the Islamic Republic named him as the Supreme Leader for Life and entrusted him with the duty to rule.

Another aspect of formal Shi'i expression is the madrasa. These religious centres started off as private educational endeavours in early Islamic history, but gradually developed into wider institutions of learning supported by rulers and other men of power and, therefore, took on a political aspect. In fact, as discussed in Chapter 1, they evolved to become powerful political centres that actively engaged with developments of state and society. Indeed, the Safavids built the Shi'i *madrasa*s to help propagate their new faith. In the twentieth century, madrasas played a crucial role in the Constitutional Revolution of 1906 and in the overthrow of the Pahlavi Shah in 1979. The *ijtihad* (effort to ascertain correct doctrine) practised by Shi'i ulama gives them more flexibility in dealing with contemporary issues. Indeed,

> The craft of the law remains central to religious learning and practice for the Shi'a as much as for the Sunni world. Yet, Shi'i learning seems to have retained more of the philosophical, reflective and

even mystical elements of medieval Islam than its Sunni counterpart, which has been more inclined to legalistic and textual limitations on reflection.[5]

It is this very philosophical and reflective element within Shi'ism that allows for a critical approach to the faith from within. The growth of the clergy's power has not always been accepted without debate, even within clerical and religious circles. Here, I will discuss some contemporary debates on the role of the clergy, before turning to filmic discourses on the topic.

It was not just opponents of the Revolution who criticised the clergy for arrogating to themselves the power to rule. Rather, from very early on, when the notion of a ruling cleric was first introduced there were those within the clergy who disagreed with the idea, maintaining that it was better to leave the running of the state to kings. As Keddie observes,

> many of the disagreements now found amongst scholars in the West concerning the role of the ulama at various times have their roots in the fact that there was almost never a single line followed by all the ulama, and hence it is often possible to quote ulama, even during one period, on several sides of the same issue.[6]

As Hasan Yousefi Eshkevari, a reformist cleric in Iran explains, 'It cannot be said that the clergy collectively are coterminous with the Islamic Republic'.[7]

Difficult as it was to criticise the religious establishment in the political climate of the Islamic Republic, it did not remain unchallenged. For instance, Ayatollah Shariat-Madari was the first *marja'* to criticise the doctrine of *velayat-e faqih,* which resulted in his defrocking in 1982 and subsequent house arrest until his death in 1986. After the Revolution, even those who had proposed the idea of a ruling clergy came, in time, to revise their views, for example on the specific doctrine of *velayat-e faqih*. As this notion evolved over the years, differences of opinion arose even among those clerics who had initially supported it. Ayatollah Montazeri, Khomeini's designated heir, is yet another example. Even though he 'played an instrumental role in inserting the *velayat-e faqih* into the constitution' he was later dismissed for being critical of governmental policies and practices as well as being unwilling to 'keep silent in the face of what [he] saw to be contrary to his religious beliefs'.[8]

Moreover, a new religious modernist movement emerged from 'within the same ideological circles that shaped the revolution'.[9] This intellectual movement, headed by Abdolkarim Soroush, questioned the religious establishment and the power that the clergy had given themselves. Mir-Hosseini and Tapper[10] discuss the influence of Soroush's theory of the relativity of religious knowledge on numerous intellectuals who came to form the foundation of New Religious Thinking in Iran. These included Mashallah Shamsolvaezin and Shahla Sherkat, editors of *Kiyan* and *Zanan* respectively. Both these monthly journals were established in 1991 and became a platform for Islamic dissent within Iran. *Kiyan* published many of Soroush's articles and speeches, including his article, *'Horriyat va row-haniyat'* [Freedom and the Clerical Establishment], which questioned the clerical monopoly of religious truth and refuted the clergy's claims to be the sole interpreters of religious knowledge.[11] Soroush, a close ally of the Islamic Republic during its conception and early years, turned into one of its most outspoken critics. He has since been disfavoured for his criticism of the theological, philosophical and political underpinnings of the regime. He subsequently lost his job, was barred from teaching, and received numerous death-threats. His public lectures were violently disrupted on many occasions and he ultimately left Iran in the mid 1990s to write and lecture in Europe and North America. His visits to Iran since then have been brief and he has refrained from public speeches.

Soroush criticised the clerics' monopoly of Islam, voicing concerns over the power of the religious seminaries, or *howzeh*s, and their close connection with the centre of power. In a talk he gave in 1992 at the University of Isfahan, he said:

> After the revolution the clergy took over the nation's management and formulated its governing political theory (the guardianship of the juriconsult), which requires a Hawzeh-trained clergyman with the rank of the grand juriconsult to be the supreme leader of the country ... it is self-evident that the religious government entails the empowerment of the clergy and the Hawzeh; the religious disciples actually empower those who possess them.[12]

Soroush argues that historically, this empowerment of the clergy and their claim to be the sole interpreters of religion has been one of the main areas of contention between the clergy and the philosophers, mystics and poets who did accept this claim. He goes on to state the numerous instances in which the latter group have denounced the power alliances of the juriconsults, and the associated dangers of corruption and abuse.[13]

More recently, in October 2000, another cleric mentioned earlier, Hasan Yousefi Eshkevari, was charged with 'apostasy, waging war against God, and other offences resulting from his participation in the [2000 Berlin] conference'.[14] From 6–9 April 2000 Eshkevari, along with a number of prominent reformists, attended the Berlin Conference entitled *Iran after the Elections, and the Dynamics of Reform in the Islamic Republic.* The conference was disrupted by two Iranian opposition groups in exile and as Mir-Hosseini and Tapper state, the conference 'became notorious in Iran for two things: disruptions by "naked" men and women, and the outspokenness of some of the panellists from Iran' both of which were filmed by the Iranian Television (IRIB) crew, under the conservatives' control.[15] The carefully edited film was broadcast in Iran to bring the reformists into disrepute. Many of the participants, including Eshkevari, were arrested upon their return.

Eshkevari's outspoken views on the mutability of social rulings brought him a death sentence, later commuted to five years in prison. Eshkevari identified three problems with the form of the Islamic Republic: first, he said, it broke its promise to the people and instead of being an Islamic Republic, it became a clerical Republic. The second was that the Islamic government became a *fiqhi* and, therefore, sectarian government for it relied solely on the Shi'i school of thought. This, he stated, is different from a religious government that is not solely confined to the Shi'i *fiqh* in all its affairs, including 'decision-making in the executive, the legislative and the judicial powers',[16] for which there is not always an answer in *fiqh.* It also excludes the four schools of Sunni thought and the possibility of their co-existence, for it deems them irrelevant to a society which in fact does include Sunni Muslims. The third problem was that, for the first time in history, the Shi'a institution of *marja'iyat* became a governmental institution. As a result, the *marja'*s lost their independence from the government and subsequently their independence from the political development of the state. Instead, he asserts, the *marja'*s, who were subjects until recently, had become rulers.[17]

The clergy's growth of authority over the years made them powerful as never before. As mentioned earlier, however, historically, not all clerics endorsed the idea of endowing the clergy with various religious or political powers. As we have also seen, the differences between the Usuli and Akhbari schools of thought in the nineteenth century were one example of disagreement on the religious empowerment of the clergy. In fact, the clergy were never unanimous in their views, particularly when their right to rule was concerned. Thus, not only did the Islamic Republic develop the most nuanced arguments on the legitimacy of the doctrine of *velayat-e faqih*, it also unwittingly produced some of its finest intellectuals, who critically engaged with the doctrine. These critics were not limited to a small group of secular intellectuals but, more strikingly, extended to many who arose from within the allies of the regime, including some of the clergy.

The relative freedom of expression attained during the initial years of Khatami's presidency (1997–2005) provided the space for more open debate. Arjomand (2000) states that the reconstitution of the Expediency Council in early 1997 and its role as an advisory board on major policies of the regime, was in fact a demotion of the president, who subsequently lost his power to determine state policies. Despite the difficulty of implementing new legislation, Khatami succeeded in reopening a discussion of constitutional principles, and his government spokesman and Minister of Culture at the time, 'Ataollah Mohajerani, withdrew many of the restrictions on the press. Consequently, and 'most importantly of all, the taboo on the discussion and questioning of the principle of theocratic government in the press, was broken for good'.[18]

However, any criticism of clerical power and its legitimacy was forcefully suppressed. Nevertheless, the harsh clampdown on publications that disseminated such 'seditious' views, and the arrest and intimidation of their authors, did little to suppress the ideas. Shahidi refers to the period between 1997–2000 as a time during which the greatest achievement of the Iranian press was to introduce 'concepts such as "citizenship", "civil society", "pluralism", "transparency", "accountability", and "the rights of women, children, and minorities" into the country's political vocabulary'.[19] It is in this context of larger intellectual debates about the role of the clergy in Iran that we must locate films such as *The Lizard* and *Under the Moonlight* and study their significance.

Parables on the World of the Clergy

Both *Under the Moonlight* and *The Lizard* function as parables. They not only depict the world of the clergy in its current form within Iranian society, but also include a moral vision of how it ought to be. Through Seyyed's eyes in *Under the Moonlight* and Reza's in *The Lizard,* we enter these two worlds and are at once presented with the contradictions between them. In examining the contemporary role of the clergy, these filmic discourses evoke the debates of intellectuals who have critically engaged with the doctrines that empower the clergy. Interestingly, even though both films discuss many similar issues, *Under the Moonlight* was screened without much controversy whereas *The Lizard* was forced to pull out of cinemas within a month of its release.

Religion Serving the Clergy

Under the Moonlight is the first post-Revolutionary film that critically examines the status of the clergy within society. It is about a young seminarian, Seyyed Hasan, who is approaching the end of his studies at the seminary and preparing to don clerical attire. He appears hesitant to take on the clerical role, and only half-heartedly proceeds with the preparations because of persistent pressures from his father and teachers. However, a street urchin, Joojeh, steals his supplies and Seyyed's pursuit of the boy leads him to an unfamiliar world of social outcasts who have set up a makeshift camp under a highway bridge in Tehran.

Under the Moonlight begins with a contrast between the life of the clergy and that of the public. As Seyyed, the seminarian student, looks out of the window of an overcrowded, hot, public bus, he sees a cleric on the highway waiting for his driver to finish a tyre-change. Such comparative sequences are scattered throughout the film and illustrate the difference between the upper world of the seminary in which Seyyed resides and the lower world of the under-bridge camp where the outcasts live. The sheltered life of the seminarian students, within the confines of an elegant edifice replete with beautiful gardens and ponds, is in stark contrast to the rough lives of the homeless. This is particularly evident in the case of the child character Joojeh who, in the guise of a street vendor, steals and traffics in drugs in order to earn a living. We also see some of the clerics acting against what they preach. The hypocrisy of the seminary's senior cleric is emphasised by the juxtaposition of his complaints about the seminary's electricity bill as a waste of money and, therefore, against the ethical principles of Islam, with his desire to obtain a mobile phone despite its high cost. He is depicted in various scenes throughout the film either going through invoices and bills, or being constantly on his mobile phone arranging or closing deals.

Soroush has variously criticised the clergy's dependence on religion as a source of income. He states that the clergy 'are not defined by their erudition or their virtues but their dependency on religion for their livelihood'.[20] For him, being a cleric must not constitute a job or profession, for religion then becomes a means to an end. Consequently, instead of defending and pursuing religious knowledge, the clergy are in danger of defending their professional interests to maximise their income. He thus argues that

> individuals who represent the greatest potential for corruption are those who, after receiving their religious education, base their livelihood on the cultivation and defense of a particular notion of Islam. Their livelihood depends upon the successful advancement of this religious interpretation, and to maximize the former they may compromise the latter.[21]

In *Under the Moonlight,* the clergy seem more concerned at maintaining their façade of piety than at striving towards the value systems they preach. The senior cleric, for example, complains about seminarian students who drink Coke on the streets together or grow their hair long, and asserts that this is unbecoming for a cleric in robe. However, when faced with the suffering of people such as the homeless, he prefers to close his eyes to it. In the senior cleric's view, it is the times that have changed and Seyyed should not feel responsible for any of it. He says, 'It was not supposed to be this way. I don't know where we went wrong or which sin we are paying off.' In fact, he exempts himself from taking any action by delegating these social problems to Divine Will and reading them as acts of punishment. The film, therefore, subtly depicts the deviation of the clergy's concern from the well-being of society to a self-centred preservation of their status.

The clergy thus appear to have forgotten an important part of their duty. They have failed to look out for those in need. The homeless living under the bridge are a 'collection' as they call themselves. They have both the physically and mentally disabled amongst themselves, led by a figure called Rostam. As his name indicates, Rostam acts as a *javanmard* in the group, a man of integrity, honour and chivalry. As Adelkhah states in her detailed analysis of the social and ethical code of *javanmardi* in modern-day Iran, one of the older references of *javanmard* is to a selfless man 'possessing fully the quality of a man (*mardanegi*), referring to his courage, honour, modesty, humility and rectitude'.[22] Rostam evokes the physical strength and heroism of his namesake in Ferdowsi's *Shahnameh*, the tenth-century Persian epic. The Rostam of *Shahnameh* is one of its best-known heroes, a great warrior and champion. The Rostam of *Under the Moonlight* was a wrestler in his younger days, around whom crowds would gather to watch him break free from heavy chains. His self-effacement, another important component of a *javanmard*, is also evident in the way he looks out for the welfare of his friends and shares what little he has with them. In fact, despite their miserable conditions, the people in the group care for each other deeply. Indeed, the love and care shown by and amongst these outcasts by far exceeds that of the world of the seminary. Many other Iranian films have also highlighted the plight of the underprivileged. However, *Under the Moonlight* differs from them in that the conditions of the destitute are contrasted not with the affluent living in the north of Tehran, but with the clergy in the seminary.

This contrast can also be read as a subtle reference to the unrealised dream of social justice promised by Khomeini before and during the early days of the Revolution. Khomeini had pledged to defend the rights of the oppressed classes (*mostaza'fin*) by bringing about social justice and narrowing the gap between the rich and poor. Even though proposals on the welfare of these oppressed were drafted and put to the first parliament of the Islamic Republic, they remained ultimately unsustainable in the social and political climate of the Revolution.[23] However, the social and financial status of close allies of the regime, including some clergy, continued to improve noticeably.

Under the Moonlight thus highlights the marginalisation and alienation of the very same people who were promised a just rule by the Islamic Republic. Not only have the rights of these people not been defended, but their living conditions have also deteriorated – a point evident from their nostalgic references to the past. Their presence in the film is, therefore, a reference to the dark reality of the conditions of the marginalised and the failure of the Revolution to fulfil its promise of social justice.

Clergy Serving the Public

Even though *Under the Moonlight* is critical of the current position of the clergy in Iran, it is important to note that it does not in any way attempt to denounce the religious institutions or the clergy per se. Instead, it reflects on the purpose and role of the clergy in society, which appear to have been misunderstood not only by the public but also by some of the clergy themselves. Seyyed's grandfather serves as an example of the noble role of the clergy. He, and not the seminarian teachers, remains an inspiration to Seyyed. We learn that the grandfather was a simple man who lived in the village and earned his living by working in the fields. He practised what he preached and was, therefore, a trusted member of the community in which he lived. For him, the good of society took precedence over his personal interests. As Seyyed himself puts it, his reluctance to don clerical robes stems from a fear of not deserving the honour. It is clear that for him, the honour lies in humbly serving the people, and he fears being incapable of fulfilling this noble calling.

Most importantly, this film revolves around Seyyed's quest. As such, he interprets the unfolding of events as a Divine sign. Thus, when Joojeh steals his supplies, he initially considers it as God's way of telling him not to proceed with finalising his education as a cleric. However, his search for Joojeh turns into the spiritual journey through which he finally realises his purpose in life. Interestingly, this happens after Rostam includes Seyyed in his letter to God asking Him to answer their pleas. Seyyed wakes up the next morning under the open-topped dome of the mosque with a white dove flying out into the light.

When Seyyed fails to appear at the enrobing ceremony, his roommate, who has already worn the clerical robes, hurries to try and persuade Seyyed to join him. He dismisses Seyyed's justifications and sounds the real reason: it is clear that Seyyed is hesitant because he has become suspicious of the clergy. As his roommate says, 'Do you think they are royal robes? No! They are working clothes! There are good and bad people in all types of work, why don't you try and be one of the good ones? You used to say that even if you are able to guide one person, then you must wear the robe!'

The phrase 'royal robes', can be read as a reference to those within the clergy who have taken on royal lifestyles and who have thus been criticised by dissident clerics. Ayatollah Montazeri had also voiced his concerns on the royal robes of the *vali-ye faqih*.[24] Breaking nearly ten years of political silence in November 1997, a few months after Khatami's landslide victory in the presidential elections, he gave a sermon in Qom criticising the corruption of the *velayat-e faqih* and the justifications for its authoritarian rule. In his words, '*Velayat-e faqih* does not mean having a royal organisation and ceremonial travels that cost billions and the like. These things are not compatible with the *vali-ye faqih*'.[25]

Mohsen Kadivar, another dissident cleric and a senior student of Montazeri, who spent a few years in the prisons of the Islamic Republic for his criticism of the doctrine of *velayat-e faqih,* compares the Islamic

Republic with the absolute monarchy they had intended to end.[26] The Islamic Republic, he states, failed to eliminate monarchical oppression and instead 'succeeded in transforming the face of monarchy in Iran; autocratic rule and monarchical relations have remained intact, and are reproduced in the form of the absolute *velayat-e faqih*'.[27] In comparing democratic rule with that of the *velayat-e faqih*, he states that the rule of the *faqih* does not provide the public with equal access to power within the public domain and subsequently alienates them within this sphere.[28]

The Parable of The Lizard

Even though *The Lizard* is a different film from *Under the Moonlight* in both genre and approach, the issues it raises are very similar. *The Lizard* is about a convicted thief, Reza, known as Reza Marmulak or Reza the Lizard. When he is taken to hospital after an attempted suicide in prison, he succeeds in stealing the robes of a cleric hospitalised next to him. The rest of the film is about Reza's attempts to escape the country while being trapped in the role of a cleric. Like *Under the Moonlight*, *The Lizard* functions as a parable. It also examines the relevance of theological reasoning to everyday real life and explores the role of the clergy, their relationship with the laity, and the notion of forced religious morals.

The storyline of *The Lizard* is a familiar comedy plot of the incongruity of displacement. A criminal dressed as a cleric and forced to act

Figure 3   *The Lizard* (*Marmulak*, Kamal Tabrizi, 2004). Obliged to lead the communal prayers en route to the village, Reza Marmulak fidgets.

as such has been depicted in various earlier films, going as far back as Charlie Chaplin's 1923 film *The Pilgrim*, which, like *The Lizard*, told a very similar story of an escaped convict grabbing the clothes of a bathing clergyman and subsequently assuming his identity. However, during its time it was received with a 'shocked indignation' in some parts.[29] Over 80 years later, this storyline still caused heated reactions amongst audiences, authorities and particularly the clergy, in Iran.

The Lizard was never officially banned but the stir it caused was enough for its creators to decide to take it off the screens. However, this did not entail defeat. The film had already succeeded on so many different levels that its withdrawal from the cinema screens did little to damage it. Financially, the film had already made a significant profit.[30] It also won several awards in the 22nd FIFF in 2004: the audience award for the most popular film, the best screenplay, and the special jury award for its lead character, Parviz Parastooyi, as well as the Interfaith Juries award.[31] It successfully spoke to the largest-ever Iranian audience on a sensitive issue such as the clergy. Additionally, even though it was aimed at domestic audiences, it succeeded in transcending national and cultural borders, becoming the first Iranian comedy to participate in some of the best-known international film festivals.[32] It also introduced a different style of Iranian films to foreign audiences. As some non-Iranian audiences commented, they were pleased to finally see

Figure 4 *The Lizard* (*Marmulak*, Kamal Tabrizi, 2004). As Reza Marmulak undresses in the public bath, he hurriedly tries to cover up his lizard tattoo from the sight of his ardent followers.

an Iranian film which not only had a tight narrative but also was not depressing!³³

The Lizard became the first post-Revolutionary film to position a cleric as the subject of a comedy. Even though it went on screen only for a month, it became the biggest box-office hit in the history of Iranian cinema.³⁴ The real audience of this film, however, exceeded the box-office figures. Pirated copies were very soon in circulation and almost everyone in Iran had seen it. The images of an irreligious convict pretending to be a man of God and leading the faithful made for some of the most humorous moments in film. However, the film aroused such fury amongst the clerics that they refused to acknowledge even its redemptive side, which allowed for a more favourable view of the clergy. Tabrizi, the director, narrated that in his attempts to gain the clergy's approval he arranged a private screening for them and their families.³⁵ He wanted them to see for themselves that the film was not hostile to the clergy. They were not convinced. Even though their families found it funny and were laughing heartily during the screening, the clerics seated on the other side failed to see the humour.

Like *Under the Moonlight*, *The Lizard* is also a social commentary critical of the clergy's position within society. It is, however, more daring in its approach. The film is filled with bold references that criticise the current approach to religion and its enforcement within society. Reza the Lizard

Figure 5 *The Lizard* (*Marmulak*, Kamal Tabrizi, 2004). Reza Marmulak forgets to remove his turban as he changes from his clerical robes in the public toilets.

had become Reza the Cleric. In Persian, 'lizard' has many connotations. Even though it appears to be a reference to Reza's artistry in climbing up walls, one cannot miss its other overtones, for the term also refers to a sly, scheming person who can easily change colours. This reference in the film could be easily stretched to the clergy.

The creators of *The Lizard* employed film to step onto uncharted territory. As King puts it, 'Comedy, by definition, is not usually taken seriously, a fact that sometimes gives it licence to tread in areas that might otherwise be off-limits'.[36] As mentioned earlier, the film functions as a parable and through Reza's eyes we enter both the ideal and the real worlds of the clergy. In the world as it is, Reza the Cleric benefits from a privileged status within society. He is easily exempted from paying a fine for driving in the wrong direction, and he enjoys special treatment on the train. Nevertheless, this status is also accompanied by public contempt for the clergy. For example, when dressed in clerical robes Reza finds it difficult to get a taxi to stop for him.

The world as it ought to be, however, is one that places the clergy and laity on level ground. Reza demonstrates this through his interaction with the people around him. Even if unwittingly, he succeeds in drawing people back to the mosque and gaining their respect. We see a world in which the clergy inspire and lead people to participate in the good of society, defending the helpless and weak against injustice, and tolerating human faults and weakness. Reza Marmulak, forced to act as the cleric for the village he has got off at, is unable to get in touch with Motazedi, the underground criminal who is supposed to deliver his fake passport for him to cross the border. Thus, during the day he dresses as a cleric and at night, 'disguised' in ordinary clothes, he looks for Motazedi. When Reza finally finds Motazedi's house, he finds that Motazedi has been arrested and imprisoned. The inquisitive Gholamali and his friend secretly follow Marmulak and witness not only his various visits to houses in the deprived areas but also the prayers of Motazedi's mother, who thanks him for his generosity. They interpret this 'disguised' nocturnal roaming as charitable work to help the needy. This also alludes to following the example of 'Ali, the first Shi'i imam, and his charitable acts. Indeed, 'Ali would roam the city at night in disguise and take food and sustenance to the orphans and needy. When Gholamali and his friends spread the word, the village people are so moved that they implore Marmulak to allow them to participate in his good deeds. Thus, every night they visit the poor, sick and needy and provide them with gifts and company.

Reza also displays an acute sense of justice and chivalry. He is furious with the village thugs who harass the village shopkeeper and vandalise his property, but feels it inappropriate to fight off the thugs whilst in his robes. However, he can no longer hold his peace when he finds out that the leader of the local gang of thugs has locked himself in with his ex-wife, Faezeh, to try and bully her into getting back together. To the villagers' astonishment he climbs the walls to the second floor and lets himself into the house. The villagers are then faced by a bleeding ex-husband who, despite his mass, has been clearly beaten up by the cleric. This further increases Reza's popularity, for now even the thugs and their leader develop a great respect for him.

In this visionary world, the cleric earns respect and achieves leadership not through preaching about punishment and fear, or by legal enforcement, but rather by setting an example himself. In fact, towards the end of the film, Reza ceases even to sit on the pulpit to deliver his sermons. Instead, he sits on its lowest step and suggests that together they should think about the meaning of the plural ways of reaching God. He invites people to enjoy the pleasures of life. His teachings do not oppose human desire but advise a more careful handling of such instincts. Thus, in contrast to Gholamali's father, who is concerned that singing in the mosque or interaction with the opposite sex constitute impermissible acts, Reza decrees them as permissible.

The visionary world is not limited to Reza acting as a man of God. As illustrated at the beginning of the film, his short interaction with the cleric in the hospital, also called Reza, provides an image of the clergy as it ought to be. This cleric does not arrogate to himself special privileges, evident in that he has been hospitalised in a public hospital and the fact that he earns a living through craftsmanship. As discussed earlier, Soroush emphasises the need for the clergy to earn their living through sources other than religious activity in order to maintain their integrity with the faith. The cleric in the hospital does not distance himself from Reza the Lizard, nor does he scorn the latter's contempt for the clergy. The inspirational passages he reads are not from Islamic sources but from Antoine de Saint-Exupery's *The Little Prince*. Truth, he says, is not found only in one source, but experienced through multiple interpretations.

In a theocratic state endorsing an exclusivist and official interpretation of Islam, *The Lizard* proposed a pluralistic approach – an argument comparable to Soroush's ideas of multiple interpretations of Islam. In a speech given at London's Centre for the Study of Democracy in November 2006, Soroush asserted that Islam is nothing but a series of interpretations, and interpretations are intrinsically pluralistic. However, those who have based their power on a particular interpretation of Islam are reluctant to allow other interpretations, and reject them as heresy. The pluralism of interpretation is, nevertheless, inevitable and he argues that the clerics need to engage with this aspect of Islam. Since there is no 'True' interpretation, one can correct and modify the existing ones but it is then logically impossible to possess the best interpretation. As such, Soroush proposed a plurality of 'right paths' rather than 'One Right Path'.

Both *Under the Moonlight* and *The Lizard* are social commentaries protesting not the relevance of the clergy in a believer's life, but rather criticising the role that some of them have currently undertaken in society. What Mirkarimi and Tabrizi achieve in their respective films is to raise many of these controversial issues and question the positions held by the clergy. As demonstrated in the discussion above, these discourses fall into the larger body of works that question the legitimacy of clerical power and role in society. The ideas proposed by these film-makers draw from the thought of intellectuals such as Soroush, Kadivar and Eshkevari, but are expressed through the medium of film.

Morals and Values

Seyyed's spiritual search and his hesitation at taking on the role of the clergy is depicted beautifully in *Under the Moonlight*. When he wakes up under the dome of the mosque, the white dove flying into the light and the satisfaction on his face suggest a search about to be fulfilled. That day Seyyed sells his books to feed the homeless, a symbolic act of carrying out the instructions in these books, rather than merely reading them in the confines of his seminary. A few days later, when the city cleaners are commissioned to clear the camp under the bridge, a heart-broken Seyyed complains to God, cries to him and sings to him, in a manner reminiscent of Rostam's unsophisticated and informal conversation with God, as we see earlier in the film. This poses an alternative to the prescribed formalistic discourses on the relationship between man and God.

Relevance of Seminarian Teachings

Another important point that both films raise is the relevance of seminarian teaching and the sharia to real-life situations. In *Under the Moonlight,* having witnessed the desperate situation of the street urchin, Joojeh, and his friends, it is very difficult to empathise with the seminarians advocating strict adherence to the principle of chopping off the hands of thieves. The impossibility of following all the prescribed rules in daily life is further demonstrated amongst the seminarians themselves. In fact, the ideals of the new student at the seminary, who zealously follows the religious texts, provide the comic relief of the film. For example, when the fervid student reminds Seyyed and his roommate that the religious texts consider having eggs at night to be reprehensible (*makruh*), Seyyed's friend adds some tomato sauce to it, thereby supposedly removing the reprehension and turning it into a permissible act.

The Lizard also questions the relevance of seminarian teachings to real life. This is depicted through the constant questioning of the keen young man shadowing Reza Marmulak. Most of these questions are completely irrelevant to the everyday life of Iranians, such as daily prayers at the North Pole or the religious duties of a Muslim in space. The film thus subtly implies that some of the current religious discourses are far removed from the practical affairs of life and are, therefore, of little use to society. The clergy's engagement with these matters is thus seen not only as being pointless but also as distant from the laity as Iran is from the North Pole or space. The film, therefore, suggests that people's more immediate problems could be dealt with in a way that better bridges the gap between real life and the values and ideals held dear by society.

As mentioned before, among other 'crimes' for which Eshkevari was sentenced to death, was questioning the relevance of religious rulings within today's context especially as they pertained to women. In fact, he asserted that some social rulings were mutable, for they were Arab and tribal customs. Appropriated by the Prophet, they were, therefore, subject to review. Thus, they could no longer be considered as absolute and divine decrees incumbent on Muslims, but rather changeable laws that should be reviewed within their own time and place. In the controversial Berlin Speech of 2000, Eshkevari divided social rulings into two categories. He allocated the first to rulings about worship and classified them as irrevocable. On the second he said:

> I would claim that these social rulings of Islam are mutable in essence and by their very nature, even if parts of them come from the Koran... In Islamic *fiqh* we have a principle that says that the ruling follows the subject matter... It means that when a subject

matter changes, the rulings too will change. But if the subject matter remains unchanged, the ruling will not change.[37]

Eshkevari then goes on to propose a reconsideration of certain social laws from being irrevocable principles to becoming changeable laws. In this way, religious rules are not divine rules but rather social contracts that could be changed in line with the needs of time and context. It was his specific proposal that these mutable rules included women's rights and the choice to wear the hijab, that the ruling clerics could not accept for ideological reasons.

In certain circumstances in the films, the very knowledge of the clergy is deemed irrelevant to the life of the laity. For example, on his first encounter with the homeless people, Seyyed is asked for the spelling of a word. He begins with providing the spelling, before going on to its etymology and root, but the destitute man cuts him short. He is not interested. Seyyed's learning is irrelevant to this man's problems – he just needs the spelling that any educated person should be able to provide.

God, however, remains a central part in the lives of both the seminarian and the homeless even though they differ drastically in their relationship with Him. The clergy employ a rigid and formal relationship with God in the form of prayers, worship, and praising of His attributes. The homeless people, on the other hand, employ a very casual vocabulary in speaking with Him. Rostam, who firmly believes in God and His kindness, is not afraid to use slang to protest against injustices inflicted upon the homeless. He dictates a letter to God and after complaining about His negligence of them, outlines a list of things they need from Him and includes Seyyed's name in it. As discussed earlier, according to the dominant Shi'i theology since the nineteenth century, the ulama had taken on the role of intermediaries between God and the believers. In this case, however, Rostam demonstrates his free and direct relationship with God and, ironically, he acts as an intermediary between God and Seyyed. Interestingly, Seyyed finds the answer to his search the very next morning. In *The Lizard,* Reza, the convict-acting-as-a-cleric, summarises the film's view on the laity's relationship with God in his sermon at the local prison. He states that God cannot be monopolised by good people. Instead, He is also the God of criminals, and does not differentiate amongst His men. Evil, in fact, occurs through the selfish acts of those who are unwilling to share their good fortune with the less fortunate.

These two films as a whole advocate an idea of God that is not bound to theological reasoning but rather, based on unconditional love and faith. One of the points of departure between mystics and the ulama has been the relationship of the believer with God. Rumi, the thirteenth-century Persian poet, and one of the greatest mystics of Islam, in his *Mathnawi* narrates the story of Moses and the Shepherd.[38] Moses overhears an illiterate shepherd praying to God and imploring Him to come out of hiding so that he can demonstrate his love for him, and feed Him, massage His feet, comb His hair and mend His shoes. Moses rebukes the shepherd for using blasphemous language and the shepherd is devastated to realise that his expression of love and devotion are considered sacrilegious. But Moses receives a revelation reproaching him for distancing God's sincere believer from Him, which continues: 'You were sent to join together, not to cause rift and disunion'. Rumi endorses this sincere and direct relationship with God that is independent of the mediation of the jurisprudents. As Soroush states, this recognition that there is an understanding beyond scholarly learning has long been a struggle between the mystics and the jurisconsults. 'The quarrel of some philosophers, mystics, and poets with the jurisconsults has not been merely academic but has been based on real differences of perspective on religious issues'.[39]

One of the reasons for Reza's success as a cleric in *The Lizard* is that he succeeds in communicating with people in their own language. Soroush highlights the importance of the seminary's task in training effective speakers and states that the preachers must be:

> able to guide the people using simple and accessible language, fables, examples and poems in order to convey moral commands, religious wisdom, and catechismic principles. There is now no faculty in the seminaries dedicated to the art of preaching even though this is one of the duties of the Hawzeh; this vocation falls to the talent and initiative of individuals.[40]

Forced Religious Morals

From the outset, *The Lizard* criticises the forced religious morals within Iranian society. This is depicted through the prison warden who wants to send his prisoners to heaven even if by force, as well as Gholamali's father who constantly pressures his son to memorise the Qur'an. The thick glasses of the soldier who carries out the warden's orders represent a blind following of the edicts. Interestingly, the new seminarian in *Under the Moonlight*, who is a strict observer of the literal interpretation of the religious law, also wears thick glasses. They both represent people with a narrow view of the world, one that is not gained, reasoned or drawn from experience, but rather handed down to them. These are people who receive the prescribed orders without giving them any further thought, or indeed, considering their relevance to the real world. In short, they are unable to see for themselves.

The notion of serving the public is also studied critically within contemporary Iranian society. Such service is either interpreted as punishment or abused for personal interests. The prison warden in *The Lizard,* for example, serves the prisoners through his dictatorial regime, and the police officer defines his service to the public as catching thieves and putting them into prison. Punishment, therefore, is seen as a tool of service. The parliamentary candidate on the other hand indulges in acts of generosity and service only to facilitate the fulfilment of his ambitions. The film also questions those who totally engross themselves in religious learning and subsequently distance themselves from society and service to it. This is clearly evidenced by Gholamali's father, for whom it is more important that his son memorise the Qur'an than set out on nocturnal missions serving the people and helping the needy.

The films also compare the ethical values of the laity with the enforced and institutionalised moral standards of the state. For example, *The Lizard* humanises both the clergy and the criminals, but in different ways. The criminals are not evil but help each other out in times of difficulty. Jackson, the underworld criminal and Reza Marmulak's friend, helps him to try to escape from the borders. Motazedi, who fakes passports, honours his word. As his mother says, she has brought up her child with an appropriate understanding of the forbidden and permissible acts (*halal* and *haram*). He earns his money, even if it is through unlawful work. The hospitalised cleric who helps Reza the Lizard and is an exemplar of the clergy as they ought to be, does not believe in punishment as a solution and is in fact complicit in the Lizard's escape. Later, when Reza Marmulak is forced to act as a cleric, his namesake, the cleric in the hospital, remains an important inspiration for him.

In *Under the Moonlight*, the seminarians who have devoted their lives to the worship of God and the study of the sacred texts, show little engagement with the laity outside and are almost oblivious to their suffering. The dwellers under the bridge, on the other hand, are compassionate despite being 'sinners', petty criminals, and drug-dealers. Joojeh's sister, a prostitute who attempts suicide, has already committed two of the 'great sins'. However, after being saved by Seyyed, who takes her to hospital, she in turn becomes an instrument of his salvation. Just before the enrobing ceremony, which he is unwilling to attend, and while his roommate is trying to persuade him otherwise, she delivers a parcel that contains his stolen garb – a sign that alludes to his ability to save souls.

We then see Seyyed finally dressed in the clerical robes and on his way to save Joojeh. Seyyed, a humble man who is deeply concerned with the suffering of the world around him, proceeds to take Joojeh out of the young offenders institution where he has been imprisoned. Seyyed asks to read his hand, the same trick that Joojeh had used to rob him of his supplies. This last sequence bears one of the most powerful shots of the film. Seyyed speaks in Joojeh's vocabulary and affectionately tells him that he is going to take him out of the prison and to his village with him. There is no hint of preaching or use of theological jargon in Seyyed's talk. Indeed, he believes in guiding Joojeh through love rather than disciplining him with the threat of having his hand cut off, an emphasis on saving the soul rather than punishing the body.

In *The Lizard*, the robe is seen as a taming device, as Reza Marmulak refers to it at the end of the film. However, it does not so much transform Reza as it gives him an opportunity to bring to the surface the best of his qualities. It does not in and of itself provide Reza with morals and values. In fact, from the very outset of the film it is clear that even though Reza is a criminal and has forgotten how to pray formally, he is not an immoral person or someone without values. Despite being convicted of armed robbery, he has never touched a weapon and considers bearing arms as contrary to his principles. Even though he is not an outwardly practising Muslim, he has his own Islamic principles – he does not steal during the holy months of Ramadan, Muharram and Safar. He does not endorse the unequal treatment of women or the hypocritical attitude of some men, who use religious sanctions to satisfy their sexual desires. In fact, he employs *fiqh* terminology to strongly condemn these acts. He does really pay Motazedi's mother out of kindness when he finds out that her son and sole bread-winner has been imprisoned. He does not abuse the trust of Faezeh, the young woman, even though he is obviously attracted to her. Instead, he gives up a golden opportunity for spending some time alone with her, and sacrifices his own desires to her best interests: Faezeh might have a future with her ex-husband, but not with him. In some instances, the robe is more of an impediment to his values than a vehicle through which to serve the people. For example, when the thugs beat up the old shopkeeper, Reza mumbles, 'If only Islam had not tied up my hands!' In short, his involvement with religion provided him with an opportunity to lead a more meaningful and purposeful life.

Conclusions

Both *Under the Moonlight* and *The Lizard* critically examine the role and status of the clergy, but neither of them accept or reject the religious institutions outright. The filmic discourses are in fact a continuation of an ongoing debate in Iran. Like Soroush, Eshkevar and Kadivar, the film-makers Mirkarimi and Tabrizi articulate their positions from a religious viewpoint. The films do not endorse the notion of clergy as men of power with unlimited authority over people's private and public lives, nor do they deem the clergy irrelevant to modern day Iranian society. Instead, they are an invitation to review our understanding of religion and its current role in society. In *Under the Moonlight,* Mirkarimi dares to break through the enclosed quarters of the seminary, and with an unapologetic approach examines the relationship of the seminarians with each other and with the outside world, as well as the relevance of their theological understanding to the real world. *The Lizard* highlights the enforcement of one particular interpretation of Islam and contrasts it with a pluralistic approach to the understanding of Islam. Both films propose a more fluid relationship between people, the clergy and the Divine that is not confined to the rigid boundaries of the seminarian debates. Even though the films, particularly *The Lizard,* are subversive in that they question the role of the clergy in society, they remain affirmative of the role of religion in one's life.

As discussed earlier, 'religion' is an ambiguous term for it comprises a number of interrelated ideas and practices ranging from faith and belief in supernatural powers to organised religion with a hierarchy between specialists and ordinary participants, as well as ritual – collective and stereotyped formal behaviours, usually in reference to a faith, and often organised by religious specialists. Statements about what 'religion' is or does may be true of only one or two of these three interrelated ideas and practices. Since they form an integrated system, all these various aspects need to be studied in order to arrive at a fuller understanding of 'religion'. Having explored the formalistic approach to religion in this chapter, the next chapter will examine how filmmakers employ film to discuss mystical concepts in a more personal approach to religion.

CHAPTER 4

SIGHT, SOUND AND SUFISM: MYSTICAL ISLAM IN MAJIDI'S FILMS

The energy and buzz of the annual Fajr International Film Festival at the cinema exclusively designated for film critics and journalists is palpable from its very crowded entrance. Frequented by established as well as aspiring film stars, directors, journalists and critics, the cinema is a hotbed of gossip and information. Every year, therefore, I took the opportunity to make as many contacts as I could. My efforts also meant that I sometimes had to listen to the running commentary of a new friend sitting next to me during the screenings, whilst desperately trying to concentrate on the film. Distracting as this was, I obtained some of the most interesting information during these interrupted film viewings and the smoggy café breaks. It was during one of these episodes, in FIFF 2005, that I learnt about the funding of Majid Majidi's then-latest feature film *The Willow Tree* (*Bid-e majnun*, 2005).

Majidi is one of Iran's most successful directors and his films have been well received both inside and outside of Iran. He has won numerous national and international awards, with his *Children of Heaven* (*Bacheha-ye aseman*, 1997) and *The Colour of Paradise* (*Rang-e Khoda*, 1999) turning him into a globally acclaimed director. A quick glance at the numerous pages of comments on the Internet Movie Database (IMDb), reveal the popularity of his films in the West. His films often depict man's struggle in the face of adversity. Many of the reviews speak of his films as having 'religious' or 'spiritual' overtones. Even without entering into the definitions of these two highly debatable terms one can easily see why Majidi made a highly suitable candidate to receive funding from Farabi's Spiritual Cinema Centre.

Despite its source of funding, *The Willow Tree* appeared in the Iranian Cinema category of the 23rd FIFF, not that of Spiritual Cinema. I learnt from my informant – a Farabi insider – that Majidi had refused to enter the film in the latter section because he feared the loss of his Iranian audiences at the box office. The label *'ma'nagara'*, he believed, would discourage his viewers from seeing the film, and therefore, jeopardise the work. This nugget of information spoke volumes about the dynamics of Iranian cinema and Iranian society at large. It demonstrated how just the branding of a product that reflected the aspirations of the Islamic Republic might lead to public rejection. The threat was serious enough for Majidi, a popular and well-established film-maker, not to take the risk.

The Willow Tree was nominated in 10 categories in the Festival and won four awards, including Best Director, Best Actor, Best Sound Recording and Audience Choice. Ironically, however, the highest number of awards that year went to one of only two Iranian films in the Spiritual Cinema category – Mirkarimi's *So Far, So Close* (*Kheyli dur, kheyli nazdik*, 2005), which was nominated in 13 categories, won six awards and was the runner-up for the Audience Choice award. It also did well at the box office during general release. Majidi's fears may well have been unfounded.

Regardless of the categories in which they are grouped, Majidi's films are deeply engaged with religious notions and themes. These references, however, are not explicitly religious. Rather, they are filmic depictions of man's struggle towards spiritual attainment, a discourse that reflects an aspect of Islamic mysticism or Sufi teachings.

Majid Majidi was born in Tehran in 1959, where he studied at the Institute of Dramatic Arts. After the Revolution, he began his career in the performing arts as an actor in the Centre for Islamic Art and Thought (*Howzeh andisheh va honar-e Islami*) and the Art Centre of the Islamic Development (Propaganda) Organisation (*Howzeh honari sazman-e tablighat-e Islami*). In 1981, he began his cinematic career by acting in Manouchehr Haqani's *Justification* (*Towjih*, 1981) and by 1989 he had acted in nine films, including three by Mohsen Makhmalbaf: *Two Blind Eyes* (*Do cheshm-e bisu*, 1984), *Fleeing from Evil to God* (*Este'azeh*, 1984) and Boycott (*Baycot*, 1986). He made his own first feature film, *Baduk*, in 1992. This was followed by *Father* (*Pedar*, 1996), *Children of Heaven* (*Bacheha-ye aseman*, 1997), *The Colour of Paradise* (*Rang-e Khoda*, 1999), *The Willow Tree* (*Bid-e majnun*, 2005), and *The Song of Sparrows* (*Avaz-e gonjeshkha*, 2008).

Many of Majidi's films are depictions of man's spiritual attainment. In these films, Majidi depicts the abstract Sufi stations (*maqam*) and states (*ahwal*) through the characters of his films. He employs the modern medium of cinema to lend form to mystical concepts. The poetic language of his films could be read as continuing in the long line of symbolic Persian literature and poetry, in which mystics, Sufis and Muslim philosophers have written much about love, God and self-annihilation. Discussing the origins of Islamic spirituality, Sells asserts that the 'poetic heritage was another central mode of expression of early Islamic spirituality'.[1] Majidi himself highlights the significance of Persian literature and the relevance of Iranian cultural history to contemporary Iranians:

> Iran is an old country with a significant cultural history. Our literature is very rich with poets such as Hafiz, Saadi, Rumi. In their writings, these poets have always given a great importance to the human being. Contemporary cultural subjects are stemming from this tradition as well as the rituals associated with them. The manner [in which] these subjects are dealt with is influenced by the particular beliefs of the Iranians that existed and continue to exist nowadays. These days, the world, and in particular the Western world, is in a period of disruption with the past. Human being[s] and traditional moral values, dear to people, seem to have been lost in the process.[2]

Thus, his filmic discourses, though modern in form, are deeply rooted in medieval Iranian mystical discourse, and particularly its poetry. They are also a reminder that Shi'i Iranian religious expressions are not limited to sacred texts, but also draw from Persian mystical literature. In this chapter I will examine Majidi's *The Colour of Paradise*, *Baran* (2001), and *The Willow Tree*, each of which are filmic discourses that reflect some of the key mystical teachings in Islam. To this end, I will explore the Sufi theme of pain and suffering in *The Colour of Paradise* and *The Willow Tree*. In the section that follows, I will look specifically at *Baran*, drawing out its depiction of the various stages of the Sufi state of 'love' that culminates in self-annihilation. I will also analyse how Majidi's films poetically engage with the Sufi stations and states as ways of spiritual attainment.

The Mystical Approach

The teachings of Islam are generally associated firstly with the Qur'an and the hadith and, secondly, with their application to Muslim societies generally and the lives of believers in particular. Consequently, many discussions on Islam as a religion are restricted mainly to its theories and practice. Reducing Islam in this way, however, runs the risk of overlooking another, more interiorised dimension of Islam, that of religious experience, which is equally – if not more – significant in many Islamic interpretations.

The mystical approach to Islam provides an alternative discourse that allows for a more personal approach than the Islam of the clerics and lawmen. As Kynsh argues, it is misleading to talk about a 'spiritual essence' of Sufism as though this were a trans-historical concept. In fact, such concepts have evolved over time and have been articulated variously by different Sufi masters.[3]

With the early expansion of Islam beyond its original Arabian context, Muslims faced various intellectual and social upheavals. Sufism was one such response to these challenges, one that dialogued with new ideas, practices and ways of thought.[4] After the fall of the Mongol Ilkhanids in Iran in the fourteenth century and the political upheavals that followed, Iran witnessed a spread of Shi'ism and Sufism. The development of Sufi *tariqa*s, or paths, gave rise to popular piety in the veneration of saints and saint cults as well as the hierarchically organised Sufi institutions with special chains of transmission from master to disciple.

Mysticism in Islam cannot be studied in isolation from its broader religious, social and cultural contexts. In fact, Sufism 'has been inextricably entwined with the overall development of Islamic devotional practices, theological ideas, esthetics, and religious and social institutions'.[5] Moreover, even though they might not have originated within Shi'ism, they have influenced many current Shi'i understandings and articulations in Iran. As Nasr asserts 'the esoteric dimension of Islam ... in one way or another colours the whole structure of Shi'ism in both its esoteric and even its exoteric aspect'.[6] However, since this is not a study of Sufism per se, here I will only summarise some major Sufi concepts, particularly their Persian articulations, in order to discuss their application in some of the films discussed in the chapter.

There is an array of views on what exactly constitutes mysticism in Islam and whether Sufism is connected to Islam at all. In discussing the difficulties of defining the term 'mysticism', Schimmel recalls the famous story in Rumi's *Mathnawi* about the blind men who were asked to describe what they were touching, without knowing that it was an elephant. Just as each one of them described it differently according to the part of the body that they had touched so, too, has Sufism, the generally accepted name for Islamic mysticism, been defined in different ways.[7] Chittick also argues that one cannot find a consensus within the Islamic texts as to the definition of the word *sufi* and that 'authors commonly argued about both its meaning and its legitimacy'.[8]

The Sufis referred to the first two codified categories of knowledge and law, the Qur'an and hadith, as the 'Way' or *tariqa,* which led to a third element. This element 'not set down so explicitly in the Koran or Hadith', is 'spiritual realisation, or the ascending stages of human perfection resulting in proximity to God'.[9] Those who aspire to follow the mystic path strive to pass from the finite to the infinite, 'from that which seems to that which is, out of all lower forms of reality to that which is Supremely Real, and, in the end, to become Being itself'.[10]

According to Schimmel, mysticism can be defined as 'love of the Absolute – for the power that separates true mysticism from mere asceticism is love. Divine love makes the seeker capable of bearing, even of enjoying, all the pains and afflictions that God showers upon him in order to test him and to purify his soul'.[11] The mystic emphasises the role of the heart in understanding the ineffable reality, which neither reason nor philosophy can reveal.[12] Indeed, the Qur'anic verse 53: 11 'The heart did not lie in what it saw' is often invoked as proof 'that the locus of spiritual vision and mystical knowledge is the heart'.[13]

Smith identifies four postulates on which mysticism bases its claims of the soul's ability to undertake this journey. The first is intuition or the soul's ability to see by a spiritual sense. 'Reality, in its highest form, cannot be understood by intelligence, but only by something above it' and through intuition man can 'perceive things hidden from reason'. The second is the inward light or Divine spark 'that seeks reunion with the Eternal Flame', for only if the soul is itself a partaker of the Divine can it know God. The third is going beyond the self, which is required for the purification from the self: 'The soul must be stripped of the veils of selfishness and sensuality if it is to see clearly the Divine vision'. Lastly, love is the guide and inspiration of the soul in its ascent to God.[14]

The predecessors of the Sufi movements

> strove to achieve a psychological and experiential proximity with God through self-imposed deprivations (especially abstinence from food and sex), self-effacing humility, supererogatory religious practices, long vigils, pious meditation on the meaning of the Qur'anic text and a single-minded concentration on the divine object.[15]

Attaining proximity to God remained one of the constant goals throughout Sufism, even as various, and at times contradictory, approaches were identified as ways of achieving this closeness. For example, seclusion was propagated by some as essential in attaining proximity while others encouraged an active involvement with worldly affairs.[16]

In explaining the appeal of Islamic mysticism from the early period of Islam, Mottahedeh states that Muslim mystics

> had created a vivid form of spirituality that grasped the imagination not only of Muslims but also of non-Muslims; and conversion to Islam both within the lands ruled by Muslims and in lands far beyond, whether in Central Asia, Central Africa, or elsewhere, took place more often through the efforts of Sufis than through those of any other representatives of Islam.[17]

As Lings[18] observes, however, there are those who regard Sufism as independent of Islam, arguing that it has borrowed from other non-Islamic traditions such as Buddhism and Hinduism, or because Sufi beliefs and practices, regardless of their origins, do not necessarily fit into their particular definition of Islam. And there are yet others, more recently, who consider themselves to be Sufis but not connected to any religion, let alone Islam. Lings points to thousands in the Western world 'who, while claiming to be "Sufis", maintain that Sufism is independent of any particular religion and that it has always existed.' Lings asserts that in doing so, 'they unwittingly reduce it ... [and] ... fail to notice that by robbing it of its particularity and therefore its originality, they also deprive it of all impetus'.[19] For him, therefore, it is quite clear that 'Sufism is nothing other than Islamic mysticism, which means that it is the central and most powerful current of that tidal wave that constitutes the Revelation of Islam'.[20]

The authorities of the Islamic Republic, even today, highly disapprove of the term Sufism, condemning its institutions and practices as unIslamic. In order to reconcile with the undeniable existence of esoteric perspectives in Islam – which form an essential part of Persian culture and literature – the term *'irfan*, loosely translated as gnosis – has become the preferred term in the Islamic Republic. This might be because gnosis does not denote a separate school of thought or institution, and thus does not pose a potential, rival threat to the Islamic Republic's interpretation of Islam and its authority. Rather, it alludes to an independent understanding attained through personal search and practice. Whilst poets such as Rumi and Hafez are renowned, especially in the West, as Sufis, the Islamic Republic refers to them as gnostics (*'urafa*).[21] Regardless of whether they are labelled as gnostic or Sufi, it is nevertheless important to note the significance of these mystical approaches to the understanding and practices of Iranians.

In one of my interviews in 2004 with Abdollah Esfandiyari, head of the Spiritual Cinema Centre of the Farabi Cinema Foundation, he mentioned the increased appeal of *darvishi*, a Persian term also used to refer to Sufism, particularly since the victory of the Islamic Republic. He went on to say how these Sufi groups have misled many, abusing their positions and robbing people of their money, with some Sufi masters even entering into unlawful relations with their female disciples. He said he had seen a documentary where the adherents of these groups had talked about their misfortunes, warning people about the dangers of following Sufi groups. Yet he recognised the appeal of Sufism in the quest for inner meaning. *Ma'nagara* cinema, Esfandiyari said, was an attempt to look at that which is beyond the surface and at the mysteries of the world.

Since it is impossible to come up with an absolute definition, I have used Sufism here to refer to a mystical dimension within Islam that seeks a direct personal experience of the Divine. I also explore Persian poetry as an important expression of Sufi thought in my analysis of the films discussed here. Persian Sufi literature composed over the last millennium is diverse and extensive. It ranges from Qur'anic commentaries, didactic metaphysical works, and ethical treatises, to poetry composed in a wide range of classical forms. However, 'the greatest masterpieces of this literature appeared as poetry and because of their great beauty and spiritual quality [they have] left their imprint on the whole of Persian culture'.[22]

Historically, Persian poetry has played a significant role in the expression of Sufi concepts and ideas in Iran. The works of Sufism's greatest poets,

Farid al-Din 'Attar (twelfth-thirteenth century), Jalal al-Din Rumi (thirteenth century), and Nur al-Din Jami (fifteenth century) are just the most eminent examples, which are still recited and relevant to Iranians several centuries after their composition. It is notable that many of these great Sufi poets were negative about the art of poetry, regarding it as subordinate to religion. However, as Lewisohn argues, 'an esoteric *double entendre* is never far away in any discussion of poetry among Sufis' and in fact the 'subordination of Poetry to Prophecy, of Art to Love, is, indeed, the central fact in Sufi aesthetics'.[23] But even if being a poet was to be the lowest degree of the Sufi (since his spiritual mastership was by far the higher status), and even if poetry was subordinate to religious practices and metaphysics, it nevertheless remained the most popular medium of Sufi expression.

Knysh draws interesting parallels between poetry and mysticism. He argues that there is an affinity between poetry and mysticism, as both

> convey subtle experiences that elude conceptualization in a rational discourse which by its very nature requires lucidity and a rigid, invariable relations [sic] between the signifier and the signified... Both carry emotional rather than fictional content; both depend, in great part, on a stream of subtle associations for their effect.[24]

Moreover, the open-endedness of poetic language, in contrast to the argumentative language of science and logic, gives it an elasticity that allows it to refer to multiple signifieds. This, in turn, allows readers to create meaning, even if the poem was written in distant times. The mystical experience compels the mystic to share his unique perspective with others even though it is too ineffable or subtle to be precisely conveyed to others. The characteristics of poetry make it the preferred vehicle for mystical experiences in certain religious traditions.[25]

Sufi poetry deals with a variety of subjects. However, beauty, divine love and complete annihilation of man in God are recurrent themes in the works of many masters including those mentioned above. Rumi's works, and particularly his collection of poems, is a combination of mystical experience with poetic inspiration. Rumi's encounter with the wandering dervish, Shams al-Din Muhammad Tabrizi, transformed him from 'a sober jurisprudent to an intoxicated celebrant of the mysteries of Divine Love'.[26] Shams discouraged his pupil from relying on the formal education he had received and emphasised love as the surest way to God, hence the many verses that Rumi dedicates to love in his poetry. Rumi's intense love (*'ishq*) for Shams inspired him to find a paradigm of his love of God.²⁷ Rumi's view of the relationship between God and man is subtle, with

> the process of the mystical annihilation of man in the divine essence (*fana'*)... never complete. As the flame of a candle continues to exist despite being outshined by the radiance of the sun, so does a mystical man retain his identity despite the overpowering presence of his Lord.²⁸

The various states and stations within Sufism have been explored most extensively within Persian poetry. Sufism influenced many aspects of Iranian culture and thought, including poetry, painting, music and philosophy. Persian poetry, however, remained the most prominent medium of Sufi expression. In a comparison of Persian poetry and other Persian arts, particularly painting and architecture, Yarshater considers poetry to stand out amongst all other Persian arts. Poetry is

> not only the fullest expression of artistic and aesthetic explorations of the people, but also the compendium of their deepest thoughts and religious sentiments. By engaging the most comprehensive artistic and intellectual interests of people, poetry constitutes the broadest stage for the manifestation of a Persian *Weltanschauung*.²⁹

Many of the Sufi stations and states, including divine love, self-annihilation and inner sight are explored in Persian poetry. This unrivalled art form, however, was to inform another, namely film. As Saeed-Vafa asserts, it appears that as a result of political censorship, cultural or personal taboos, or spiritual experience, codes and signs are inevitably employed in Iranian poetry, narrative and visual arts to convey incommunicable ideas. Thus, the 'mysteries of the system and the universe are understood and conveyed only through metaphor'.³⁰

In this chapter, I will examine how Majidi employs the medium of film to articulate mystical concepts such as love, God, suffering and annihilation, and their relevance to the modern-day lives of ordinary people.

Pain and Suffering

Suffering is one of the main topics in Majidi's films. His lead characters, who are mostly children, are afflicted either by poverty, disability or both. His debut feature *Baduk* (1992), concerns the slavery of two lonely, impoverished and orphaned young siblings. The film depicts the struggles of these two children against kidnappers and drug-traffickers, who rob them of their freedom, childhood, and finally each other. In Majidi's later films, the bad-guy figures blur. Instead of having the good protagonist against the evil antagonist, his heroes are ordinary people who fight the challenges of life in extraordinary ways.

In 1998, his *Children of Heaven* (1997) was the first Iranian film to be nominated for an Academy Award for Best Foreign Language Film. *Children of Heaven* is also about a brother and sister living in poverty, but this time the siblings live with a loving and caring family in the urban setting of Tehran. These two children, 'Ali and Zahra, fight their poverty with remarkable courage and maturity. The film looks at this daily struggle, which turns into 'Ali's quest with constant searching and running throughout the film. Initially, 'Ali runs to find his sister's shoes. The film then proceeds with both of them running to share 'Ali's only pair of worn-out shoes to school. The chase then concludes with 'Ali's attempt to win third prize in the running competition – a pair of trainers – for his sister. Through the film's simple narrative, Majidi relates the greatness and strength of the human spirit, determination, humility and sacrifice that manifests itself through the acts of these small children. In his later films, Majidi explores the themes of pain and suffering further: the lead characters in both *The Colour of Paradise* and *The Willow Tree* deal with physical disability and through them, the films demonstrate man's suffering in a mystical and Sufi context.

The Colour of Paradise

The Colour of Paradise (1999) is about the struggles of Mohammad Reza, a blind 11-year-old, deprived of paternal love. Having lost his mother when he was six, he lives far away from his village, at a boarding school for the visually impaired in Tehran. When the school closes for the summer holidays his father, Hashem, reluctantly takes him back to the village. There, his two young sisters and paternal grandmother shower him with much love and affection. His father, however, appears to be ashamed of him and considers him the major obstacle to his remarriage to the young woman he desires; he is, therefore, desperate to get rid of him.

The Colour of Paradise depicts Mohammad Reza's acute sense of awareness of the world around him and its beauties, contrasting it with his father's obliviousness and 'blindness' to the same. The film, therefore,

Sight, Sound and Sufism

Figure 6 *Colour of Paradise* (Majid Majidi, 1999). Mohammad Reza running through the village fields with his sisters.

is as much about the inner blindness and struggles of the father as the struggles of his son. Mohammad Reza's greatest challenge, however, is not overcoming his handicap, but securing the love of a father who cannot come to terms with his son's disability or, in fact, the miseries of his life. Thus, the colourful surroundings of Mohammad Reza as opposed to the dull, grey setting of the father's workplace also indicate the contrastingly different worlds in which they live.

Mohammad Reza's blindness has not cut him off from the world. Instead, through touch and hearing he has developed a remarkably keen sensitivity. More importantly, he has the ability to temporarily detach himself from worldly affairs, and to listen to and contemplate nature and his surroundings. Throughout the film, Mohammad Reza hears the sounds of birds and nature when everyone else around him seems to be unconscious of them. He can sense the trouble of a chick fallen from its nest by its chirping. When his father negotiates the price of the small carpet he wants to sell to the merchant, Mohammad Reza easily blocks off the men's voices and the classical music playing in the store to listen to the pigeons and doves singing above. Once back in his village, he listens to the woodpeckers in the forest and tries to decipher the notes of their chirping. At school, he listens to his grandmother's voice on the recorded tape and connects with her through the recording. He hears what most people around him fail to hear.

In many classical Sufi texts the sense of hearing precedes the sense of seeing.[31] The Prophet Muhammad, for example, received the Revelation through hearing. When asked about the experience he likened it to the sounds of caravan bells. Bukhari documents the following hadith from Ayesheh, the Prophet's wife:

> Al-Harith bin Hisham asked Allah's Apostle 'O Allah's Apostle! How is the Divine Inspiration revealed to you?' Allah's Apostle replied, 'Sometimes it is (revealed) like the ringing of a bell, this form of Inspiration is the hardest of all and then this state passes off after I have grasped what is inspired. Sometimes the Angel comes in the form of a man and talks to me and I grasp whatever he says.' 'Aisha added: Verily I saw the Prophet being inspired Divinely on a very cold day and noticed the sweat dropping from his forehead (as the Inspiration was over).[32]

Mohammad Reza and his father Hashem have both suffered in various ways. However, each of them deals with their afflictions in a different manner, which also informs their different approaches to life. The implied shortsightedness of the father has allowed him to focus only on his miseries, turning him into an embittered soul. Hashem is afraid that Mohammad Reza's blindness might hinder his own marriage prospects and his only chance of attaining happiness. Thus, his initial reluctance to let Mohammad Reza appear publicly in the village, and later his eagerness to get rid of him, are not really out of shame for his son's disability. In fact, he does not express the same concerns outside the village setting, for example, when Mohammad Reza is present at his workplace with his co-workers or when they are travelling in Tehran. Mohammad Reza, however, is capable of surviving the society in which he lives despite its occasional hostility. Even though initially teased by the village children, Mohammad Reza succeeds in amazing them when he attends the village school and reads out the school text fluently in Braille. Except for his father, he enjoys a very close and loving relationship with his family. He participates in village life with his grandmother and two sisters who are only too happy to have him around.

Hashem, however, seems incapable of seeing all the love and beauty that already exists in his own life. Whilst all other members of his family bring great joy and happiness to one other, the father has totally deprived himself of it, choosing only to see his loss. His outburst at the grandmother when she leaves home because he had taken Mohammad Reza away is very telling:

> You want me to get stuck with taking care of a blind child? Why does that God of yours, Who is Great, not help me out of this misery? What should I be grateful to Him for? For things that I do not have? For my miseries? For a blind child? For a lost wife? I lost my father when I was young. Who cared for me? Who loved me?

This complaint against God is also voiced by Mohammad Reza. When he is tricked by his father and is left with the blind carpenter in a place far away from the village, the distraught boy opens up his heart to the carpenter:

> Nobody loves me, not even granny, because I'm blind. Everyone wants to run away from me. All other village children go to the village school except for me, who has to go to the special school for blind people at the other end of the world... our teacher says that God loves blind people more, but I said if He did so, He wouldn't make us blind so that we couldn't see Him. He said God is not visible, He is everywhere, you can see Him everywhere, you can see Him through your fingertips. Now I look for Him everywhere, so that one day my hands might touch Him and I can tell Him everything – even all the secrets in my heart.

Human suffering is one of the important themes discussed in Sufi literature. As an aspect of human life, various people respond to suffering differently. In Sufism, suffering is welcomed as a process through which the human soul is purified; it is the precursor to a greater joy. Rumi's famous poem about the chickpeas cooking in the pot of boiling water is a metaphor for the suffering of the human soul that matures through the process. The uncooked chickpeas keep jumping up in the pot trying to evade the fire, but the woman keeps pushing them back down in with her ladle. They ask her why she keeps torturing them, since she had already shown her appreciation by buying them. She responds:

> I do not cook you because I dislike you: I want you to gain taste and savor.

> You will become food and then mix with the spirit. You do not suffer tribulation because you are despicable.³³

Even though Mohammad Reza also complains about God and not being loved, his approach to his suffering differs greatly from that of his father. Mohammad Reza searches for God everywhere, to talk to Him and share his secrets with Him. A man does not become fortunate or unfortunate because he is spared or burdened with suffering; rather it is his response to suffering that makes him fortunate or unfortunate and shows his worth.

> God makes an unfortunate man suffer and he flees from Him in ingratitude,
> But when He sends suffering to a fortunate man, he moves closer to Him.³⁴

The father, by contrast, gets further and further away from God and can only see what he has lost. The greatest torture, however, *is* to be far from God.

> The cruelty of Time and of every suffering that exists is easier than distance from God and heedlessness.
> For that cruelty will pass, but distance from Him will not. No one possesses good fortune but he who takes to Him an aware spirit.³⁵

Analysing Rumi's body of literature, Chittick maintains that in the tribulations that man faces, his attachment to self results in suffering. These afflictions however are 'all Mercy hidden in the guise of Wrath'. They provide man with the opportunity to separate himself from the Self and get closer to God. 'The fundamental problem of most men is that they do not realize that every hardship and pain they undergo is only a shadow of their separation from God'.³⁶ These sufferings provide man with the necessary rituals of purification through which he is liberated from his Self and the world. Trying to avoid suffering is in fact an attempt to flee God. One 'must not flee pain and heartache – which come to him from God – but his own self. The only way to flee from suffering is to seek refuge from one's own ego with God'.³⁷

Hashem can no longer appreciate what he does have, but rather allows things that he does not have to overshadow his life. Eventually he starts to lose all that he did have but refused to see. As Rumi says, 'No one has ever fled from suffering without finding something worse in return'.[38] Indeed, Mohammad Reza's grandmother dies more from grief than from her illness, and Hashem's fiancée's family breaks off the engagement, considering the marriage inauspicious. The sudden burden of these new afflictions awakens Hashem. He goes back to the carpenter and after much hesitation finally asks to take Mohammad Reza back home. On their way, Mohammad Reza falls into the river while crossing the bridge. Hashem pauses for a long time – as though momentarily welcoming the situation that would rid him of this unwanted encumbrance – before plunging into the river to save his son. This delayed reaction, however, means that the strong river currents have swiftly taken Mohammad Reza out of reach.

When Hashem regains consciousness and finds Mohammad Reza washed up on the seashore, it is the first time that we see him hold his son. This last scene of Mohammad Reza and Hashem is similar to one of the most famous epic tableaus of Rostam and Sohrab, immortalised in the *Shahnameh*. As in the Persian tragedy of Rostam and Sohrab, the father's attempt to make reparations is too late. Rostam, not knowing that his opponent Sohrab is his own son, strikes the fatal wound, only to immediately realise the truth. His desperate attempts to save his son and the remedy with which he returns to heal his wound are all too late. Sohrab dies just before his father brings the remedy. Thus, the famous Persian proverb of 'the remedy after Sohrab's death' (*nush daru ba'd-e marg-e Sohrab*), which refers to a belated and futile attempt to make amends, can be read in Hashem's belated expression of love for his son. Indeed, even though Hashem throws himself into the water and endangers his own life to save that of his son, this act of selflessness comes to naught. Mohammad Reza's illuminated hand, even though understood by many reviewers as a happy ending, is read more plausibly as union with the Divine when he finally touches/ sees God.

In fact, most of Majidi's films do not have a happy ending in the conventional style of the protagonist achieving his desires. Rather, in most cases the 'vague' endings could be read as the higher spiritual attainment of the protagonist. Thus, even though 'Ali does not win the trainers in *Children of Heaven*, and Mohammad Reza does not gain his father's love and acceptance, their experiences transform them in the path to a higher level of being in the ascending stages of human perfection.

The Willow Tree

Majidi's *The Willow Tree* (2005)[39] also has a blind protagonist, this time Yusuf, a middle-aged professor of literature and mysticism in Tehran. The lead character is married and enjoys the love and support of his family, particularly that of his wife, Roya. Their calm and happy life is threatened when he is diagnosed with a tumour. Yusuf travels to France for an operation and, in a twist of fate, learns not only that the tumour is benign, but also that he is regaining his eyesight after almost 38 years. He returns to Tehran, but this new experience changes everything in his life.

Some Western reviews of *The Willow Tree* have read the film as a philosophical journey of existentialism,[40] to which Majidi responds: 'We were very aware of Existentialism when we wrote it. It was core for what the film is about. But also, because the philosophy of Iran is linked to the Metaphysical and Spirituality the film has two sides'.[41]

The Willow Tree makes intertextual references to *The Colour of Paradise*. In a way, Mohammad Reza's unanswered question about God's love in *The Colour of Paradise* is addressed in *The Willow Tree*. Before his trip to France, Yusuf writes a letter to God, pleading with Him to show mercy and to cure his tumour. He reminds God how he had not complained about suffering from the darkness of sight and says:

> I want to say a few words to you, or have you forgotten me? The one whom You deprived of Your beauties and he didn't complain. Instead of light and brightness I sank into darkness and did not complain. I was content with this little paradise of mine and was enjoying it. Were all these years of suffering and difficulty not enough that You want to add to my suffering? I do not know whether or not I will ever make it back to my family. I do not know whether or not this illness will put me down. I do not know who[m] to take my complaint against You. But I beseech You to show me some of Your kindness. Do not take away the opportunity of this life from me.

After the operation he is blessed with more than he asks for. Not only is his life spared, but there is also a possibility of regaining his sight. Once again he implores God for yet another opportunity:

> I know I made a mistake, and my first mistake was that I did not know You well enough. Now I know that You haven't erased my name from Your book of kindness, that You haven't forgotten me, that You are with me and looking after me. But I so wish that you would complete Your kindness. Now that You've been there for me and brought me halfway, I beg of You to finish it well. Trust me! I appreciate light more than others. If I come out of darkness, I will be with You until the end.

One more time Yusuf's prayers are answered. However, he fails his test miserably and God's 'act of kindness', therefore, turns out to become his suffering. His heart begins to desire what his eyes see, and his enlightened heart quickly sinks into darkness. He begins to lose his love and respect for things that he had held sacred before his trip. At the beginning of the film Yusuf compares his wife Roya to the heavenly angels. Her unconditional love for him is compared to Rumi's unquestioning love for Shams. After regaining his sight, however, he lusts after a much younger and more glamorous woman and loses all appreciation for his family and the happy and respectful life that he had enjoyed so far.

The world and all its distractions overwhelm Yusuf. He allows his hungry eyes to dictate his life and the course they take. As he tells his mother in an outburst, he no longer needs anyone. He spends many long hours exploring the city and its gleaming consumerism. The glitter eventually overpowers his divine spark, turning him into a lost soul. He disregards his years of research and study on philosophy and mysticism as a pile of rubbish and resigns his occupation as a respected professor. Roya, his wife, can no longer take his unkind behaviour towards her. She leaves him, taking their daughter with her. Yusuf's mother falls critically ill with worry about her son's transformation and is hospitalised. And the home, which he had once imagined as a little paradise, now makes him sick. The image of his house, covered with the ashes of books and pictures that he burns in his garden towards the end of the film, is reminiscent of a hell that he has created with his own hands. Most importantly, he loses his closeness to God, and his 'fortunate' recovery ultimately results in great loneliness.

The film compares sufferings that are beyond man's control and, therefore, attributed to God, with self-inflicted afflictions, such as those that Yusuf experiences after he regains his sight. As mentioned earlier in this chapter, the real suffering in the Sufi context is attachment to the Self and the further the distance between man and God, the more his suffering. Yusuf's blessed eyesight increases his separation from God and his obedience to his ego. His heart, which had once been home to the love of God, is instead filled with the emptiness and desires of the outside world. Only when God withdraws his mercy, and Yusuf begins to once again lose his eyesight, does he return to God, talking to him, repenting and pleading for one more opportunity in life. As Rumi states, 'separation is to suffer His absence, majesty and severity (*qahr*). But mercy prevails over wrath, so every cruelty (*jafa'*) of the Beloved is in fact an act of faithfulness (*wafa'*). In showing their sincerity, God's lovers welcome the pain (*dard*) of the dregs (*durd*) along with the joy of the wine'.[42]

Mohammad Reza's puzzle in *The Colour of Paradise* – that 'if God loved us, he wouldn't make us blind' – is addressed in *The Willow Tree*. It turns out that Yusuf's blindness was a blessing in the disguise of suffering. As a blind man, he had been a respected professor who had dedicated his life to the study of mysticism and enjoyed the support of a loving family. God's love for him far outweighed his loss of physical sight. He enjoyed inner sight and peace as well as love and respect within both his private and social life. God's love for him, however, did not stop during the period of his separation from Him. When Yusuf loses his eyesight for the second time and begs God for another opportunity in life, he seeks not just the recovery of his sight, but an opportunity for repentance. As mentioned earlier, repentance is the first station on the Sufi path which, the eleventh-century Sufi, Hujwiri, states is followed by other stations such as conversion, renunciation and trust in God. The film ends with Yusuf effectively at the beginning of the Sufi path.

Self-Sacrifice and the Alchemy of Love

Whilst most Sufis agreed that the goal of the mystical path was achieving the *haqiqa* or Ultimate Reality or God, the various states and stations that led to this destination were not always defined in the same way. As we shall see shortly, this meant that what was characterised as a Sufi station in one definition of a particular Sufi master or group was at times recognised as a Sufi state in another. However, stations and states were recognised by the majority as undisputable necessities in the Sufi path. These stations and states stand between the lover and the Beloved and the lover has to traverse them before reaching his Beloved. In outlining the similarities of the Sufi and Shi'i doctrines, including the spiritual and gnostic stations, Nasr stresses how the 'spiritual stations of the Prophet and the Imams leading to union with God can be considered as the final goal towards which Shi'ite piety strives and upon which the whole spiritual structure of Shi'ism is based'.[43]

In the earliest formal exposition of Sufism in Persian, *Kashf al-mahjub*, the previously-mentioned Sufi 'Ali b. Uthman al-Jullabi al-Hujwiri states:

> The term 'spiritual station' (*maqam*) denotes one's 'standing' and 'rising' in the Way of God, not the devotee's dwelling there, and his fulfilment of the obligations relevant to that station until he completely realizes it as far as is humanly possible. It is not allowable that the devotee take leave of that station until he completely meets its requirements and fulfils its obligations. In this respect, the first station is 'repentance,' then 'conversion,' then 'renunciation,' then 'trust in God,' and so on. Hence, no one may lay claim to knowing 'conversion' without first experiencing 'repentance,' nor pretend to 'trust in God' without 'renunciation'.[44]

According to Hujwiri, following the stations on the Way are the mystic states (*ahwal*) of ecstasy bestowed upon the seeker's soul as signs of favour and grace to encourage him on his path. They are the gift of God alone, and in no way depend upon the mystic's own striving.[45] In short, whilst the seeker completes each station through his strict endeavours, the state is a gift that is endowed upon him through God's grace; he can have no active role in attaining it.

Rumi does not set out to give a systematic definition of each station and state. Like the three dimensions of Sufism, his works can be broadly divided into three categories. The first two are knowledge (*'ilm*) and action (*'amal*), or law and practice. Rumi refers to the third category not merely as a destination, but rather as a process that includes 'stations' (*maqamat*) and 'spiritual states' (*ahwal*). The believer is compared to a traveller who undergoes these inner experiences during his journey. This dimension

> concerns all the 'virtues' (*akhlaq*) the Sufi must acquire in keeping with the Prophet's saying, 'Assume the virtues of God!' If acquiring

virtues means 'attaining to God,' this is because they do not belong to man. The discipline of the Way coupled with God's grace and guidance results in a process of purification whereby the veil of human nature is gradually removed from the mirror of the primordial human substance, made in the image of God, or, in the Prophet's words, 'upon the Form of the All-Merciful.' Any perfection achieved by man is God's perfection reflected within him.[46]

The Sufi stations and states on the mystical path culminate in self-sacrifice and love. There are abundant references to these themes in Persian literature, and particularly in poetry. Rumi, 'Attar, Sa'di, Jami and Hafez's compositions are just a few examples of poetry filled with themes of love, sacrifice and self-annihilation. These poetic metaphors do not just refer to divine love. Jami's poetic rendition of the love story of Leyli and Majnun, for example, transforms human love into a vehicle and symbol of divine love.[47] Majidi explores these concepts through the vocabulary of love in modern times. His poetic discourse in *Baran* is a magnificent depiction of the various stages of the Sufi state of 'love'.

Baran is about a young Azeri man, Latif, who works on a building site in Tehran. His relatively easy job of catering and shopping for the labourers allows him to avoid the more arduous manual labour. When Najaf, an illegal Afghan labourer, falls from the second floor of the building and injures his leg, his young son, Rahmat, tries to replace his father to earn a living for the family. However, Rahmat proves too weak and incompetent. Subsequently, Memar, the construction supervisor, swaps Latif and Rahmat's jobs, forcing Latif to take on the hard labour he had so far managed to avoid.

Latif is furious at this new arrangement and takes all his anger out on Rahmat, who never utters a word. He grudgingly shows Rahmat the ropes and introduces him to the shop from which he used to buy groceries for the workers. The shopkeeper keeps Latif's birth certificate to guarantee the goods sold to him on credit. Latif takes the opportunity of being away from the site to slap Rahmat hard on the face on their way to the shop. Rahmat's only response is to pick up a stone and aim it at Latif but not throw it at him. To Latif's great disappointment, Rahmat's tea and lunch spreads are very soon welcomed enthusiastically by the men, and he is the only one who dines alone. In a fit, Latif goes to the tiny pantry where Rahmat is based and smashes everything, creating a huge mess. Rahmat, as usual, does not utter a word; a position he maintains

Figure 7 *Baran* (Majid Majidi, 2001). The moment when the wind blows the curtain, revealing Baran's reflection and, therefore, true identity, to Latif.

consistently throughout the movie. Instead, Latif's outrage allows Rahmat to clean up and rearrange the room from inside out, turning it into his own space. Latif, increasingly consumed by hatred for Rahmat and not satiated with these acts of revenge, waits one early morning on the rooftop in ambush for Rahmat and Soltan (an old Afghan worker who introduced Rahmat to Memar) and throws wet stucco at them. Later that day, when Latif is working from across the pantry, the wind blows aside the curtain at the entrance of the pantry and in the dim reflection of a mirror, he sees the image of a girl combing her long hair and tying it up. He creeps up behind the curtain to get a closer look and only then realises that Rahmat is, in fact, a girl disguised as a boy.

Latif is overwhelmed and bewildered when faced with the truth of Rahmat's identity. The unveiling of truth, and in this case, the two layers of unveiling − of the curtain lifted at the pantry entrance because of the wind and Rahmat's unveiling of her headcover − enables him to see the beauty hidden from him. His subsequent attempts to make amends do not simply arise from the shame and pain he feels for his previous selfish behaviour. Rather, he falls in love with Baran, which is Rahmat's real name. His blind and selfish acts were, therefore, a result of his ignorance, through which he failed to appreciate real beauty and truth. As Hujwiri states, 'All veils come from ignorance; when ignorance has passed away, the veils vanish and this life, by means of gnosis becomes one with the life to come'.[48] Once having entered the path, the Sufi undergoes a process of inward transformation. Similarly, this revelatory incident becomes the beginning of Latif's inward transformation. The following day, we see Latif breaking a wall in the construction site and making holes into it, like two eyes that let in light, a symbolic reference to Latif's newly acquired ability to see. As Smith argues, gnosis

> means the Vision, for when the eye of the soul is stripped of all the veils which hindered it from seeing God, then it beholds the reality of the Divine attributes by its own inner light, which goes far beyond the light which is given to perfect faith, for gnosis, as we have seen, belongs to a sphere quite other than of faith.[49]

The film follows Latif's inner journey, with various stages analogous to the Sufi stages, which is crucial in Sufi doctrine for 'the goal, which is to reach God, cannot be achieved except through the states and stations'.[50] At the beginning of the film Latif gave the impression of boyish insouciance and hot-temperedness; now he turns into a considerate man who channels all his anger into protecting Baran. When a worker throws back at her the cigarette she has bought for him, demanding a different brand, Latif jumps in and has a fight with him. When another worker walks into the pantry demanding tea outside break-time, Latif's blood boils and he forces the man to leave the pantry. When the government inspectors, alerted about Memar's employment of illegal Afghan workers, chase Baran in the street, Latif gets involved and takes the beating to give Baran enough time to escape. Interestingly this appears to happen on the very same street on which he had slapped her earlier. Latif is arrested and later bailed out of jail by Memar.

Discussing Rumi's philosophy of 'attainment' to God, Chittick argues that once the disciple has entered the Way, this third dimension of spiritual realisation is not a simple, one-step process. Rather, 'this third dimension of Sufi teaching deals with all the inner experiences undergone by the traveler on his journey'.[51] In this way, 'once having actualized wakefulness, the traveler moves on to repentance and then to self-examination; or once having achieved humility, he ascends to chivalry and then to expansion'.[52] Latif's acts clearly demonstrate these various stages of his inner journey, including wakefulness, repentance, humility and chivalry.

Thus, when Latif takes the beating and imprisonment for Baran's sake, he takes the first steps, in Rumi's terms, in chivalry and expansion.

However, these acts of redemption and sacrifice only prove to be the beginning of his long ordeal in loving Baran. Even though he is awakened from his ignorance and succeeds in overcoming many of his selfish desires, the greatest test still remains – the ability to overcome his ego. In Sufism, the ego is the final and most opaque veil that stands between man and his Beloved. '[The] Veil between man and God is not heaven and earth, but your assumptions and ego are your veil. Remove that from the way and you shall reach God'.[53] This annihilation of self is also an essential aspect of Rumi's philosophy. He asserts that it is only through the annihilation of selfhood that one can attain 'his true self, which is existence and "subsistence" within God'.[54]

After Baran's near arrest, Memar can no longer risk employing Afghans. Baran, along with all the other Afghan workers, is dismissed. This marks the beginning of Latif's restlessness in his separation from his beloved. Not knowing where to find her and unable to share his pain with anyone, he distances himself further and further from the world around him. The only trace of her left behind is a hairpin with a few strands of her hair caught in it, which he finds on the rooftop where she used to feed the pigeons. He treasures the hairpin like dear life and carries it with him everywhere. Again, this echoes a verse from 'Attar:

From her tresses, if I were to get a tip of her hair
I would treasure it like my eyes and attend to it like my life[55]

Latif begins searching for her in the secluded area outside the city where many Afghan families dwell. Despite being very close to her, he fails to see her even though she sees him. During his search he finds Soltan, the Afghan friend who had brought Baran to the construction site. He finds out from him that Rahmat works as a 'rock collector', removing heavy rocks from the river. After witnessing the extreme conditions under which Baran works, Latif becomes even more restless. He is desperate to save Baran from the arduous conditions in which she lives. After much pleading with Memar, he collects his pending salary for a year from Memar and takes it to Soltan. He asks Soltan to give the money to Najaf, Baran's father, without mentioning its source. Najaf, however, decides to gift the money back to Soltan so that he can return to Afghanistan and the family awaiting him.

Latif is devastated when he finds this out, not because he has lost all his earnings but because he seems unable to make a difference to Baran's difficult life. His acts of self-annihilation and non-existence are evident through this generous and selfless giving of all his material wealth for Baran. Latif takes the note that Soltan had left for him pledging to pay him back as soon as possible, and casts it into a stream. He had never considered the money's return and willingly accepted poverty for his love. The concept of poverty and giving away of one's material wealth is repeatedly employed in many Sufi teachings. As Chittick states:

> Rumi often employs the term 'poverty' in a context showing that it is synonymous with 'annihilation' and 'non-existence', the dervish is he who is 'poor' because he has nothing of 'his own'. He is totally empty of selfhood. The true 'poor man' is in truth the richest of all men, since not existing himself, he subsists through the Self. This then is the significance of the Prophet's saying, 'Poverty is my pride'.[56]

In Sufi teachings, love leads to man's annihilation, which is a necessary step in union with God. 'As long as man continues to live under the illusion of the real existence of his own ego, his own selfhood, he is far from God. Only through negation of himself can he attain to union with Him'.[57] Latif's self-annihilation culminates in doing away with his identity. With no money left except for a few notes of his pocket cash, he buys wooden crutches for Najaf and leaves them by their house door. He overhears Najaf sobbing for the death of his brother, killed in the war in Afghanistan, and his desire to return to help his brother's family.

When Memar refuses Najaf's request for a loan, Latif takes matters into his own hands. With nothing left, Latif sells his national identity card – the most important document an Iranian needs to hold to be recognised as a legal entity by the state – to black-market traffickers. With this act, therefore, he gives up the last trace of his identity, a metaphor that can be read as a complete annihilation of the self. On true love, Smith quotes the tenth-century Abu Abdallah al-Qurashi:

> 'True Love,' said Abu Abdallah al-Qurashi (*ob.* A.D. 941), 'means to give all that thou hast to Him Whom thou lovest, so that nothing remains to thee of thine own'. And this meant not only the sacrifice of personal possessions, which might be a cause of separation

between the lover and his Beloved, and the giving up of the personal will, but a complete self-surrender. Only the lover who is emptied of self can hope to be the dwelling-place of the Divine.[58]

Latif hands over to Najaf the money he receives from selling his identity, and pretends it was sent by Memar. Najaf is overjoyed and plans to leave for Afghanistan the following day. In effect, he uses this last belonging of Latif to separate him forever from his beloved. Latif runs aimlessly around the town and ends up at the local shrine. He leaves his cap, with Baran's hairpin on it by the pond and is drawn inside the shrine. It is as though the Divine has called for him. The shrine, which is referred to as Imamzadeh Sho'ayb, could be read as a Qur'anic reference to Moses who after fleeing from Egypt to Midian, is now a stranger with nothing on him. Moses implores God: 'My Lord! I am needy of whatever good Thou sendest down for me'.[59] It is then the daughters of the Prophet Sho'ayb bring their father's invitation to him. Moses not only finds shelter, but also companionsip of one of Sho'ayb's daughters who is given to him in marriage.[60]

As mentioned earlier, unlike the Sufi stations, which require man's concerted efforts, the Sufi states are 'usually said to consist of spiritual graces bestowed directly by God and outside of man's power of

Figure 8 *Baran* (Majid Majidi, 2001). Baran opening the door to Latif when he goes to deliver to her father, Najaf, the money he has raised from selling his ID card.

acquisition'.⁶¹ Latif's acts of selflessness thus far can be read as ascending the hierarchical Sufi stations. His experience in the shrine, however, tells of the grace of having entered the Sufi state, reflected in the contentment in his face as he sees his beloved off the next day. He kneels in front of her to help her pick up the vegetables she has dropped on the ground just before she is to leave. And it is at this moment that he finally, albeit briefly, succeeds in fully gazing upon the face of his beloved. As Smith argues, pure love guides the mystic from one station to another

> until he comes to the end of the first stage of the Way, when the mirror of the soul has become as pure from self as flame from smoke, and is fitted to reflect the Light of God, by which it is illuminated in the second stage, that of ecstasy; and now the mystic enters upon that third stage of attainment, which is indeed the end of his journey. There he receives that mystic knowledge of the Divine, the gnosis (*ma'rifa*), which will enable him to see God face to face, and in seeing Him, to become one with Him.⁶²

Through this film, Majidi demonstrates Latif's inner journey and maturity from nonchalant boy to selfless lover. As in Qur'an 33:50 where the mercy of God is compared to the rain that revives the earth after its death:

> Then contemplate (O man!) the memorials of Allah's Mercy! How He gives life to the earth after its death: verily the same will give life to the men who are dead: for He has power over all things.

So, too, does Latif's beloved become the *baran-e rahmat* (rain of mercy) that pours over him and graces him. After she leaves, the only trace left of her is a footprint in the mud, which steadily fills up with the pouring rain that begins just as she departs. Aside from the metaphor with the Qur'anic verse, this reference could also be read vis-à-vis Rumi's reference to this world as a rain-filled footprint.⁶³ According to Rumi,

> because Love pertains to the experiential dimension of Sufism, not the theoretical, it must be experienced to be understood. It cannot be explained in words, any more than the true nature of one's attachment to a beloved of this world can be set down on paper'.⁶⁴

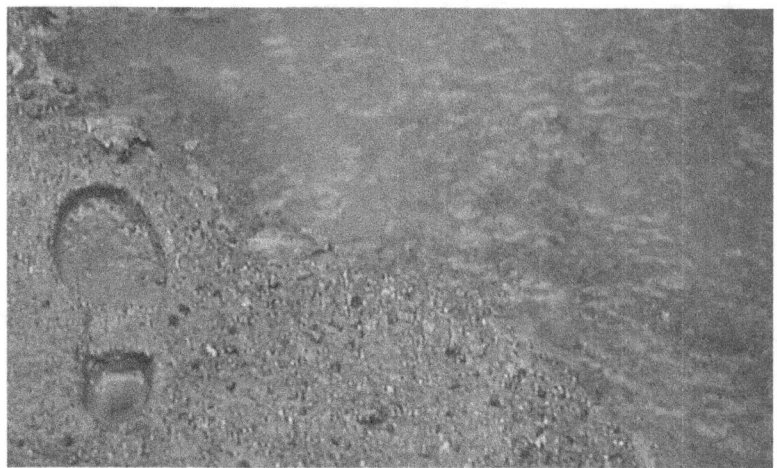

Figure 9 *Baran* (Majid Majidi, 2001). A footprint, the only remaining trace of Baran, steadily filling with rain.

Similarly, Majidi's narrative provides us with a glimpse of this transformative experience, and allows us to see that which cannot be articulated through the narrow confines of words.

Conclusions

Sufism's early appearance within Islamic history, the vast amount of literature it has produced over the centuries as well as its pervasive influence on Muslim culture and society makes it an undeniably significant approach within Islam. Persian literature, and particularly its poetry, played a significant role in the expression of Sufi ideas. Numerous works explore the Sufi states and stations, and the mastery with which many of them have been composed, has rendered their authors immortal. As diverse as these approaches can be, man's spiritual attainment and his proximity to God remain at the core of any Sufi teaching. One can write volumes on Sufism, but this chapter focused selectively on those arguments that have been expressed in the works of Majidi in order to show their filmic expressions.

Majidi's films are a reflection of Iranian Shi'i religious expressions, which are not limited to the sacred texts, but also draw from the works of great mystical masters. Majidi demonstrates how the Shi'i and particularly Iranian Shi'i expression of religion is deeply rooted not only in its sacred texts but also in the artistic and cultural expression of the people. With their poetic language, Majidi's works are filmic discourses on man's journey to spiritual attainment and his proximity to God. The four Sufi postulates – intuition, inward light, going beyond self and love – are all explored in Majidi's three films discussed above. In *The Colour of Paradise*, Mohammad Reza's intuition and inward light is contrasted with his father's inward blindness and lack of intuition. They live in different worlds even as they share the same time and space. This leads to the very different ways in which each of them approaches pain and suffering. In *The Willow Tree,* Yusuf's intuition and inward light during the long period of his blindness had allowed him to live in a paradise of peace and happiness, a state which he rapidly loses after the gleam of the outside world blinds his inward light. *Baran* is a filmic discourse on the various Sufi stations and states in which love becomes the guide to the soul's journey and its ascent to God. *Baran*'s narrative relates the various Sufi stages: drawing the curtains of ignorance and stripping off the veils of selfishness and sensuality to see the Divine vision. In all these films, spiritual attainment requires no special rank or distinction, or indeed, any understanding and study of the textual sources, and includes the ordinary man. In fact, none of the characters, except for Yusuf, are formally educated in mystical knowledge. Most of Majidi's protagonists undergoing these spiritual journeys are either children or barely-educated adults from an impoverished social class.

Majidi's works bring these age-old mystical notions to the silver screen and apply them to the modern-day lives of ordinary people. Just as Rumi, 'Attar, Sa'di and Jami's works are not a mere collection of stories and poetry but imbued and embedded with Sufi teachings and meanings, Majidi's films are similarly not just simple stories of destitute or disabled people. Instead, they are layered with Sufi concepts that allow his viewers to share the spiritual experiences of his characters. He reifies these abstract concepts through the medium of film and draws their relevance to today's modern world much as they were at the time of their articulation many centuries ago. The modern-day focus on the Muslim interpretation of self-annihilation is often understood in terms of violent acts of terror and destruction such as suicide attacks. In the Sufi context of Islam, sacrificing oneself, however, is not and was not ever defined as dogmatic reactions seeking to wreak havoc on lives and livelihoods at the touch of a button. It is, in fact, a long and challenging process of sacrificing one's desires for the betterment of another, of practising patience, forgiveness and love. What Majidi succeeds in doing is to produce a modern discourse which is rooted in the medieval Iranian mystical discourse of Islam and acts as a reminder of Sufi notions. Like the stories of Leyli and Majnun, the Simurgh and the *Mathnawi*, Majidi also narrates stories, but through the medium of film and with contemporary and ordinary Iranians as his heroes.

Having explored formalistic approaches to religion through film in the previous chapter, and mystical and personal approaches in this chapter, in the next chapter I will study how cinema gives new life to a Shi'i expression that is communal and public, but unpopular with the formalistic approach propounded by the religious authorities.

CHAPTER 5

CINEMA AS A RESERVOIR FOR CULTURAL MEMORY

In February 2007, BBC Persian Radio reported on the latest trends of music and mobile ringtones in Iran during the month of Muharram, particularly those heard during the ninth and tenth day of Muharram (Tasu'a and 'Ashura respectively). These did not fall into any of the two broad music categories popular in Iran – pop music, including Western and Iranian pop, or classical Iranian music. Rather, they were *nowheh-khani* (singing *nowheh*). *Nowheh* are lyrics mourning Imam Husayn, the third Shi'i imam, martyred at Karbala in the seventh century. One young man played the two different *nowheh* ringtones he had on his mobile phone for the interviewer. He explained that one *nowheh* was set as his general ringtone and the other was assigned to his '*jujeh*' (lit. 'chick'/girlfriend). Other interviewees also said that they changed over their mobile ringtones and their car CDs to *nowheh* to keep with the mood of this period.

Most interesting, however, was the interview with Hossein Tohi, an Iranian rapper, whose music is part of the Iranian underground music scene. A computer student, Tohi (Hossein's self-styled name meaning 'empty' in Persian) was born in 1986. Even though a number of rappers have emerged in Iran, only a few have gained official authorisation. The majority of the rap-Farsi (Persian rap) singers remain part of the underground scene and disseminate their work mainly through the internet. Hossein Tohi relates how he woke up one morning in the early days of Muharram 2007 and felt like writing about Imam Husayn. He asked his composer friend, Mahdiyar, who was familiar with Eastern music, to compose music for his rap. The end result could be called rap-*nowheh*, with its lyrics praising the Imam and mourning his death, sung in rap-Farsi to music that also employed the traditional percussions used in *nowheh*. Tohi, however, refuses to refer to it as *nowheh* and instead prefers to call it simply a rap about Imam Husayn and his companions.[1] Here is an extract of his rap about Imam Husayn, the first Muharram Rap[2]:

> The minute your name is mentioned, oh Master! [Imam Husayn],
> I do not know why my tears start running and the love in my heart increases.
> You are the greatest of martyrs and noblemen,
> It has been years since your death
> But your name still remains alive, oh Master!
> I pray I will have the opportunity
> Barefoot to come and visit your shrine.
> Or for you to come at night to my land,
> And visit me in my dreams.
> You know that I carry your name,
> And would never want to stay away from you.
> Let me be your servant at your shrine,
> Or maybe you still do not find it deserving and, therefore, that is for the best.
> We beat our chests for you during Muharram,
> And in one voice say 'Oh, Husayn!' when we are with one another.
> Oh Master! Do have a look at us and put your hand on our shoulders,
> Take some of the burden from our shoulders.
> The truth is that I'm terrified,
> That you will leave me alone on the first night of my death...

The programme continued its report on the many different kinds of music produced over that past year for Muharram. These employ various music genres – some a fusion of the traditional *nowheh* music and others just pure pop. Is this, as the interviewer asked, an updating of the Muharram mourning? However we define this music, this new form of lamenting for Imam Husayn has certainly attracted a large number of youth, making quite untenable the claim that listening to *nowheh* is an outdated practice of the older, or more traditional, generation. In fact, the amalgam of Shi'i religious concepts and modern musical genres has enabled a new medium of expression through which Iranian youth can more easily explore their Shi'i identity. However, trying to attract the youth to *nowheh* is not always considered a good enough excuse for 'reinventing' or 'modernising' traditional religious practices. Daneshmand is just one adherent of this latter school of thought.

Hojjatol Islam Mehdi Daneshmand is an Iranian cleric and author of a number of books on religion. He is a frequent public speaker and delivers sermons in different parts of Iran. Daneshmand is highly entertaining, with a great talent for doing impressions and, unusually for a cleric, has no compunction about swearing during his speeches. The reach of his sermons now extends beyond the mosques and other public sessions, thanks to the virtual world of the internet and particularly YouTube. Some of his clips on YouTube have received hundreds of thousands of hits. Given the fact that the clips are in Persian and not subtitled, one can safely assume that most of his virtual audience is also Iranian. Not all of these audiences, however, can be classified as enthusiastic viewers, as some of the obscenities left in the comments section testify. My main interest in Daneshmand's speeches, however, revolves around his references to the commemorative practices of Muharram, for they reflect an important sample of the current official religious attitudes towards them.

Daneshmand is critical of many aspects of these commemorative practices of Muharram. He particularly takes issue with the *maddah*s. *Maddah*s, literally eulogists, like the *rowzeh-khan*s narrate stories of the Prophet, imams and saints. *Maddah*s are not necessarily trained in the madrasas and draw their material from a broad spectrum of literature, including their own compositions. Daneshmand criticises the ways in which many of the current *maddah*s praise the Shi'i imams and the family of the Prophet. He holds these 'ignorant and uneducated' *maddah*s responsible for providing the Sunnis with the ammunition to condemn Shi'i rituals and practices. The internet, he states, is rife with Sunni sites that are anti-Shi'a and they use extracts from these *maddah*s to prove that the Shi'a are heretics. His own selective extracts from the *maddah*s provide him with the perfect foil for condemning those religious ceremonies that are held independently of the ulama. Not only are the *maddah*s, therefore, framed as uneducated, uninformed and bereft of any religious knowledge, but more dangerously, their ignorance offers the enemies of Shi'ism an excuse to revile it! The audiences of these *maddah*s are not spared either. Daneshmand holds them equally responsible for attending these sessions and keeping quiet during such disgrace, which brings untold shame upon religion:

> A bunch of uneducated no-goods get together and chant 'Husayn, Husayn!' ... You beating your chest for three hours, how many sermons of Imam Husayn have you studied? How many books have you studied on Imam Husayn?
>
> ... I was in one of the provinces and I actually disrupted the session. The *maddah* there was singing: 'Hasan [Husayn's elder brother and preceding imam] has one dot [a reference to the dots in the Arabic/Persian alphabet], Husayn has three dots, Fatemeh [Husayn's mother, the Prophet's daughter] has one dot, Zaynab [Husayn's sister] has five dots, Wah! Wah! ...' I said, 'Shut it, and why are you [the audience] wailing?' ... CDs of these sessions are made and then put on the internet and the Sunnis come and show it around and say: 'See! This is the share of the Shi'a [their contribution to Islam] ....' What is this you [the *maddah*s] are saying? Don't you have brains? ... Didn't Zaynab have sermons? Didn't she have speeches? ... What kind of a *rowzeh* is this that you are feeding people in the name of religion?[3]

In another speech, he further criticises mourning sessions set up independently of the ulama which, therefore, result in heretical and blasphemous talk. The extract below, taken from his sermons, is yet another example of the tension between the laity and the clergy discussed in Chapters 1 and 3. Religion, Daneshmand implies, should remain within the domain of the clergy whose prerogative it is to authorise religious rituals and practices. It is certainly not for the *maddah*s to bring in music as an accompaniment to their singing. For Daneshmand, the entire practice, whether it is the lyrics, the *maddah*s or the audience clapping their hands together, is problematic. It should be noted however, that the very fact that the Ministry of Culture and Islamic Guidance broadcasts *nowheh*s with music, if not necessarily the exact ones that Daneshmand points to, on national radio and television, gives them some degree of legitimacy, if not outright endorsement. At the very least, it points to the plurality of practice sanctioned by the state even as it attempts to strike a delicate balance between filling in a gap 'demanded' by the laity, and being cognisant of the concerns of more conservative elements within the state who fear the erosion of their power and influence. As we shall see below, Daneshmand is conscious of this perceived sanction and addresses it squarely:

> A few *maddah*s, who have studied under only-God-knows-which-master, string together some rubbish so that they can supposedly attract the youth to them.
>
> ... When not even one *'alim* [singular of ulama] is present in [organising and guiding] your gathering, it is no surprise that the result is this kind of catastrophe.

Daneshmand then goes on to provide an example of lyric he had heard a *maddah* sing:

> 'I who hold on to the love of Husayn,
>
> Am only the dog of Husayn'
>
> For God's sake, what kind of a lyric is this?
>
> ... They say 'la ilaha illa Husayn' [There is no God but Husayn] ... They've no clue what they're saying. This is blasphemy!!!
>
> ... Tapes of this group of uncouth *maddah*s, who have distanced themselves from the ulama, are being distributed in Zahidan [a province bordering Pakistan], in the Arab countries, in Saudi Arabia. This has closed the mouths of [i.e. silenced] the [Shi'i] ulama. They [the anti-Shi'a Sunnis] say you are heretics! You consider Fatima and Husayn as God!!! ... The reputation of religion is not in the hands of these few maddahs.
>
> They sing their *maddahi*s with the keyboard, with *santoor* [a traditional string instrument].
>
> You've taken the bloody music into the pulpit, into the mihrab and into *rowzeh* as well!!!
>
> The Ministry of [Culture and] Islamic Guidance ... has spent millions and trillions of tomans on *daf* and *tonbak* [both traditional percussion instruments]. What does it want from mihrab and religion? Leave Husayn alone ... leave religion alone ... leave the keyboard for the television and radio, and the Ministry of Culture and Islamic Guidance. Wherever there are *tonbak*s, all the cameras are ready and present, but they don't want to have anything to do with a session of such grandeur [pointing to his own session] ...

I have to say that religion has a master ... Husayn's head did not go on top of the spear so that I and you could get together now in his sessions and clap our hands and whistle, play the *santoor*, take the *santoor* inside the mihrab. Whoever has heard of *maddahi* with flute?! They justify that the Islamic Republic of Iran Broadcasting shows it [these *maddahi*s]; the Islamic Republic of Iran Broadcasting shows a lot of things, like the struggle of the fittest in the jungle, should you imitate? ... The Islamic Republic of Iran Broadcasting is not a source of emulation (*marja'-e taqlid*), the radio is not a source of emulation, they cannot be the source of emulation, they cannot show jurisprudence.[4]

Many Shi'i practices such as pilgrimage to the shrines of the imams and saints, and visual representations of the imams and the prophets, have been condemned by mainstream Sunnis.[5] Shi'as, however, have not necessarily thus shied away from rituals that may be perceived as 'unIslamic' by the Sunnis. Daneshmand's concerns about such 'malpractices' do not appear to stem solely from anxiety about believers losing salvation, but also about the disrepute that they can bring Shi'ism. This constant awareness of the 'Other's' perception and condemnation of 'Self' appears to precipitate attempts to comply and reconcile with what is acceptable to that 'normative' view, and, in turn, to shape local practices. One could even question if Sunni normativity is replacing Shi'i sensibilities. It is, therefore, pertinent to ask if the recent banning (in the Muharram of 2007) of certain practices, some of which had been observed for centuries in Iran, is a reaction to anti-Shi'a propaganda or a political discourse used to strategically condemn rival factions.

The official bans in 2007 included public displays of the images of the imams, the carrying of *alam*s (standards) during the mourning processions and the playing of instruments as part of the commemorative ceremonies. It is, however, debatable whether individual Shi'a themselves will remove the pictures of the imams from their homes, shops or cafes. But for now, another video clip on YouTube very tellingly streams a *maddah* beating his chest and singing passionately in a very crowded mourning session: 'They can say whatever they want, I am the dog in Zaynab's alley!', upon which the congregation beat their chests and repeat this refrain after him.[6] Interestingly, a fragment of a silk and gold carpet dating from 1600–1625, and on display at the British Museum's exhibition in 2009 entitled *Shah 'Abbas: The Remaking of Iran*, bears *waqf* inscriptions referring to the Shah as 'the dog of this shrine'. Indeed, the exhibition catalogue cites additional references where Shah 'Abbas is referred to as 'the dog of 'Ali ibn Abi Talib' or 'the dog of the shrine'.[7] One can, therefore, safely assume that the phrase 'dog of Husayn' has been in currency for a long time within the Shi'i Iranian vocabulary and is not a recent innovation as Daneshmand would have it. The question posed above regarding Shi'i sensibilities and Sunni normativity is obviously far more complex and requires further research which lies outside the scope of this study. However, it is clear that the current commemorative events of Muharram are not just about Husayn and his message. Even though *ta'ziyeh* (the passion play) traditionally offered an opportunity to criticise the injustices of the privileged, a theme that will be discussed later in this chapter, recent events suggest new developments of the Muharram sessions. Interestingly, the Muharram commemorations have themselves turned into a battle for authority in defining what these commemorations do and do not entail. It is the official versus the popular discourse on Husayn, a battle that is not so easily won on either side.

Aside from the general populace, the events of Karbala and the martyrdom of Husayn have also inspired many film-makers. The notion of martyrdom in its specific Shi'i tradition has been heavily employed in the war films made about the Iran-Iraq war, referred to as Sacred Defence Cinema (*Sinama-ye defa'-e moqaddas*). As we saw in the Introduction, other than a few exceptions, these are usually propagandist films, a genre that has already been extensively studied. In this chapter I will explore the ways in which film provides a new medium of expression for one of the oldest Shi'i narratives, highlighting the continuing impact of Husayn's story on Shi'i believers. I will first examine the various approaches to commemorating the death of Husayn, who is fundamental to Shi'i Iranian identity and has captured both the laity's imagination and the clergy's attention. As such I will proceed to discuss the origins and development as well as the characteristics of *ta'ziyeh*, the oldest and until the modern period the 'only' Islamic drama, which re-enacts the events of Karbala. Next, I will examine how two filmmakers employ elements from *ta'ziyeh* in their filmic narratives. Like *ta'ziyeh*, many of these films include the historical and mythological in their narratives. In the final section, I will study how Kiarostami captures the continuing relevance of the martyrdom of Husayn in the Iranian Shi'i context.

The Figure of Husayn and Iranian Shi'i Identity

Husayn b. 'Ali was the grandson of the Prophet Muhammad, and the third Shi'i imam. After the death of the first Shi'i imam, 'Ali, the Shi'a followed Hasan, his eldest son as their imam. Upon his death – or murder, according to Shi'a tradition, by the order of the Umayyad caliph, Mu'awiya, in 669 – 'Ali's second son, Husayn was to succeed as the third Shi'a imam. The *Shi'at 'Ali* who were displeased with their Sunni Umayyad rulers persistently invited Husayn to rise against the Umayyads. In 680, Mu'awiya passed away and was succeeded by his son, Yazid. The *Shi'at 'Ali* of Kufa, who had begun a rebellion against the new caliph, sent messages to Husayn asking him to lead them and take over the caliphate of Yazid. Husayn accepted their invitation and set out from Mecca for Kufa. He was accompanied only by members of his family and close companions. However, when Yazid sent an army of 4000 men to stop Husayn on his way, the Kufans failed to stand by their oath of allegiance and did not come to his aid.

Husayn refused to pay homage to Yazid and, on the second day of Muharram, was forced to camp at Karbala, a desert place without fortifications or water. Yazid's army closed off Husayn's access to water by installing 500 men on the way to the Euphrates.[8] Husayn and his companions were made to suffer from thirst for three days. On 'Ashura, the 10th day of Muharram, under the command of Shimr (also referred to as Shamir) Yazid's army attacked Husayn's camp. By afternoon, they had slaughtered Husayn and all his men, including young children. The martyrs of Karbala numbered 72. Shimr would have also killed Husayn's sick boy, Zayn al-'Abidin, who had had to remain in his tent. However, Ibn Sa'd, Yazid's commander, restrained him and forbade anyone from entering that tent. As we shall see, the tragic death of Husayn and his companions at Karbala near Kufa in 680 'played an important role in the consolidation of the Shi'i ethos',[9] becoming the central historical event in the lives and consciousness of the Shi'a

Husayn: Sayyid al-Shuhada', *Master of the Martyrs*

David Cook outlines a number of factors that characterise the figure of the martyr. The martyr must have 'belief in one belief system and possess a willingness to defy another belief system'.[10] His martyrdom is more effective if this particular belief system is under attack or in a minority position, whether politically or culturally. 'By demonstrating publicly that there is something in the subordinated or persecuted belief system worth dying for, the value other believers place upon it is augmented, and that belief system is highlighted'.[11] The audience also plays an important role in the martyrdom narrative and in ensuring the success of martyrdom itself, for they are instrumental in shaping the historical memory of the martyr. This audience does not need to be physically present during the pre-martyrdom suffering or at the moment of martyrdom, but must have access to the information. 'Ideally for the martyrdom to succeed, there must be an absolute evil upon which the audience can focus their revulsion'.[12] This can be a ruling power or its representative that is oppressive or at least conceived to be as such within the narrative.

One can easily trace all of the above elements in the narrative of Husayn. Husayn, the grandson of the Prophet, refused to give in to the Umayyad usurpers and their unjust rule. In fact, his 'martyrdom epitomized the essential illegitimacy of the Umayyad rulers, who contrasted unfavourably with his pious lifestyle'.[13] He was demonstrating a willingness to defy the Umayyad belief-system. He was in a position of minority, as leader of a political group of the *Shi'at 'Ali*, as well as in terms of the military might of his enemies who attacked him. The first audience is Husayn's family, particularly his sister Zaynab, who is taken captive to the court of Yazid in Damascus. History has recorded the eloquent speech she delivers in Yazid's court, condemning his actions at the unjust murder of Husayn. The community itself also becomes the audience. This can be traced back to the *tawwabun* (Penitents), who gathered to lament his death four years after his murder. As discussed below, this continued over the centuries and found various forms of expression. The absolute evil, Yazid, the Umayyad ruler, and Shimr, the killer, became the subject of absolute hate and revulsion for the Shi'i mourners, epitomising all that is evil, cruel and repulsive.

The figures of Husayn and his opponents have been invoked not just in narrating the events of Karbala in the commemorative processions or in the religious ceremonies of *rowzeh-khani*, but also in addressing contemporary historic moments. In fact, Khomeini's rhetoric, both during the struggles to overthrow the Shah and after the success of the Revolution, relied heavily on these religious icons. The corrupt regime of the Shah, he stated, was the present *taqut*, a Qur'anic reference to the idolatrous and tyrannical Pharaohs. Khomeini thus implied that he was the Moses of his time, who was to free the people from the enslavement of the unjust rulers. The 'unIslamic' reign of the Pahlavi Shah was to end so that the Muslim community and umma could be preserved. However, soon after the Revolution, when another Muslim country, Iraq, attacked Iran, the rhetoric changed: it was no longer that of a Muslim umma against idolaters and heretics. Rather Husayn once again became the mobilising figure in uniting Iranians to defend their country against the tyrannical Saddam and his Arab armies. Suddenly, Iranian nationalism was once again relevant to the Islamic Republic, which had hitherto tried to downplay it in favour of a wider Islamic identity. The historical Sunni-Shi'a differences returned to the forefront.

Husayn remains the only figure whose death has been commemorated so extensively in Iran. He plays a pivotal role in the formation of Iran's Shi'i identity. His martyrdom has turned him into one of the greatest mythical figures of Iranian narrative – a narrative that has been appropriated by various factions at different periods. Thus, Khomeini employed this narrative in his anti-Shah rebellions from 1961 onwards. He created a new image of Husayn that 'was to be not only the object of mourning and pity, but the example of courage and resistance. His image was redefined from one of passive suffering to one of protest against tyranny'.[14] The story of Husayn also found expression amongst both laity and clergy, such as *pardeh-khani*, *ta'ziyeh* and *rowzeh-khani*, which will be discussed below. The former expressions allowed the laity a personal and direct engagement with religion as well as resulted in the creation of certain religious rituals which historically have not always met with the approval of the clergy.

Commemorating Husayn

Four years after the death of Husayn, a small group of *Shi'at 'Ali* from Kufa gathered at Karbala to lament his murder as an act of repentance for failing to come to his aid. This group called themselves *tawwabun* or 'Penitents.' This event was significant for various reasons. Firstly, even though lamentation as an act of atonement already existed in the Mediterranean religions such as Zoroastrianism, Manichaeism, Christianity and Judaism, this was the first time that it was practised within an Islamic framework. 'Indeed, the collective lamentations of the Penitents at Karbala were the first documented rituals of what would eventually become a wholly new religious tradition'.[15] More importantly, it is from this time onwards that the *Shi'at 'Ali*, who as a group had sought the political leadership of the Muslims from within the *ahl al-bayt*, or family of the Prophet, came to evolve into a distinct religious tradition called Shi'ism.

> Put simply, the memory of Karbala was slowly transforming the Shi'atu Ali from a political faction with the aim of restoring the

leadership of the community to the family of the Prophet, into an utterly distinct religious sect in Islam: *Shi'ism*, a religion founded on the ideal of the righteous believer who, following in the footsteps of the martyrs at Karbala, willingly sacrifices himself in the struggle for justice against oppression.[16]

A number of scholars have thus linked Shi'a identity with Persian ethnicity, noting that the Persian struggle against Arab domination traces its roots back to the events of Karbala:

> Husayn's refusal to admit the legitimacy of the Umayyad caliphate had been a stance that he shared with the people of Kufa, 'Ali's capital. Many Kufans were liberated slaves and Persian prisoners of war who had risen in revolt against the distinctly Arab character of Umayyad rule'.[17]

It is not only Iranians who project this link from within, but also Arabs from outside, who even today associate it back to the Abbasid period and the Shu'ubiya movement – a literary movement that 'was formed to assert the cultural superiority of the Persians to the Arabs, and to influence the official culture of the 'Abbasid Caliphate'.[18] Indeed, Nasr asserts that the Arab 'treatment of Shias as outsiders – as "lesser Arabs" – has always found justification in the accusation that they are Iranian, and that their demand for rights is nothing more than a modern-day reenactment of the Iranian-led *sho'oubi* revolt against Arab rule in the early centuries of Islam'.[19]

The first recorded public commemoration of Muharram has been traced to the 10th century Persian Shi'i Buyid ruler, Mu'izz al-Dawla, who enforced it in Baghdad in 963. All businesses were closed during the 10 days of Muharram and people were asked to participate in the lamentations for Husayn.[20] The practice, did not, however, survive long after the fall of the Buyid dynasty in 1055. The religious sessions known as *rowzeh-khani*, or reading religious sermons about the events of Karbala, popular among the Iranian Shi'a today, are traced back to the Safavid period. Husayn Kashefi's (d. 1504) composition of *Rowzat al-shuhada'* (Paradise of Martyrs), a literary masterpiece, became a popular text for *rowzeh-khani*:

> Originally, it was customary to recite or chant a chapter from *The Garden of the Martyrs* in public each day during the first ten days of Muharram. Gradually, it was staged during the whole month

of Muharram and the following month of Safar, eventually to be performed all year round.[21]

As discussed in Chapter 1, one of the religious functions that madrasa graduates of the first cycle are able to perform is reading and reciting the stories of Karbala during the mourning ceremonies of the month of Muharram. These sessions are held either at the mosques, the private quarters of individuals or *tekiyeh*s, and are a means of generating income for the clergy.

It was also during the Safavid period that significant mourning processions, along with standards (*alam*s), horses and drums, were led on the streets during the first 10 days of Muharram. These were also accompanied by some theatrical elements. The battle of Karbala also provided the 'prototype for the only indigenous dramatic form in the world of Islam'.[22] This drama, in which the tragic events of Karbala are re-enacted, is referred to as *ta'ziyeh*, or passion play. The term '*ta'ziyeh*' itself 'literally means expressions of sympathy, mourning and consolation'.[23]

Figure 10 A *ta'ziyeh* troupe in the roles of (left to right) Malek-e Ashtar's father, the teacher of Hasan and Husayn, Fatemeh, an extra, Malek-e Ashtar, Hasan, Husayn, and the Prophet Muhammad. The re-enactment of *ta'ziyeh* includes stories other than the martyrdom of Husayn. Here, the story of Malek-e Ashtar's conversion to Islam is performed. Photo: Pejman Pak. Tehran, August 2010.

CINEMA AS A RESERVOIR 135

Some scholars have traced back the roots of *ta'ziyeh* to earlier pre-Islamic Iranian rituals. The similarities between *ta'ziyeh* and particularly *Siyawush-khani* has led many to believe that *ta'ziyeh* was rooted in these ancient practices.[24] According to Iranian cultural tradition, Siyawush, the son of Kaykawus, the Persian emperor, was falsely accused by his stepmother, Sudabeh, of raping her. To prove his innocence, Siyawush had to undergo a trial by fire. He emerged unharmed out of this trial and was thus cleared of any wrongdoing. Later, he commanded his father's army against the invading forces of Afrasiyab, the king of Turan. Nevertheless, when Siyawush accepted the peace proposal offered by Afrasiyab, his father Kaykawus dismissed him and the peace treaty. Consequently, Siyawush joined Afrasiyab, who accepted him with open arms and even gave his own daughter to him in marriage. Siyawush's popularity and rising power displeased Afrasiyab's brother, who went on to instigate Siyawush's death.

Siyawush's innocent death some few thousand years ago was lamented by men and women and marked by many elegies. Minstrels would sing and recite these elegies, commemorating Siyawush's death. An archaeological discovery in the ruins of the city of Panjikent, 68 km from Samarqand, provided further evidence of the connection between *Siyawush-khani* and the mourning rituals of Husayn. The discovery was of a wall painting dating back to around 300 BC. It depicts Siyawush in a large coffin,

Figure 11 A *pardeh-khani* in Tehran, August 2010. Photo: Pejman Pak.

with a number of men and women surrounding the coffin, beating their faces, heads and chests. The resemblance of this depiction to the Shi'i Iranian mourning rites for Husayn is striking,[25] rites that are also present in *ta'ziyeh* performances.

Ta'ziyeh also appears to have evolved from a number of earlier pre-Islamic visual and performing arts such as *pardeh-khani* (story-chanting) and *naqqali* (storytelling). In *pardeh-khani,* the narrator uses a *pardeh* or painted screen that usually illustrates the various episodes of his narration. Screens used for the mourning of Husayn usually have depictions of the battle of Karbala, with some Qur'anic references and at times even stories from the national epic of *Shahnameh*. The *pardeh-khan* then sings and recites the story, pointing to the illustrations on the screen to elucidate the scene. Later, *ta'ziyeh* drew heavily from these depictions, as well as from the elegies of *pardeh-khani, naqqali* and *rowzeh-khani* themselves and the techniques of *naqqali* recitation.

Despite its religious motifs, *ta'ziyeh* did not at first meet with the approval of all the ulama. They objected to it on various theological grounds that condemned human representation in art, and the contentious issue of music.[26] Moreover, it allowed women to watch the play, providing a new space for their public appearance and participation. Most importantly, however, its great popularity became a threat to *rowzeh-khani,* a ceremony that was customarily organised by the ulama, and from which they earned an income. However, others such as Mirza Abu'l Qasim Qommi (d. 1815), a prominent religious authority living during the reign of Fath 'Ali Shah (r. 1797–1834), supported *ta'ziyeh*. In a *fatwa* (religious decision), he 'unequivocally expressed the opinion that not only were religious plays lawful and not prohibited but that they were among the greatest of religious works'.[27] This is comparable to the decision Khomeini was forced to make about cinema. With the Islamic Republic's victory in 1979, the ulama chose to endorse cinema by appropriating it for their own political purposes. While Khomeini opposed cinema's 'misuse', its adoption 'became an ideological tool to combat Pahlavi culture'.[28]

Ta'ziyeh: the only Islamic Drama

Ta'ziyeh started out as an outdoor performance, with simplicity of dialogue, props and *mise-en-scene*. With its growing popularity, however, the need for a permanent place was all too evident, and resulted in the building of the *tekiyeh*s. These were modelled after the local caravanserais,

Figure 12 The famous Ostad Torabi performing *naqqali* (storytelling) of the *Shahnameh*. Photo: Pejman Pak. Tehran, August 2010.

which were square or rectangular buildings with rooms on the perimeter overlooking a vast yard in the middle. The pond traditionally located at the centre of the yard was covered or replaced by a raised stage on which the actors would perform, surrounded on all sides by the audience.

Audience participation is one of the main features of *ta'ziyeh*. As Pelly observes,

> If the success of a drama is to be measured by the effects which it produces upon the people for whom it is composed, or upon the audience before whom it is represented, no play has ever surpassed the tragedy known in the Mussulman world as that of Hasan and Husain.[29]

People cry and sympathise with the sufferings of the imam and curse his enemies in the play. The actors are called *shabih* or dramatisers. Each of the actors have the suffix '-*khan*' i.e. 'reader' (of the manuscript) attached to their titles. Thus, each follower of Husayn is referred to as *mazlum-khan* (the reader of the oppressed), each of his enemies as *mokhalef-khan*

Figure 13 Musicians playing for *ta'ziyeh* as well as *naqqali*. Among other things, the music cues the passage of time, sets the battle scenes and is an important component of the drama. Photo: Pejman Pak. Tehran, August 2010.

Figure 14 A *mokhalef-khan* in the role of Qanbar's uncle, an idolator, who promises his daughter's hand in marriage to Qanbar on the condition that the latter kills 'Ali. Photo: Pejman Pak. Tehran, August 2010.

(the reader of the opposition), the actor playing Husayn as *Husayn-khan* (the reader of Husayn) and Shimr, Husayn's slayer, *Shimr-khan* (the reader of Shimr). This serves to remind the audience that these individuals are, in fact, actors playing out the roles and not actually Shimr or Husayn. Thus, during the performance, the actor playing Shimr would himself cry, inviting the audience to join in his sobs, as he prepared to behead Husayn.[30]

Music and poetry were an integral part of the *ta'ziyeh* performance. *Ta'ziyeh* scripts took the form of poetry. Unlike the poetry of the great Persian masters, *ta'ziyeh* was written in a language accessible to ordinary people. As Beyzaie emphasises, it was not a performance of poetry, but rather a performance employing poetry as its language.[31] The poetic framework of *ta'ziyeh* drew from *marsiyeh* (poetry composed to lament the passing away of a beloved person) and the content of its constituent stories drew heavily from the various kinds of *naqqali*. In fact, the two distinct styles of *naqqali* are evident in *ta'ziyeh* dialogue. The melancholic words sung in a particular Iranian metre by the *mazlum-khans* (the readers of the oppressed) are remnants of the religious *naqqali*, and the exaggerated recitation of *mokhalef-khans* (readers of the opposition), replete with

Figure 15 A *mokhalef-khan* in the role of Malek-e Ashtar before his conversion to Islam. *Mazlum-khan*s and *mokhalef-khan*s are not allowed to move across their respective groups and usually remain confined to these roles for life. For example, the actor playing the imam(s) will continue to play a *mazlum-khan*. Similarly, the above actor could only act as a *mokhalef-khan*, even if his character converted into a friend of the Prophet or the imam(s) by the end of the play. As such, on the first day of the three-day performance, he was a *mokhalef-khan* acting the role of Qanbar, who converts by the end of the performance and only briefly plays the role of a *mazlum-khan*. The next day, the role of Qanbar is played not by him but by another actor who is a *mazlum-khan*. The above actor then continued in the role of another *mokhalef-khan*, this time as Malek-e Ashtar, before his conversion to Islam. Photo: Pejman Pak. Tehran, August 2010.

Figure 16 *Mazlum-khan* Qanbar. Photo: Pejman Pak. Tehran, August 2010.

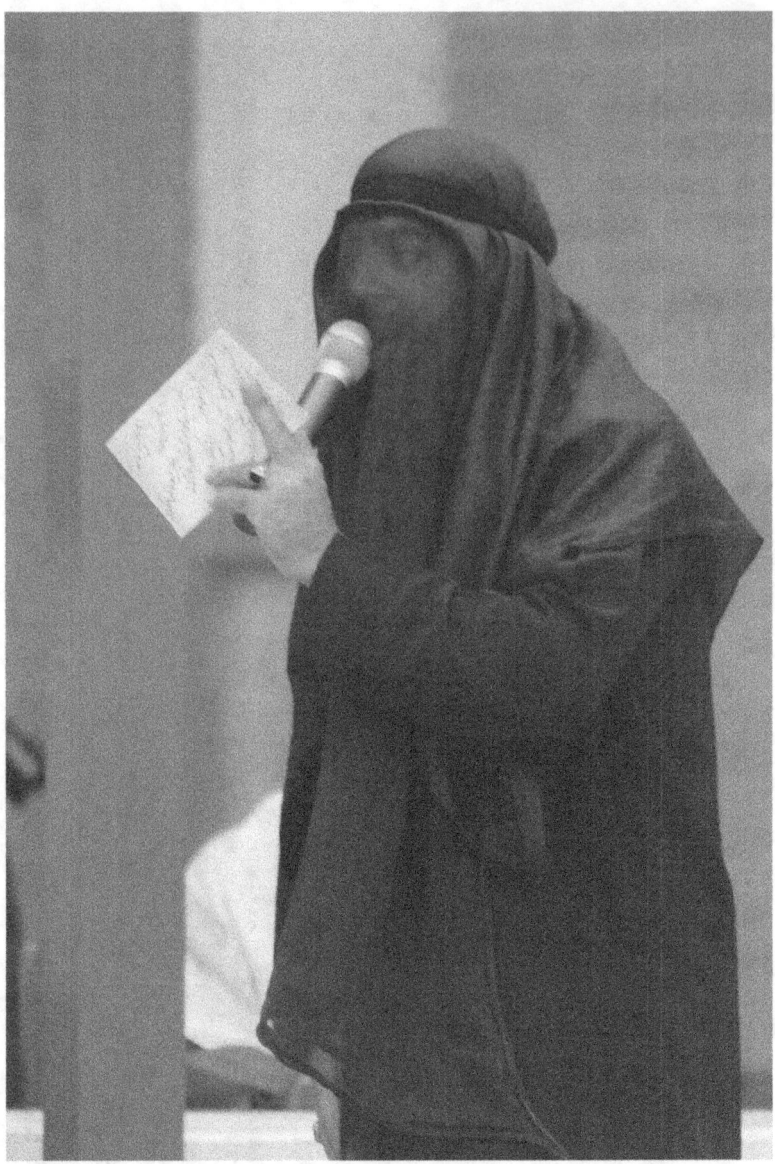

Figure 17 A *mazlum-khan* in the role of Fatemeh, the daughter of the Prophet, singing his lines. Traditionally, the role of women is played by men as women are not permitted to perform in *ta'ziyeh*. Photo: Pejman Pak. Tehran, August 2010.

gesticulation and grandeur, is a remnant of epic *naqqali*.³² There were thus rules according to which the actors would recite the poetry. Those playing the followers of Husayn, the *mazlum-khan*s, were usually required to have a good voice and read or sing their parts beautifully. The enemies of Husayn, on the other hand, were not required to sing, and instead shouted out their parts.

Ta'ziyeh made its way into the court and in the upper echelons of society. It reached its peak under Qajar patronage, a period referred to as the golden age of *ta'ziyeh*. Moreover, the emerging new social class of merchants and politicians also supported *ta'ziyeh*. In his travels to Europe, Nasir al-Din Shah Qajar (r. 1848–1896) developed a taste for European theatre. He wanted a playhouse similar in architectural style to the Royal Albert Hall in London. Subsequently, in 1869, he ordered the building of the magnificent Takiyeh-Dowlat in Tehran, located on the southeastern side of Golestan Palace. But even before it was completed, there were protests from the religious strata about the types of performances it might hold. The Shah ultimately designated the building for *ta'ziyeh* performances.³³

The Takiyeh-Dowlat, the greatest playhouse ever to have been built in Iran, accommodated approximately 20,000 people. During the Qajar period when *ta'ziyeh* enjoyed royal patronage, many of the court scene props were provided by the palace. This transformed the traditionally simple performance into one with extravagant costumes and *mise-en-scene*. The dialogues correspondingly evolved along more elaborate lines. Jewels from the king's treasury would be used for the actors' costumes in order to give the performance a more real feel. Camels and various other animals were also brought onto the stage. The court women would personally sew and knit the costumes of actors (all men) playing the female roles of Yazid's court.³⁴ During the 10 days of Muharram, there were two daily *ta'ziyeh* performances – one in the afternoon, the other in the evening. There are records of the attendance of foreign dignitaries and their families, who were invited to watch *ta'ziyeh* every day except on 'Ashura. Non-Muslims were prohibited from watching *ta'ziyeh* or indeed the martyrdom of Husayn on 'Ashura.³⁵

Whilst *ta'ziyeh* was performed in great grandeur and pomp in the court, it retained its simpler forms in smaller towns and villages. By the time of Muhammad Shah Qajar (r. 1907–1909) and Ahmad Shah Qajar

(r. 1909–1925), who were increasingly becoming Westernised, *ta'ziyeh* gradually came to lose its royal patronage.36 Many years later, Takiyeh-Dowlat fell by the wayside under Reza Shah's modernisation project, which included a ban on *ta'ziyeh* performances. After the demolition of Takiyeh-Dowlat, *ta'ziyeh* was pushed out of the bigger cities and into the suburbs and villages, where performers went in the hope of finding an audience. It is important to note that the decline of theatre was not limited to Iran, but extended throughout the world. According to Chelkowski, this worldwide crisis in theatre was the result of the 'advancement of film and television in the post-World War II period, together with a decline of religious ritual'.37

Several Iranian film-makers, however, have engaged with *ta'ziyeh* in their films. Through their re-interpretation of this older form of performing art, they have – even if inadvertently – reintroduced *ta'ziyeh* to their audiences. One can, therefore, argue that despite the destruction of Takiyeh-Dowlat, the symbol of *ta'ziyeh*'s glorious period, the cinema screens revived some of the recognition and significance that *ta'ziyeh* once enjoyed. In the following sections, I will discuss the works of two very different film-makers, Bahram Beyzaie and Abbas Kiarostami, and their employment of *ta'ziyeh* in film.

Beyzaie: a Film-maker Rooted in 'Historical Genealogy'

Bahram Beyzaie was born in Tehran in 1938. He is a distinguished playwright, screenwriter, film and theatre director, film editor as well as a scholar of the Iranian performing arts. He left his studies at the University of Tehran incomplete, and began his own independent research on Iranian theatre, epic literature, including Ferdowsi's *Shahnameh*, and the traditional plays of *ta'ziyeh*. His research also encompassed a study of pre-Islamic Persian history and Persian painting. Later, he extended his studies to Eastern art and spent a decade writing about this, as well as Iranian theatre and cinema. He made his first short film, *Uncle Moustache (Amu Sibilu)* in 1969, and in 1971 he produced and directed his first feature film *Downpour (Ragbar)*.

Beyzaie is one of the Iranian *auteur* directors whose works have been studied both inside and outside Iran. He states that his fascination for the traditional Iranian arts – which is reflected in his cinematic works – stems from an interest in the lesser-studied field of understanding the lives of ordinary people.38 He clearly deems the familiarity of the film-maker with historical genealogy to be a necessary component:

> ... many people still do not know why it is necessary to be rooted in a historical genealogy of one sort or another ... In fact, when we look at some of the greatest films ever made, we note that the film-maker has a literary, or visual, or theatrical history which is instrumental in his cinema. In Japanese cinema, in particular, you see the strong presence of Japanese theatre. It seems that in many instances, if one were to show a person walking in the street or any other daily activity, one need not have historical documentation to validate that act. Yet in other circumstances we need a more contemporary and philosophical expression of the history and culture of the past.[39]

An Unknown 'Modernist' Film-Maker

Beyzaie's deep knowledge of the Iranian performing arts, history and culture as well as his numerous contributions to the literary and art scene of the country over four decades have not, however, earned him an easy place within the field. A number of his films and plays have been banned by the government. These include *Ballad of Tara* (*Cherike-ye Tara*, 1979) and *Death of Yazdgerd* (*Marg-e Yazdgerd*, 1982), which have not yet received screening permits in Iran. His outspoken philosophical views cost him his tenure at the University of Tehran, shortly after the Islamic Revolution. Despite creating some of the masterpieces of Iranian cinema, he has not gained due recognition outside Iran. While Western scholarship in Iranian cinema has increased over the last two decades, very few scholars – mostly those with an Iranian background studying Iranian cinema – have paid attention to his work.

A simple search on Amazon.com and the Internet Movie Database, IMDb.com, is enough to indicate the meagre international recognition of his films. A search of Iranian DVDs on Amazon.com returned 46 films.[40] While many Makhmalbaf, Kiarostami, Mehrjui and Majidi titles were listed, there was no trace of Beyzaie's films. The Internet Movie Database – self-styled the Earth's Biggest Movie Database – catalogues all 13 short and feature films directed by Beyzaie. However, the paucity of user comments hints at the limited international scope of his audiences and distribution of his films. Only four of his 13 films have received comments; *Rabid Killing* (*Sagkoshi,* 2001) has five comments, but the other three have received only one comment each. By comparison, Majidi's *The Colour of Paradise* (1999) alone had received 67 comments on IMDb. One commentator, Lalit Rao, reviewing Beyzaie's *Maybe Another Time* (*Shayad vaqti digar,* 1988), complains about the difficulty of finding his films, stating,

> I would like to explicitly remark that it is a great shame that almost all the films by Bahram Beyzaie have not been distributed widely on DVD. What are the DVD labels like Artificial Eye, Criterion Collection, Kino, New Yorker Films or Facets doing?[41]

Another commentator, Mehdi, liked *Rabid Killing*, but did not recommend it to non-Iranians:

> This film points to some kind of customs and cultures in Iran [and] needs you to be an Iranian if you want to realize it. [F]or whom they are outside of Iran and they've heard about Iranian cinema this could not be an interesting movie. [B]ecause they will not get what is going on.[42]

Many critics also regularly refer to this inaccessibility of Beyzaie's work, particularly for those who are unfamiliar with Persian history and culture. Beyzaie, in turn, has expressed his frustration with those who have labelled his films abstruse.[43] While some critics regard Beyzaie's work as too specific to Persian culture, Maddadpur, the Iranian scholar whose work was analysed extensively in Chapter 2, regards his works as the best example of a 'Westoxicated' art, where myth and truth are mixed together. According to him, Beyzaie is incomprehensible to both his audience and the intellectuals who sing his praise.[44] On the other hand, Dabashi, another critic also studied in Chapter 2, believes that Beyzaie manages to channel his attraction to Persian mysticism in a constructive direction.[45] Even as critics and scholars disagree on whether or not Beyzaie is Western or exclusively Iranian, a mythologist or a neo-realist, accessible or indecipherable, one cannot deny the significance of his work in any serious study of Iranian cinema.

Beyzaie's obscurity on the international scene and his interest and use of traditional performing arts in cinema can be compared to the Japanese film-maker Yasujiro Ozu (1903–1963). Noel Burch argues that with the revival of the modernist movements in cinema in the 1950s and 1960s, modernist film-makers looked eastwards for models of filmmaking.[46] This included Japanese cinema and the introduction of directors such as Akira Kurosawa to the West in the early 1950s. Japanese cinema was rooted in its earlier traditional performing arts and 'derived from the aesthetic which emerged from the court culture of the Heian era (794– 1185) and which became the basis of Japan's traditional arts'.[47] Ozu was one of the directors posthumously referred to as 'the greatest director of his generation in Japan'. His works, however, were considered 'too Japanese' to be included in international film festivals during his own time and were only reintroduced later in the 1970s.[48] Indeed, as with Ozu, one can argue that some of Beyzaie's works have not made it to the international festivals because they also are considered to be 'too Iranian' for recent festival tastes. It is, therefore, possible that whilst pre- and post-Revolutionary governments might have been less tolerant of his critical views, the international scene might have snubbed him for his heavy use of Iranian mythology and/or unfamiliar traditional theatrical forms.

Beyzaie's use of theatre in cinema is not unprecedented. In fact, in its earliest forms, cinema was used to 'capture theatrical performances, such as pageants representing the life of Christ'.[49] Moreover, as early as the 1920s Brecht proposed the use of *Verfremdungseffekt*, translated as 'a distancing effect', or 'alienation effect' in film. He achieved this in his own films and they 'became a model of "presentational theatre", showing how to incorporate such antinaturalistic effects as direct address, impersonal recitation of lines and frank displays of the mechanics of lighting and staging'.[50] Interestingly, *ta'ziyeh* also employs various distancing techniques, such as speaking to the audience and referring to the actors as 'readers of' the characters they play. As mentioned earlier, in *ta'ziyeh* the 'reader of' the murderer of Imam Husayn (*Shimr-khan*), who is a Shia in real life, cries when he kills him and recites elegies to that effect, reminding the audience that what they see is just a performance. Beyzaie uses many of the theatrical forms of *ta'ziyeh* in his films, which distance the audience through the 'alienation effects' just discussed.

Like film history generally, Iranian cinema has experienced various movements, which have oscillated between coming close to theatrical forms and moving away from them. Beyzaie's cinema is towards the former extreme. While works of other film-makers whether national or international who have broken away from conventional styles of filmmaking such as Kiarostami, Makhmalbaf, Majidi, Resnais, Antonioni, Godard and Ozu might have received international recognition and exhibition (whether posthumously or in their own lifetimes) Beyzaie's works still remain largely unknown and undefined. There is evidence hinting that he faces greater challenges than others in obtaining the necessary local authorisation for the production, exhibition and distribution of his films and their international participation. Farahmand lists a series of incidents in which Beyzaie's films and his attendance at international festivals were cancelled by Iranian authorities. These include Beyzaie's jury membership at the 16th Turin International Film Festival in November 1999, a film retrospective in his honour at the same festival, and the omission of his episode from the version of the *Tales of Kish* (*Qeseha-ye Kish*, Makhmalbaf, Jalili and Taqavi, 1999) screened in Cannes.[51] This marginalisation clearly cannot simply be due to his filmmaking techniques, which break away from the conventional Hollywood style. In fact, Iranian cinema has been recognised and lauded on the international scene for its distinctly different style of film-making. Beyzaie's reliance on the cultural and historical context of his subjects does not render his films incomprehensible any more than Majidi's reliance on Persian mysticism does, and audiences of his many-layered films might well draw different levels of meaning from them. The term 'modernist film-maker' that I assign to Beyzaie in the section heading is more to challenge the usual preconceived assumptions about him than to categorise him as such. It is also to challenge the idea that Beyzaie is 'too local' and 'culturally parochial' to comprehend. Here, I will examine two of Beyzaie's works that draw from both the form and the content of *ta'ziyeh* in their narratives.

A Retelling of Karbala through Ta'ziyeh *and Film*

Beyzaie has consistently maintained that it is his passion for understanding ordinary people and their cultural and historical roots that has driven his work and research. His screenplay *The Day of Incident* (*Ruz-e vaqe'eh*), which he wrote in 1984, recounts one of the most important Shi'i Iranian narratives, the story of Karbala. *The Day of Incident* was not just an attempt to put *ta'ziyeh* on screen or to document a dying tradition. Instead, Beyzaie successfully brings these two elements, film and *ta'ziyeh*, together and employs both the Western, secular medium and an Iranian religious tradition to retell the martyrdom of Husayn and his companions. Even though it is based on the historical incident of Karbala, it makes no claims to be a historical film. Instead, like *ta'ziyeh*, it encompasses in its narrative the larger Islamic historical and mythological elements as well as those that are specifically Iranian. Despite Beyzaie's numerous attempts to make the film, he failed to obtain the necessary permits. Finally, in 1994, the film was given to Shahram Asadi to direct. Beyzaie's solid script, however, did much to turn it into one of the best narratives on the events of Karbala, a narrative that is remarkably influenced by the elements of *ta'ziyeh*.

The Day of Incident won four awards, including best film in the 13th Fajr International Film Festival in 1994. Even though he was nominated, Beyzaie did not win the best screenplay. Ten years later, in 2004, during the opening ceremony of the 22nd FIFF and on the occasion of the 25th anniversary of the Islamic Revolution, the achievements of those Iranians 'who have been the source of pride for Iranian cinema'[52] were celebrated under three categories: Sacred Defence Cinema (*Sinama-ye defa'-e moqaddas*), The Cinema of Revolutionary Ideals (*Sinama-ye armanha-ye enqelab*) and Religious Cinema (*Sinama-ye dini*). The first two categories have arguably been exhausted of their topics from the early days of post-Revolution cinema, with various events held to recognise and celebrate them. The third category of religious cinema, however, had not received serious attention before. This was evident from the fact that, unlike the other two categories, only one film, *The Day of Incident* (Asadi, 1994)

Figure 18 *The Day of Incident* (*Ruz-e vaqe'eh*, Shahram Asadi, 1994). Rahila and 'Abd Allah.

swept all the commendations for Religious Cinema, with no other films in the running. It was also thought-provoking to note that only *The Day of Incident* seemed to fit this newly created category (this was a year before the introduction of the Spiritual Cinema category in 2005). Beyzaie was also commended – albeit ten years late – for his screenplay. He was not present at the ceremony to collect his award.

The Day of Incident is set in the seventh century, in an unidentified Arab land. Through the love of Rahila, a Muslim girl, a Christian referred to only as 'Abd Allah converts to Islam. Rahila's father, having rejected 'Abd Allah 37 times, finally agrees to give him his daughter's hand in marriage. This, however, is met with strong tribal opposition. Despite this reproach, preparations are made for an elaborate wedding on the ninth of Muharram. The big day arrives but during the celebrations 'Abd Allah hears a voice asking for help. He asks the guests if anyone had called out for help, but no one else seems to have heard the voice. He keeps on hearing these words: 'Is there anyone who will come to my aid? Tomorrow Christ will be crucified in Neynava.' Just before the marriage rites are performed, he abruptly leaves the gathering, mounts his horse and gallops towards the desert. This causes a huge stir amongst the guests – it is clearly an unforgivable insult and a stain on their Arab honour and reputation.

On his journey to find Karbala and Husayn, 'Abd Allah encounters various people and has to surmount many life-threatening challenges. He finally arrives at the scene of Karbala at noon of the tenth of Muharram. The enemy, however, have already entered Husayn's camp, looting and burning everything, and rejoicing over their victim's dead bodies. They hold spears atop which rest the heads of those they have slain. The place is filled with smoke, dust and shrieks of women and children. Suddenly, two suns appear in the sky and 'Abd Allah, blinded by the light, cries out that if he were not meant to arrive in time, why was he summoned in the first place? He then blacks out. When he wakes up later, he sees a woman's figure – bound but wrapped in light. She addresses him as *javanmard*, and asks him to return with their message. 'Abd Allah returns to Rahila's town to tell everyone what he saw.

In his book on the performing arts of Iran, Beyzaie states that during Nasir al-Din Shah's reign (1848–1896), when *ta'ziyeh* reached its peak in terms of its artistic and entertainment values, it was divided into two parts: the *pish-vaqe'eh*, or 'before the incident' and the *vaqe'eh* or 'incident' itself. The *pish-vaqe'eh* usually consisted of lighter performances and varied from love stories to satire. It was usually an opportunity to criticise those in positions of power,[53] or to enact stories with titles such as 'Queen Sheba's meeting with Solomon', 'Fatemeh's attendance at a Quraysh wedding', and so on. This was then followed by the *vaqe'eh*, which was three times as long and focused on the events of Karbala.[54] Thus, the *ta'ziyeh* performance would make people laugh and cry at the same time. It was both a joyous and sad occasion.

The title of the film, *Ruz-e vaqe'eh*, can be read as paying homage to these earlier forms of *ta'ziyeh*. The film draws from *pish vaqe'eh* and *vaqe'eh* in *ta'ziyeh*, by starting with a love story. Interestingly the wedding scenes comprise roughly one third of the entire film (27 out of 95 minutes). More importantly, the wedding dances and music with which the film begins are in sharp contrast to the current more sombre forms of commemorating Muharram in modern-day Iran under the Islamic Republic. Like *pish vaqe'eh* in *ta'ziyeh*, the first part of the film provides an opportunity to criticise those who use their privileged social status to inflict injustice on the dispossessed. The *pish vaqe'eh* in *ta'ziyeh* provided the space to criticise the feudal landlords. In *The Day of Incident,* the opponents of 'Abd Allah's marriage to Rahila are sceptical of his true intentions in converting from

Figure 19 'Abd Allah wanders in the desert in *The Day of Incident* (*Ruz-e vaqe'eh*, Shahram Asadi, 1994).

Christianity to Islam. They claim that since they have been Muslims for three generations it is beneath them to intermarry with new converts or, for that matter, with one whose very conversion is under question. The film, therefore, provides a critical look at the Islamic elite of the time. In the early development of Islam, *sabiqa* (priority) became one of the most important signs of distinction that resulted in the formation of a new Islamic elite within the emerging umma (community).[55] Those in Rahila's tribe who constantly question 'Abd Allah's faith in Islam and regard their three generations of Muslim-ness as a privilege and a licence to marginalise those outside this circle can be seen as subtly satirising of the current Muslim leaders of Iran who use their position as holders of the 'true interpretation' of Islam as a device to silence all others.

'Abd Allah's character also raises interesting issues about Iranian Shi'i identity. His origin and ethnicity remain vague throughout the film, but certain references suggest to the viewer – particularly an Iranian one – that 'Abd Allah is most likely Iranian. The fact that he is not an Arab is mentioned at several junctures of the film. Even though his conversion is regarded with suspicion by many, he refuses to deny Christ or his own history and identity. This has clear parallels to the Persian conversions after the Arab invasion of Iran in 663. The early Islamic conquests resulted in the political and administrative union of vast regions extending from North Africa to the Persian Empire. Like many other conquered regions during this period, Iran was Islamicised. However, it remained the only territory to resist Arabisation. Similarly, 'Abd Allah embraces Islam without repudiating everything about his previous identity. Instead, he employs his own vocabulary and existing framework to interpret and understand the new faith.

In the specific context of the rationale for conversion, the Arabs' suspicions about 'Abd Allah can be compared to the reactions of the early Muslims when faced with early Iranian conversions. Although non-Muslims were not required to convert to Islam after the Muslim conquests, they were nonetheless 'obliged to pay the *jizya,* or poll-tax and so adopt an inferior but secure role in the new order of things'.[56] Thus, the subsequent conversions of Persians were sometimes interpreted as a tax-evading strategy rather than sincere declarations of faith. A non-Muslim wishing to profess the faith of Islam was only required to pronounce the *shahada* three times. Indeed, no other formal procedure was necessary to become Muslim. This simple oral ritual roused the suspicion of many – both Muslims and non-Muslims – about the sincerity of the converts. The

Arab tribe in the film alleges that 'Abd Allah's conversion was just out of his love for Rahila rather than a true profession of faith, but scepticism about his conversion is not limited to his fiancé's tribe; indeed, it is shared amongst his own people. In the opening scene of the film, a Christian monk asks 'Abd Allah if he has indeed become an apostate because 'the Arabs are now the conquerors of all conquerors.'

'Abd Allah displays all the characteristics of a *javanmard*, a Persian term for a man of integrity who is also brave, noble and chivalrous. As mentioned in Chapter 3, *javanmard* refers to a man possessing the qualities of 'courage, honour, modesty, humility and rectitude'.[57] It has been argued that the idea of *javanmard* is linked with 'a number of rebellions throughout Iran's history'.[58] In this context, Adelkhah goes so far as to ask whether the concept of *javanmard* was indeed 'a case of a movement to assert identity, a national resistance movement against Arab occupation?'[59] If it is, the term *javanmard* stands in stark contrast to the term '*ahl-e Kufeh*', 'the Kufans'. In Persian, this is a metaphor for unfaithful people, derived from specific reference to the Kufans who had invited the Imam Husayn to Kufa to liberate them from the oppressive Umayyad caliphate, but then spectacularly failed to stand by their oath of allegiance. The allegory of 'the Kufans' has also been consistently used in the Islamic Republic's propagandist slogans since the early days of the Revolution: 'We are not the Kufans / for 'Ali to remain alone'.[60] This is yet again another example of how the story of Husayn is used for political agendas.

'Abd Allah's response to the call for help is an act of *javanmardi*. Once summoned, regardless of the consequences, he selflessly stands by his oath of allegiance. When he meets the woman enveloped in light – most probably Zaynab, Husayn's sister – she refers to him as *javanmard*. It is she who elucidates 'Abd Allah's mission. He was summoned not to fight with Husayn, but to bear witness to the tragedy and become the carrier of Husayn's message. Remembering the story of Husayn so that history will not forget his message and sacrifice is an important Shi'i practice. In this context, as discussed earlier, the martyrdom of Husayn is a narrative that is deeply rooted within the Iranian Shi'i tradition.

Beyzaie employs the techniques of an older performing art to depict an important religious event. *Ta'ziyeh* informs the narrative structure of *The Day of Incident*. As we have seen, the two distinct parts of the film can be compared to *pish vaqe'eh* and *vaqe'eh* in *ta'ziyeh*. Like *ta'ziyeh*, the film is not just about the martyrdom of Husayn but includes the lighter story of 'Abd Allah and Rahila's love. This also provides the opportunity

Figure 20 A battle scene in a *ta'ziyeh* between Qanbar (left) before his conversion to Islam and Imam 'Ali (in green). *Mazlum-khan*s usually incorporate the colour green in their costumes. Photo: Pejman Pak. Tehran, August 2010.

Figure 21 *Ta'ziyeh* performance. Having kidnapped Hasan and Husayn, Malek-e Ashtar prepares to kill them Photo: Pejman Pak. Tehran, August 2010.

to criticise the biases of the privileged just as *ta'ziyeh* would those in positions of power. The film also makes references to Iranian ideals such as *javanmardi*, a value that was incorporated in their religious traditions. It also emphasises the Shi'i obligation of upholding Husayn's message. Thus, Beyzaie does not just enact the events of Karbala on screen. In fact, very little is dedicated to the events of Karbala itself. Instead, he emphasises the impact of Husayn's martyrdom in the lives of the Shi'a and in the formation of their religious identity.

The *ta'ziyeh* motifs are, however, restricted in *The Day of Incident*. The overall dramatic aspects of the film would have certainly looked different had Beyzaie himself directed it. Nonetheless, as we shall see shortly, *The Travellers* (*Mosaferan*, 1992) provided Beyzaie with the opportunity to write and direct a film that employed many *ta'ziyeh* motifs, even though it was a story set in modern times and not that of the martyrdom of Husayn.

Narrating a Modern Tragedy through Ta'ziyeh

The Travellers (1992) won six awards in the 10th FIFF in 1992 including the Special Jury Award, Best Actress in a Leading Role, Best Actress in a Supporting Role, Best Actor in a Supporting Role, Best Cinematography and Best Sound. Beyzaie was nominated for Best Directing and Best Editing but did not win. The simple story of *The Travellers* provides various levels of meaning. It is about a wedding celebration that is tragically turned into a mourning ceremony. Mahtab (the bride's sister), her husband and two sons set out from a city in the north of Iran to attend the wedding in Tehran. They are also carrying the wedding mirror that a family traditionally places on the wedding spread. They are all, however, killed in a road accident. While the news comes as a devastating blow to everyone, the grandmother alone refuses to acknowledge their death. She adamantly awaits their arrival and the mirror they had promised to bring for the wedding. At the grandmother's insistence, the bride finally agrees to change from her mourning clothes into her wedding gown. To the utter astonishment of the guests, the deceased family enters the house surrounded in an aura of light, with Mahtab carrying the promised mirror.

One of the most striking elements of *ta'ziyeh* is the complete lack of suspense in the story and performance. Both the spectators and the actors know the tragic ending. They know that Imam Husayn and his companions will be killed and his family taken captive. It is, therefore, unimportant to keep this a secret to retain the story's suspense. Similarly, at the beginning of *The Travellers*, Mahtab faces the camera and tells the audience that she and her family are on their way to Tehran to attend her sister's wedding. She then goes on to say that none of them will make it, that they will all die, thus giving away the ending of the story right at the beginning of the film. Moreover, like the performance of *ta'ziyeh* and unlike the commonly used shot/reverse camera angle, Mahtab faces the audience and speaks to them directly.[61] The dramatic acting in the film is also a departure from the preferred realist or neo-realist styles in filmmaking. Instead, the acting of the various actors is a tribute to the different traditional performing arts of Iran including *pardeh-khani*, *naqqali* and *ta'ziyeh*. The constant circular movements of the camera throughout the film simulate the *ta'ziyeh* arena, which is traditionally a round stage with spectators gathered all around it.

In his literature on the Iranian performing arts, Beyzaie provides a detailed description of how deaths are staged in *ta'ziyeh*. The method of depicting the tragic deaths in *The Travellers* can be compared to the conventions in *ta'ziyeh*. Beyzaie states that in *ta'ziyeh*, the injured actor leaves on horseback, usually followed by a few men. Soon after, the horse returns without its rider but pierced by numerous arrows. The return of the riderless horse is an old metaphor in Persian literature that indicates the rider's death. The actual moment of Imam Husayn's martyrdom is also hidden from the spectators' eyes, even though it occurs on stage. Traditionally, 10 people from the opposing army surround the imam, gradually tightening the circle around him. Suddenly, they throw themselves upon him and freeze in this position. Then the Shimr-reader, who is weeping loudly and inviting the audience to also cry (he is, after all, a Shi'i believer in real life), storms into the middle of the circle and murders the imam. At this moment, because the imam cannot be seen even though he is on stage, pigeons are released into the sky. They symbolise both the ascent of Imam Husayn's soul into the heavens and the messengers who carry the news of his death.[62]

In *The Travellers*, the exact moment of the tragic deaths is also hidden from the audience. The viewer is aware from very early on in the film that the family will not make it to Tehran. The numerous warning signs are a constant reminder of the unpleasant incident that is about to take place. The car's navigation along the dangerous and twisted roads through mountains that seem to close in on them, the dark tunnel they pass through, the musical cues that constantly change from merry beats to suspenseful tones and, finally, the tanker that approaches the camera threatening a crash but then calmly steers back onto the road, all suggest the imminence of the incident. It is only after the tanker passes that the audience sees the leak from behind it. The fire and smoke in the next sequence and the traffic lieutenant reporting on the incident all combine to inform the viewer that the fatal accident has indeed occurred. No gory details are shown, nor is there any emphasis on the bodies. Indeed, there is only one quick shot of a draped body. Instead, the tragedy is depicted through the body of the smashed car, empty but with broken and bloodstained windows, just like the riderless horse full of arrows on the *ta'ziyeh* stage.

The audience is also shielded from hearing the news of death, a pattern that is repeated throughout the film. Even when the family is informed of the death of their loved ones, the audience sees only their reaction to the devastating news rather than hearing the news itself. Although various people deliver or hear the news of death, these accounts are inaudible to the viewer. Instead, only the dramatic reactions to the news are shown. The men are usually quiet but clearly grief-stricken, the women scream, throw mud on their heads, break mirrors and crystal and tear the curtains in their displays of grief. Only the grandmother calmly refuses to accept the deaths and does not go into mourning.

One of the sequences that best alludes to the *ta'ziyeh* stage is the mourning ceremony held in the family's house. The camera constantly makes circular movements around the guests, suggesting a round stage in the centre of the room. This then becomes the centre stage for various family members, just like the *ta'ziyeh* actors, to make their speeches. When the brothers of the deceased couple give their speeches on death, they define it according to their respective professions – business and academia. The husband of Zarinkolah, the village woman who had also been in the same taxi, then enters the stage. The performative and melancholic narration of his wife's story is reminiscent of the religious *naqqali*. He narrates his wife's long desire for a child and her constant search for a cure, which ultimately led to her death, for she had been on her way to Tehran to visit yet another fertility clinic. Similarly, when the taxi driver's wife enters, like the *naqqal* (storyteller), she also gives an emotional account of her husband's story and the misery that had befallen her. In contrast, the traffic lieutenant confidently provides a technical account of the accident, analysing the various logical reasons that might have led to the collision.

Indeed, the family of the deceased can be compared to the *mazlum-khan*s (readers of the oppressed) and the truck driver and his assistant to *mokhalef-khan*s (readers of the opposing army) in *ta'ziyeh*. The latter, too, attend the mourning ceremony to pay their respects and beg for forgiveness. Initially, their appearance causes a stir amongst the guests, with the sons of the deceased taxi driver attacking them. When everyone is finally calmed down, the truck driver and his assistants sit on the floor/stage. They then begin to vociferate how despite their desperate efforts to avoid the accident, the truck had slid on the slippery road and crashed into the taxi. The loud, crude and rough voices of the driver and his assistant and their frequent use of slang and colloquial terms is very similar to the way the *mokhalef-khan*s speak in *ta'ziyeh*.

Ta'ziyeh also provides a cathartic release for its spectators, just like the family in *The Travellers*, who do not just grieve the loss of their loved ones, but also lament about their own old and inner pains. Thus, when mourning the loss of his brother and nephews, Hekmat sobs to his wife that no more male descendants are left to carry their family name, which will subsequently vanish without a trace. What surfaces, however, is Hekmat's own unhappiness at not being able to have a male child. His wife has borne him two daughters and doctors have advised against another pregnancy as it would put his wife's life at risk. Similarly, the loving relationship between Mastan and Mahu (the bride's brother), is not as perfect as it had appeared. During the mourning ceremony, Mastan faces the camera and announces that they have a disabled child who lives far away from them, and whom they can visit only once a month. The mourning ceremony, just like the *ta'ziyeh* stage, therefore, allows the open – and safe – expression of these strong emotions. The family grieve for their loss, just as *ta'ziyeh* allows spectators to openly grieve not only for Husayn's fate but also their own misfortunes.

The Travellers employs many *ta'ziyeh* forms in narrating its story. The elements of lack of suspense, veiled moments of death, its impact on the bereaved, the circular movements of camera, the delivery of the dialogues and the cathartic nature of the mourning rituals are all comparable to *ta'ziyeh*. Beyzaie employs all these features of *ta'ziyeh* to narrate a modern tragedy. *The Travellers* also allows Beyzaie, who laments the loss of older Iranian forms of performing arts, to employ the medium of film to reintroduce and reinterpret these older traditions to his audience.

In the next section I will explore how Abbas Kiarostami, whose style and approach differ dramatically from Beyzaie, engages with *ta'ziyeh* in film (biographical details for Kiarostami are provided in Chapter 6). It is not necessarily only the martyrdom of Husayn, but the story of Karbala and the rituals of *ta'ziyeh* that have informed Iranian Shi'i identity and its expressions.

Ta'ziyeh and its Spectators

In early May 2005, Abbas Kiarostami staged an installation of the *ta'ziyeh* called 'A Look to Tazieh' at the London's Victoria and Albert Museum, followed by an 'in-conversation' between him, Ahmad Karimi-Hakkak, and Geoff Andrew.[63] The installation consisted of three screens – two large screens on each side of a relatively smaller television screen in the middle. The television screen played scenes of *ta'ziyeh* performed in a remote rural area. The two large screens on either side showed spectators watching *ta'ziyeh*. These were images of men, women and children edited in such a way that their reactions corresponded precisely to the *ta'ziyeh* that was screened on the television screen. The spectators initially begin to watch the play distractedly, talking to each other, having tea, and giggling away. But gradually the drama captivates them, and as the tragedy reaches its climax, many are in tears, some sobbing or beating their chests.

This installation was a departure from Kiarostami's usual ouevre as will be evident from the analysis in the next chapter. During the post-screening discussion, Kiarostami explained his attraction to a topic that would normally not have interested him. The idea was first conceived in 1997 when he was awarded the prestigious Palme d'Or award at the Cannes International Film Festival for his *Taste of Cherry* (*Ta'm-e gilas*, 1997). When an interviewer at Cannes asked him if the distancing at the end of the film was a Brechtian influence, Kiarostami responded that it was the influence of *ta'ziyeh* rather than Brecht. The director of the Rome Theatre, who was present at that interview, was keen to know more about *ta'ziyeh* and so Kiarostami sent him a tape on his return to Tehran, which ultimately resulted in the installation at the Rome Theatre in 2003.

Kiarostami believes that the 'primitive *ta'ziyeh* of older times' was a much better performance. One could legitimately ask if this arises merely out of his fascination with the older, more simple and, therefore, exotic aspects of culture and society. He has, in fact, been frequently criticised for his choice of subjects and locations, particularly by some in the Iranian diaspora who read his films as an attempt to win foreign audiences and awards by depicting Iran as 'backward'. This is a view that has time and again been argued about – but it is a discussion that I shall not enter into here. At the very least, the problem with this criticism is that it dismisses the films on the basis of very superficial readings indeed. Instead, I will first look at Kiarostami's discussion of both his experiences of *taʿziyeh* as a child and his later film-making experience, which will allow me to analyse his work better. Kiarostami is a great orator and knows how to engage with his audience. His talk during the discussion was frequently punctuated with outbursts of laughter, particularly from the Iranian audience. Sadly, much of the humour was lost in translation. Here I have noted down excerpts from his talk,[64] which will shed light not only on Kiarostami's interpretation of *taʿziyeh*, but also on its evolution in modern Iran:

> My earliest memory of *taʿziyeh* was watching it when I was four or five on my father's shoulders. Much has changed in the last 50 years. Like all other things, when there are better facilities the results are far worse. *Taʿziyeh* has become far more performative and far worse. It was much better when it was performed with the minimum of equipment. I found the *taʿziyeh* that you just watched in one of the remote areas of Iran. Everything in *taʿziyeh* has become so modern that it has lost the newness, honesty and sincerity which was once present in *taʿziyeh*.
>
> One of my childhood memories of *taʿziyeh* is a battle scene between Imam Husayn and Yazid [sic].[65] The swords they were using must have been made of tinplate, because they were very primitive and flimsy. During the battle, one of the swords got bent. The other one took it from him and straightened it with a stone and handed it back. I was astonished to see that even though they were enemies and fighting with each other, they also enjoyed a friendly relationship. This is an important theme that runs through all *taʿziyeh*s ... The dialogues, for example, bear this interesting duality, something that I picked up through my repetitious viewings of the rushes. In a verse such as *manam ke ba lagad mizanam be sanduq-e ʿelm-e ladoni* (It is me who kicks your chest, the chest of divine knowledge), the character acts both as friend and enemy. That is, even though I am kicking you, I also acknowledge that you are the bearer of divine knowledge.

Kiarostami's later experience of making the *ta'ziyeh* installation was equally, if not more, fascinating. He stated that he was more interested in the audience watching *ta'ziyeh* than the performance itself. He wanted to know who they were, where they came from, and more importantly, to watch a people that one does not usually get or think to observe. The main challenge, however, was not the presence of the camera in front of the spectators. In fact, Kiarostami said, they would get so engrossed in the *ta'ziyeh* that they would rarely notice the camera and those behind it would even stretch and position themselves to look over it for a better view of the stage. Instead, it was filming the segregated audience that proved very challenging for Kiarostami. The women who were sitting on the top-floor balcony did not allow the male cameramen to go upstairs. As a result, the only camerawoman he had did not record enough footage of the women watching *ta'ziyeh*. When it came to editing, Kiarostami was 40 minutes short of footage of the female audience. He thought creatively of a resolution to the problem:

> We had to wait for another Muharram, next year. I thought of a solution but wasn't sure if it would work. I transferred all my footage of *ta'ziyeh* onto VHS tape and put my television in the backyard garden and covered the walls with black cloth. Then I asked one of the cleaners that worked in our neighbourhood to bring me some extras, who would sit and watch the film, and I could then intersperse their images with my previous footage. I set up the scene and put out the chairs and some 16 of them arrived by minibus. They entered in silence and sat on the chairs and without giving any explanations, I started the VHS player. They began watching the film in my backyard and by minute 40 they started to cry. All the good shots that you just saw of women crying are the ones from my garden!
>
> However, the fact that they were watching it on TV and not 'live' did not take away anything from the reality of the meaning of the process itself. In fact one could see it as an extension of the distancing that occurs in *ta'ziyeh*. It [the mediated form] was no longer important for them. In fact, at some points the sun was so bright that you could barely see anything, but they still continued to cry by just hearing the words. Interestingly, once everything was finished I was embarrassed to pay them. I

thought, they've come and cried and I have to say, 'Here is this much for your crying'. I had the money in my hand inside my pocket, but not knowing what to do I went to the driver and thanked him and said goodbye to each of them. The woman who was their organiser came up to me and said, 'It has come to this much.' I was perplexed, not knowing what was genuine – the crying..., the money...?! Then she also asked for her husband's fees. I said, 'But he wasn't there crying in the garden,' to which she responded, 'No, but he's been waiting here in the minibus!' So he was paid without even crying and I was completely confused!

Then again we were short of footage, so I asked for another 15 new faces. This time the organiser brought 30 women with her, 15 of whom were the old faces. I told her that I had already shot their faces, to which she responded, 'Well, they've come along anyway!' So we sat the old crowd on the side and the new ones in front of the camera. We served them tea and sweets and then got started. After a while I noticed the old ones who didn't have the camera on them were much more emotional and weeping far more than the new batch! [Audience is laughing heartily by now] Whatever I'm saying is the truth! Once they were finished, their organiser came to me and charged even for the old group saying that they had done their share of crying anyway! Despite all of this, it is very difficult and complex to find out what is happening in their heads... I didn't say all of this just to make you laugh! I wanted to demonstrate how people are far more complex than it appears... there is so much contradiction in Iran.

Kiarostami's *ta'ziyeh* was produced as a response to Western curiosity about this performing art. His installation is an invitation to look beyond the stage performances, and directs our gaze to the spectators. In fact, Kiarostami's approach to introducing *ta'ziyeh* is a clear departure from the traditional emphasis on the characteristics of script and performance. The larger-than-life images of the spectator, and the relatively smaller screen of the performance itself, make it very clear that he is more interested in the spectators watching *ta'ziyeh* and its effect on them than *ta'ziyeh* itself. It is a statement that defines *ta'ziyeh* as an ensemble, of which the spectators are an integral part. In his own words,

'Ta'ziyeh is strictly linked to its audience – the event is actually created by the rapport between actors and spectators'.[66] Kiarostami thus demonstrates that it is this link between the performance and the spectator that makes *ta'ziyeh* very different from any other drama or performance. The men and women who begin watching the play passively – some whispering, talking, giggling or even dozing off – become increasingly active and engaged, sobbing and beating their chests as they approach the epilogue.

Kiarostami's deployment of *ta'ziyeh* in film is not an attempt to preserve or revive this old, 'dying' performing art. In fact, he is not interested in a newer, more performative and technically advanced form of *ta'ziyeh* either. Rather, he maintains that it is the newness, honesty and sincerity of the old that is lost with the modern interventions. However, it would be a disservice not to acknowledge the very modern interventions that allow him to capture what he classifies as 'the best female shots of the film' from the paid spectators. The video screening enables him to 're-enact' a performance outside its usual time and space to achieve the desired reactions. Nevertheless, Kiarostami's search for a location in which the *ta'ziyeh* is closer to the 'primitive *ta'ziyeh* of the older times' points to the fact that he, too, even if subconsciously or inadvertently, is trying to capture and hold on to a glimpse of an older tradition that is swiftly evolving and developing into newer forms. In this sense, his installation could be seen as preserving the older performing art.

Conclusions

The complexity of the modern Iranian Shi'i Muslim points to the problem of dichotomising religious traditions and modernity. Whether it is a *rowzeh* that turns into a mobile ringtone or an underground rap singer who 'updates' the traditional *rowzeh-khani* into a rap about Muharram, the boundaries of tradition and modernity, religious and secular are no longer clear-cut. It is no longer possible to define the space for religious traditions as restricted to the mosques and the clergy. Nor are the secular and modern totally separate from religion. Religion finds a new medium of expression through modern secular inventions such as the internet, which allows a cleric such as Daneshmand to expand his sermons to include a virtual audience. The internet has also enabled Sunni-Shi'i conflict discourse to occupy and engage with a new medium, with each group posting evidence of the heretical character of the other. As shown in this chapter, it is no longer possible to ignore this growing interaction between religious traditions and modernity.

It is within this evolving context of religious traditions that *ta'ziyeh*, which originated in much older pre-Islamic forms of performance, has survived its many centuries of eventful history. It has been condemned by some ulama as unIslamic, endorsed by others; flourished under royal patronage, and been banned and ignored for being 'backward' during the rule of the Pahlavis. It has moved from the greatest performance halls in cities to remote rural plateaus. Thus, the lifeblood of *ta'ziyeh* has historically been held largely in the hands of the religious and ruling authorities and more recently continues to cause concern amongst them for the reputation of religion.

Films provided *ta'ziyeh* with a new space controlled by the artist rather than those in positions of power. The film-maker Beyzaie employs many *ta'ziyeh* elements, in terms of both form and content, in writing and making his films. In Beyzaie's reinterpretation, *ta'ziyeh* is employed to narrate one of the most powerful Iranian Shi'i narratives. *Ta'ziyeh* informs the narrative structure of *The Day of Incident*, and its motifs are applied to narrate a modern-day tragedy in *The Travellers*. In this way, Beyzaie not only revives the old performing art but also demonstrates its relevance to the modern Iranian imagination. Like *ta'ziyeh*, his films encompass the historical, the mythological, the national and the religious as they relate to Iranian society and culture. For his part, Kiarostami illustrates in his installation that the idiosyncrasies of *ta'ziyeh* are not limited to its performative aspects but, more importantly, lie in the effect it has on its spectators. What Kiarostami captures through his images of the spectators is the continuing impact of the story of Husayn's martyrdom on Shi'i believers. One of the most powerful narratives in Iran, the story still manages to capture the imagination of its audience, whether present at the performance or paid to watch a televised version. Both Beyzaie's films and Kiarostami's installation are particularly important in the face of the evolving traditions of the Muharram ceremonies discussed above. They act as a reservoir of a tradition within a context where there is a growing concern about the 'Other's' perception of 'Islamic' practices, which includes the omission of some of these older traditions.

Having explored the popular expression of religion in this chapter, as well as the formalistic and mystical approaches in Chapters 3 and

4 respectively, the final chapter will further examine the works of Kiarostami whose films, I argue, are philosophical texts that, among other things, deliberate upon the question of religion, including some of the approaches discussed thus far.

CHAPTER 6

THINKING FILMS: KIAROSTAMI, A POETIC PHILOSOPHER

In 2005, I presented a paper at a three-day conference entitled *Abbas Kiarostami: Image, Voice and Vision* at the Victoria & Albert Museum, part of a London-wide series of events held in Kiarostami's honour.[1] Having made an ethno-documentary film on Iranian asylum seekers in Turkey in 2002, I was keen also to attend the nine-day intensive film workshop at the French Institute that was part of this series of events. To my dismay, my application to the workshop was declined. At the end of the conference, all the speakers were invited to an Italian dinner with Kiarostami. He was seated at the far end of the long table from where I was sitting, and I did not get a chance to speak with him. Later, one of the organisers called me and said that Kiarostami was intrigued to hear that I had presented a paper on his films and religion, and that he would like to meet me.

My subsequent conversation with Kiarostami proved to be highly engaging. He was genuinely surprised to hear that someone was looking at religion in his films. As far as he was concerned, his films were not at all religious and he did not know if he would even label himself religious. I explained that I was not looking at his films as religious works, but rather that I was exploring his approach and references to religion. He found this very interesting and said that as far as he knew, no one else had looked at this aspect of his films. After this long and productive conversation, Kiarostami said that we would need more time to talk about his films and that it would be good if I could attend the workshop at the French Institute. I told him that I had already applied and been rejected.

He advised me to just turn up on the day and say that I had an invitation from Kiarostami. And sure enough, I was admitted!

Most of the students came from a film-making background, and very soon word was out that I, along with a couple of other invitees, were not part of the main student pool. Kiarostami, however, treated us equally and expected the same from all of us, so much so that it was difficult to differentiate between the bona fide students and the 'gate-crashers' while doing the work. During those nine days, Kiarostami discussed his methods of film-making, such as the use of non-actors, the advantages and challenges of these methods and the general difficulties of producing and distributing films. He also shared the experiences of his other students at previous workshops in Italy and Brazil. We were then asked to make a short film on digital video on the topic of lifts, using the techniques he had introduced to us. By the end of it I had a one-and-a-half minute short film and acted in two other shorts, all of which were screened at the Ciné Lumière on the last day. But more excitingly, these nine days afforded me the opportunity to learn directly from him. Before this, I had known Kiarostami only through his films, his poetry and his photographs. The workshop was, therefore, a remarkable opportunity to gain further insights into his approach and deepen my understanding of his work.

Kiarostami's films are often studied for their humanistic, universal and sometimes spiritual and other idiosyncratic references,[2] but they are seldom known for their treatment of religion. In my interviews with Iranian film-makers, critics and authorities of the industry in Iran on the topic of religion and spirituality in cinema, many names were invoked but not once was Kiarostami mentioned in this regard. Even when I suggested his films as a possibility within this category, they were all very surprised. Most of them dismissed the idea immediately and others just exclaimed, 'Really?!' before moving on to other topics, not really seeing the point in discussing religion in Kiarostami's films.

Kiarostami is certainly not known for his religious life or background. Moreover, if by religion and cinema we mean taking a theological approach that attempts to detect parallels between religious doctrines and the ideas conveyed in film, or the depiction of the lives of saints and founders of religion, then Kiarostami's work would obviously not fall within this category of study.[3]

One could argue that if Kiarostami himself was intrigued by my study of religion and spirituality in his films, then the surprise this proposal aroused in others was completely understandable. However, unlike the response of the critics, Kiarostami's surprise was not because he felt his works are far removed from religious references. It was simply that no one had previously paid any serious attention to this aspect of his films. He explained that the problem arises when religion is understood only as that which is defined by a sole authority. Faith and belief, however, go beyond these limited definitions. When asked in an interview with *The Guardian* whether or not he has religious faith, Kiarostami stated:

> I can't answer this. I think religion is very personal and the tragedy for our country is that the personal aspect has been destroyed. It would be the easiest thing in the world for me to say that I am religious, but I won't. This most personal aspect of our lives has become the tool of the government's power. The value of people is equated with their religiosity.[4]

It would be an overstatement to assert that religion is the main concern of Kiarostami's films, but the premise that he avoids religious references altogether does not hold water either. Kiarostami does not shy away from referring to religion by touching on traditional belief systems, social taboos, and more importantly showing, as Bird states, 'man's struggle to discern the divine presence'.[5] Like some other Iranian film-makers, such as Majidi, Kiarostami also employs the poetic style to explore man's struggle towards spiritual attainment.

Many critics, especially in the West, read Kiarostami's works as alluding to the spiritual. However, these references are limited mainly to parallels drawn between Sufi concepts and certain imagery in the films, such as zigzag paths and lone trees. I set out to examine the treatment of religion and spirituality in Kiarostami's works by more than merely outlining correspondences between the pictures and Sufism. Rather, I argue that Kiarostami is a poetic philosopher. His films may be read as 'poetic philosophies' that resonate with Wittgenstein's thought and the lyrical language of Iranian poets such as Sohrab Sepehry (d. 1980), Forugh Farrokhzad (d. 1967) and even as far back as Omar Khayyam (d. 1123). In this chapter, I will study Kiarostami's poetic celebration of life and its meaning, with a particular focus on the conflicts of life and death in his films. Kiarostami questions the religious and scientific convictions about the world and proposes an alternative approach to looking at the world. His approach to these issues makes for interesting comparisons with Wittgenstein's philosophy on the mystical.

Philosophy in Film

Recently, some scholars of philosophy have been attracted to films in their study and analyses of philosophical thought. Their approaches vary from studying philosophy through film to considering film as philosophy itself. Falzon proposes to study various films 'to identify philosophical positions, themes or questions that are being presented or worked through in particular films'.[6] Thus, he introduces an approach which does not intend to impose philosophy on film, but rather brings out what is happening in film. In discussing moral philosophy, for example, he focuses on the central question 'Why should we be moral?' For this, he provides a range of arguments on the topic including those proposed by Plato, Kant, utilitarianism and existentialism. According to Kant's moral theory[7] moral worth is dependent not on the consequences of our acts but on the motivations behind them. Utilitarianism, on the other hand, argues that the consequences of our acts determine what is moral. Therefore, even if an act produces some unhappiness it can be justified as good as long as the happiness and pleasure it produces in the world outweigh this unpleasantness. Existentialists differ from all of the above in that unlike Kant they do not base morality on reason or in the utilitarian spirit of human happiness. The answer does not lie with religion either, for God is not viewed as the lawgiver. Instead, existentialists argue that humans have free choice and should take full responsibility for their actions. Falzon selects particular films that deal with the question of morality in a manner that is comparable to these theories. Woody Allen's *Crimes and Misdemeanors* (1989) is one such example. When one of the characters faces the dilemma of what to do with his mistress when she threatens to expose their affair, we are introduced to a number of views as to why one should be moral.[8] Falzon studies these various perspectives, such as keeping in line with God-given moral law, the role of the conscious in people's lives and the pursuit of one's own happiness.

Goodenough[9] identifies four reasons for the philosopher's interest in film. One is the technical aspect of film itself, where the philosopher might be interested in understanding the technology, process, and social meanings of watching films. Another reason is that some films illustrate philosophical themes and issues. He refers to *The Matrix* trilogy (Wachowski brothers, 1999–2003) as a series of fantasies that provide graphic illustration of a number of philosophical issues. However, since the financial success of a film is central to its production, action becomes the primary concern of the film. Thus, content is not approached in a very philosophical way and becomes secondary to these special effects. There are other films, however, that raise philosophical issues in a serious and central way. This is the third reason for the philosopher's attraction to film. These are, as Goodenough refers to them, 'films about philosophy'. Jarman's *Wittgenstein* (1993) is one such example, where philosophical thought is explicitly discussed and constitutes the main content of the film. The last approach is Goodenough's thesis of film itself as philosophy. Drawing from Mulhall's[10] arguments, Goodenough states that films are independent forms that think seriously and systematically about philosophical arguments and issues.[11] They are different from and stronger than literary texts, for the written arguments and texts tell us about philosophy, whereas films *show* us philosophy.[12]

The film-maker's intention in showing philosophy is irrelevant to the film's ability to do philosophy. Drawing from a number of arguments on this topic, Goodenough asserts that a film is not to be considered only if it conforms to any of the existing philosophical theories. Rather, it is the kind of questions that a film poses and the kind of answers that it provides, which can be of a philosophical nature, and which, therefore, make it appropriate for this kind of study. Similarly, Litch (2002) proposes to study and discuss some of 'the enduring questions within philosophy' through feature films. In her view, whether or not the writer or director of a film intended to do philosophy is irrelevant to the possibility of a film dealing with philosophical questions. She thus states that the main criterion for the selection of films in her study is to 'present and defend an answer to one of philosophy's classic questions'.[13] For example, in her study of morality she also analyses *Crimes and Misdemeanors* (Allen, 1989) as one such film which presents one of philosophy's classic questions.

Goodenough mentions *Blade Runner* (Scott, 1982) as another such film that demonstrates the ability to think in films. He argues that this film thinks seriously about philosophical arguments and issues, including personhood and identity. A film that seriously thinks about philosophical arguments and issues should ultimately 'act as a kind of philosophical mirror, making us look to see how we see ourselves'.[14]

Even though this approach to philosophy in film does not directly fall under the study of film and religion, it is a method that can usefully be applied to this area of study. Both philosophy and religion, and specifically theology, are concerned with questions such as identity, human relationships with the world, the nature of evil, morality and so on. This approach, however, is different from the theological approach in that it does not aim to detect parallels between the theological arguments and films. Rather, it detects how films themselves can reflect on philosophy, theology or religion. When a film contemplates a theme such as morality within a particular context and studies the various understandings of morality, it does not seek to draw comparisons with theological arguments. Rather, it reflects on the theological definition of morality alongside perhaps other definitions, and thinks seriously about these arguments. Thus, this approach is a useful tool that opens up another avenue for studying how religion is dealt with in films.

The reliance on philosophy in some of the Iranian discourses regarding religion and spirituality in cinema is evident. Indeed, some Iranian critics have employed Western philosophy, such as Heidegger's, to support arguments in their approaches. Unlike the approach of philosophy in film, these Iranian studies are not about seeing how film does philosophy. As discussed earlier in Chapter 2, these Iranian critics instead employ Heidegger's ideas on technology to study the encounter of art and technology, and of Islam with modernity. Thus, despite the Western origin of their theories, they develop a uniquely Iranian approach and one that is rooted in a much older history of Iranian intellectuals who employed Heidegger to provide a philosophical understanding of their disenchantment with modernity and the Pahlavis' modernising projects. In this chapter, I have employed a philosophical framework to study the engagement of Kiarostami's films with religion and spirituality.

Kiarostami, a 'Poetic Philosopher'

It is not an exaggeration to say that Abbas Kiarostami is the most internationally acclaimed Iranian film-maker. Born in 1940 in Tehran, Kiarostami is also a poet and photographer. He studied graphic design and drawing at the University of Tehran. In 1969, he joined the Centre for the Intellectual Development of Children and Young Adults in Tehran (*Kanun parvaresh fekri kudakan va nojavanan*), where he set up and ran the film department and made his first films. He has won many international awards including the prestigious Palme d'Or at the 1997 Cannes International Film Festival for *Taste of Cherry* (*Ta'm-e gilas*). His international claim to fame began with *Where is the Friend's House?* (*Khane-ye dust kojast?*, 1987). The fact that these and all his more recent films are easily available from the main online retailers such as Amazon.com and other distributors, or media stores such as Virgin and HMV — a luxury not granted to most other Iranian film-makers — speaks volumes about his credibility in the West. It is not just film festivals and critics that have been attracted to his works, but also academia, evident in numerous publications that discuss his films at great length. Academic publications seem to be so saturated with his works that editors of various journals who have otherwise shown interest in my work have inevitably hinted that there is already so much available on Kiarostami that they prefer to publish material on other film-makers.

However, Kiarostami's popularity outside his home country has not been shared inside it. In his own context, Kiarostami is often felt to have gained undeserved recognition. As Saeed-Vafa (2002) demonstrates, some Iranians criticise his rural depictions as an effort to exoticise Iran in order to cater to international tastes and film festivals. Others argue that his films are irrelevant to the concerns of modern day Iran and overshadow the efforts of film-makers such as Beyzaie. They argue that since the reading of these latter films requires a deep knowledge of Iranian culture and mythology, they are labelled as inaccessible and undesirable for foreign audiences.[15] For them, Kiarostami's films, therefore, impede the exposure of more deserving fellow film-makers.

Even Kiarostami's 1997 success at Cannes received less attention in the Iranian media than his kiss on Catherine Deneuve's cheek when receiving the Palme d'Or. Back in his homeland, this stirred great controversy among conservatives, who condemned this as an un-Islamic gesture. Thus, instead of expecting a grand welcome and reception for having elevated his national cinema to the highest international recognition, he was forced to postpone his return until the troubled waters settled. Some have argued that the Iranian state has been supportive of Kiarostami's international appearances because of his films' apolitical and non-critical stance. However, as he has often mentioned in his recent interviews, none of his films have actually been screened in Iran since 1996. It is only a small group of students and elites within Iran who remain attracted to his works and until recently they could only watch his films through either private screenings or pirated copies, which are widely available in the country. Things seem to have improved slightly. For example, a conference entitled *Barresi zaban-e filmha-ye Kiarostami* (Examining the Language of Kiarostami's Films), held at the University of Tehran in January 2006, screened many of his films and invited him to address the students. However, despite wide rejection in his home country, his influence on many Iranian film-makers is indisputable, a fact that even his opponents admit, and which academic publications detail.

Locating Kiarostami within the Various Discourses

I am aware of the criticisms that may be levelled against drawing parallels between a Western philosopher's thinking and that of an Iranian film-maker. In fact, comparisons of Kiarostami with modernists have often been opposed as an inappropriate exploration. Indeed, should we 'complacently analyse the works of such a genuinely Iranian film-maker using a concept of 'modernity' which is so markedly Western?'[16] There are many problems inherent in the notion of a 'genuinely Iranian film-maker' and, consequently, with the irrelevance of modernity in this regard. To mention but a few, first it presumes that Iran, being a non-Western country, never experienced modernity, and, therefore, as Mir-Ehsan[17] asserts, the only way of determining Kiarostami's influences and roots would be through looking at Persian miniatures and the Iranian musical tradition. However, an argument that consistently positions Kiarostami, or for that matter any other Iranian film-maker, solely within an Iranian tradition is untenable. Secondly, this approach overlooks the obvious: the nature of the medium of cinema itself as a Western import. Thirdly, in his various interviews, Kiarostami's frequent references to Western philosophers such as Cioran, and to film-makers like Bertolucci and Fellini, clearly indicate his familiarity and engagement with Western thought.

However, it is not only the Western/Iranian comparison that provokes dissatisfaction. As discussed above, criticisms in his own context vary from protests at his exoticisation of Iran through rural settings catering to international tastes and film festivals, to impeding the exposure of more meritorious and fellow film-makers. The appeal of Kiarostami's films, they argue, stems from the fact that the films are not rooted in Iranian culture, which in turn makes them easily accessible to foreign audiences. Farahmand, referring to film-makers such as Kiarostami, argues that 'village themes and location shooting in rural landscapes not only take viewers away from urban politics, but also reinforce the exotic look of Iranian films – and increase their marketability abroad'.[18] A closer look at Kiarostami's films, however, clearly shows this criticism to be unfounded and rather limited. What it suggests, in effect, is that for these critics, only a particular genre or cinematic style qualifies as being deeply rooted in Iranian culture and tradition. As we shall see, however, Kiarostami's aesthetic and poetic approach is indeed so rooted.

Many Iranian critics have also criticised Kiarostami's works as lacking any intellectual bearings. Shahrukh Dulku asserts that they have an 'overwhelming emphasis on the instinctual and not intellectual aspects of life'.[19] In my interview with Dulku in Tehran in January 2005, he was emphatic that the greatest weakness of Iranian film-makers was their ignorance of both their tradition and of modernity. In his view, they are generally unfamiliar with the appropriate employment of technology and resort to superficial elements to convey meaning and content. This weakness results in films that suffer from a lack of harmony between form and content.

Maddadpur, another critic, whose views on spirituality and cinema were discussed in detail in Chapter 2, is one of the few to refer to religion in Kiarostami's films. In *Seyr va suluk-e sinamayi* (Cinematic Spiritual Journey, 1997), he attempts to locate cinema's position within the discourses of religion, spirituality and technology. He denies the possibility of exploring religion or spirituality in film, and asserts that an impious soul preoccupied with this-worldly life cannot transcend to other-worldly status.[20] He maintains that only the likes of the martyred Avini, who fought on the front lines in the 'Sacred Defence' during the Iran-Iraq war, are capable of depicting spirituality through film. The present avant-garde Iranian cinema, he states, has replaced the tough-guyism and eroticism of pre-Revolutionary cinema with semi-religious mysticism, lacking the slightest trace of a spiritual journey. Kiarostami, he says, is the greatest teacher and most disjunctive-minded of Iranian postmodern film-makers. He states that Kiarostami sometimes takes on the role of the open-minded theologian.[21] As though this were a final and self-explanatory decree, Maddadpur fails to analyse any of Kiarostami's films and moves on to criticise other film-makers without any further elaboration of his assertions.

Kiarostami's films, however, are neither a demonstration of cinema techniques, as Dulku might put it, nor are they a means to engage in theology, contrary to Maddadpur's belief. The problem with an approach such as Maddadpur's lies in considering films as sermons and film-makers as priests. It is the expectation that, like theologians, film-makers, too, explore the nature of God and seek the truth.

Kiarostami does, nevertheless, employ cinema's unique characteristics to make philosophical films. He is a 'poetic philosopher', a term already applied to him by Rapfogel.[22] However, other than the extract below, I have thus far found nothing by Rapfogel elaborating on this terminology in general or in reference to Kiarostami in particular. In comparing Kiarostami's and Jafar Panahi's films, Rapfogel asserts:

> Kiarostami's vision is a broader, more panoramic one. It's Panahi who takes Kiarostami's methods and innovations and directs them towards more specific, socially topical subjects. Panahi shares with Kiarostami a poetic sensibility, but he focuses it downwards, towards the street and the problems he finds there, rather than upwards and outwards – he's a poetic journalist to Kiarostami's poetic philosopher. The difference is clear from the titles of their films: *And Life Goes On* (1991) (more accurately translated as *Life and Nothing More*), *Taste of Cherry* (1997), *The Wind Will Carry Us* (1999) – these are philosophical titles for philosophical films. There's nothing pretentious or facile about them – there's conviction and true wisdom at their heart, and they're always rooted in particulars. But Kiarostami's films are unmistakably the fruit of contemplation, of abstract meditation, whereas Panahi's films spring more directly from observation.[23]

Rapfogel does not discuss further the philosophy in Kiarostami's work. Here, I aim to demonstrate how some of his films are philosophical and how they resonate with Wittgenstein's thought. The films' lyrical language is influenced by Iranian poets such as Forugh Farrokhzad, Sohrab Sepehry and Omar Khayyam – the titles *Where is the Friend's House* and *The Wind Will Carry Us* (*Bad ma ra khahad bord*, 1999) come from poems by Sepehry and Farrokhzad respectively. It is not that Kiarostami provides a filmic version of the poetry of these masters or of Wittgenstein's philosophy; indeed, nothing in his films suggests Kiarostami's familiarity with Wittgenstein's thought. However, as Read suggests when discussing works of certain film-makers, it is 'perhaps increasingly obvious that films think, that films are no longer merely to be viewed as illustrative material for pre-existing philosophies...nor as illustrative material for pre-existing ideologies or theories'.[24]

Similarly, Kiarostami's films could also be seen as films that think, not as depictions of pre-existing philosophies, but as re-thinking within the context of existing ideas, thoughts and beliefs. As such, these films contain certain philosophical concerns that parallel Wittgenstein's philosophy. Kiarostami's films could be read as 'philosophy in action', a term that Mulhall uses in discussing certain films as philosophy:

> I do not look to these films as handy or popular illustrations of views and arguments properly developed by philosophers; I see them rather as themselves reflecting on and evaluating such views and arguments, as thinking seriously and systematically about them in just the ways that philosophers do. Such films are not philosophy's raw material, not a source for its ornamentation; they are philosophical exercises, philosophy in action – film as philosophising.[25]

In studying the similarities between the approaches of Kiarostami and Wittgenstein, I have based most of my readings on Wittgenstein's *Tractatus*. Despite Wittgenstein moving away from his views on religion as articulated in the *Tractatus*, the fact that it remains widely-studied within academia says much about its continuing validity and relevance. Interestingly, even Kiarostami's works could be seen as evolving works that inform each other. He sometimes refers to a theme in one film and then picks it up again in another film to elaborate on and study it further. This could be regarded as a philosophy growing and evolving, with the films thinking and informing each other. The later films do not make his earlier approaches redundant or irrelevant. They remain as relevant and valid approaches to thinking about those particular themes.

An Alternative Approach to Religion

The engagement of modern philosophy with metaphysics involved two main trends. One, associated with Hume and Ayer, dismissed such beliefs in metaphysics as intellectually misguided, and the other, that of Kant and Wittgenstein, sought to restore a sense of its integrity and validity, but in terms different from those of medieval philosophy and theology. Ayer, a positivist, attacks metaphysics for being unverifiable and disqualifies it from sense.[26] He does not claim it to be false, but makes a far more powerful claim by dismissing it totally as nonsensical. The narrowness of this philosophy is reflected in the equation of sense with verifiability. In this way it destroys the richness of living by failing to appreciate interpretations of reality that are outside the physical world. 'Kant readily acknowledged the threat which a modern scientific worldview poses for morality and religion, yet ... he emphasised an individualism that affirmed human moral autonomy and freedom'.[27]

Wittgenstein dismisses the principle of verification as an all-encompassing tenet that could be applied to everything. According to the nature and limits of verification itself, only states of affairs are verifiable and anything beyond the facts cannot be subject to verification.[28] Hence, claiming that the mystical is not verifiable and is, therefore, nonsensical is in itself a nonsensical claim. 'Not how the world is, is the mystical, but that it is'.[29] The certainty of belief is stronger than the certainty of a scientific prediction, yet the object of belief is not predictable.

While Wittgenstein restores the validity of the mystical in metaphysics, which guides humans in their lives, he does not endorse medieval philosophy or theology. Human language, Wittgenstein asserts, is incapable of explaining the mystical. The religious, however, are tempted to make the mistake of explaining it, which only results in pseudo-explanations. The moment an explanation is offered, the mystery and wonder of the mystical is destroyed. Wittgenstein explains this as a problem of human language, inherent in which is the tendency to convert metaphysics into facts. Indeed, he states, 'Whereof one cannot speak, thereof one must be silent'.[30]

Wittgenstein explains religion as a double-edged knife, which is poetic with rich culture on the one side, and full of danger and dogmatic on the other. Notions of faith such as God, death and eternity can be talked about poetically, but cannot be talked about as facts. In trying to explain God, religion sometimes turns Him into an idol. What is mystical and can be spoken of poetically and symbolically, therefore, becomes an idol. The unutterable has to be conveyed in a different way: it has to be shown. In proposition 6.522 of his *Tractatus*, Wittgenstein maintains that 'There is indeed the inexpressible. This shows itself; it is the mystical'.[31] He does not claim that religious language is false or 'waste time garnering evidence for the falsity of religion. Rather, he focuses upon the discourses of religion and shows how it lacks the pictorial relation to the world essential for the possession of meaning'.[32] It is not only religion that becomes irrelevant to the mystical:

> Science is about empirical, contingent and verifiable matters. Metaphysics is not about contingent, empirical or verifiable matters. It is about what is absolute and necessary. But language is not geared to coping with the absolute and the necessary. As

Wittgenstein puts it, certain signs in a metaphysical proposition lack meaning ... But he did not conclude ... that this rendered metaphysics inarticulate. It is just that the articulation is somewhat different from the statement of scientific and common-sense facts.[33]

Thus, Wittgenstein aims at restoring the non-scientific form of understanding:

Among those things that 'show themselves are ethics, aesthetics, religion, the meaning of life, logic and philosophy'. In all these areas, Wittgenstein appears to believe, there are indeed truths, but none of these truths can be expressed in language; they all have to be shown, not said'.[34]

The realm of religion differs from that of the intellect. Clack mentions the two ways that Wittgenstein believed the mystical could be shown: 'a particular way of living as well as artistic creation which can mediate what is higher'.[35] The fact that the faith view does not fall into the trap of providing evidence renders it better than the religious

Figure 22 *Where is the Friend's House? (Khane-ye dust kojast?,* Abbas Kiarostami, 1987).

view in Wittgenstein's philosophy. 'Religious belief is the upshot of a kind of life, a kind of upbringing, which culminates in a certain sort of belief'.[36]

It is this philosophical outlook on religion that makes for interesting comparisons with Kiarostami's works. Kiarostami, too, as the analysis of his films in this chapter will demonstrate, alludes to the mystical in a way that resonates with Wittgenstein's thought. He does not avoid dealing with the religious view, contrary to what many of his critics claim. In fact, he presents an array of religious discourses without trying to prove them true or false before proposing an alternative approach to religion. He also contemplates the relevance of scientific knowledge to the mystical in some of his films. In fact, Kiarostami's films could be read as an endeavour towards the artistic creation that Wittgenstein refers to as being one of the ways of showing the mystical. When asked if serious art creates a desire in the spectator for some other reality, Kiarostami says:

> Yes, I believe so, because otherwise art would have no purpose. Should religion not prove successful at accomplishing that mission, art always can attempt it. They both point in the same direction. Religion points to another world, whereas art points to a better existence. One is an invitation, an offering to a faraway place, the other to a place that is close.[37]

Reading Life and Death in Kiarostami's Films

One of the main philosophical concerns in a large proportion of Kiarostami's films made in the 1990s is death and life. A search for the friend that began in *Where is the Friend's House?* (*Khane-ye dust kojast?*, 1987) continues in *And Life Goes On* (*Zendegi va digar hich*, 1992), only this time, the danger is no longer that of the barking dogs and dark alleys of Koker village but a catastrophic earthquake that has wiped out the friends and loved ones of many. Kiarostami's subsequent film, *Through the Olive Trees* (*Zir-e derakhtan-e zeytun*, 1994), also looks at the aftermath of the earthquake. These three films have been referred to as the Koker Trilogy in the West. The tens of thousands of lives that were lost to the 1990 earthquake in Iran were the starting point for a series of Kiarostami's films that have death as a prominent underlying theme.

The Traditional Discourses

Natural disasters have usually led to the theist's attempt to understand the reasons why God has afflicted people with such adversity. It is during such times that man's reasoning about the question of evil is heightened. Ingmar Bergman depicts this quest in his *The Seventh Seal* (1957) in which people try to understand why so many lives are lost to Black Death across Europe.[38] Similarly, in *And Life Goes On* and *Through the Olive Trees*, the survivors and those witnessing the aftermath of the earthquake strive to make sense of the catastrophe.

Kiarostami presents us with an array of ruminations about death, God and evil, and enables us to gain an insight into how the local people are trying to make sense of the tragedy in their own vocabulary. He does not strip them of their understanding nor does he force his own upon the viewer. When the truck driver caught up in the heavy traffic in *And Life Goes On* asks, 'What sin has this nation committed to be punished by God like this?' it is a question that assumes the earthquake to be the result of people's wrongdoing. Similarly, Husayn, in *Through the Olive Trees*, calmly interprets the deaths as a direct result of the villainy of individuals. He had fallen in love with Tahereh when working as a mason in a building right across her house. However, when he had approached her mother to ask for her hand in marriage, she had not only rejected him but also made sure that he lost his job. In Husayn's view, Tahereh's parents and his employer were killed in the earthquake for conspiring against his wish to marry Tahereh – their deaths were a punishment for breaking his heart.

Death as God's punishment for wrongdoing could be read within the context of traditional scripture and the subsequent interpretations of believers. Sura 7 of the Qur'an, 'The Heights', forewarns the faithful about disbelief in God and His Messenger:

> And if people of the townships had believed and kept from evil, surely We should have opened for them blessings from the sky and from the earth. But (unto every messenger) they gave the lie, and so We seized them on account of what they used to earn.
>
> Are the people of the townships then secure from the coming of Our wrath upon them as a night-raid while they sleep?[39]

In fact, this Qur'anic chapter relates numerous accounts of punishments inflicted on those who disobeyed God and His prophets. Thus, the people of Noah were drowned for not believing him,[40] the root of the tribe of Aad was cut down for disbelieving Hud,[41] the people of Thamud were destroyed by an earthquake for disobeying a prophet sent down to them,[42] the people of Lot destroyed by a heavenly rain poured upon them for their lewd acts,[43] the people of Midian were seized by an earthquake for disobeying Sho'ayb[44] and the Pharaoh's folk who did not follow Moses were punished with flood, locusts, vermin, blood and the drowning sea. Even Moses' own folk who were led astray were not spared and subsequently punished by an earthquake.[45] These are just some of the examples of natural disasters described in the Qur'an as a consequence of people's wrongdoing.

Inherent in suffering is the problem of evil, raised for centuries among the monotheistic religions. If God is omniscient, omnipotent and wholly good, why is there so much suffering in the world? In *And Life Goes On*, for the old Mr Ruhi, the earthquake is not a punishment sent down by God, rather it is like 'a hungry wolf that attacked a flock of sheep and ate some and spared others.' It is an event that he believes will also result in a better appreciation of life by those who survived. Mr Ruhi sees the disaster as a result of the forces of nature rather than God's intentions, endorsing the theodicy that good, and in this case a better appreciation of life, requires the existence of evil.

Similarly, the woman who has lost her seven-year-old daughter attempts to come to terms with her loss and consoles herself by saying that it was what God willed. The young boy acting as Kiarostami's son, on the other hand, is keen to retain God's goodness. He draws from the various analogies he has come across to exempt God from intending to kill an innocent seven-year-old. These range from the analogy of the hungry wolf and a better appreciation of life espoused by Mr Ruhi, to the story of Abraham and Ishmael in his own history book. This is indicative of the transmission and reinforcement of a system of knowledge and beliefs through the generations ranging from the ancient narrative of Abraham's sacrifice to what the young boy has heard from Mr Ruhi only moments before. Indeed, when the mother asks the boy where he has learnt all of this from, he says, 'Half from Mr Ruhi, half from my history book and half from myself', a response that alludes to the power of narrative and oral tradition in forming a worldview which transcends history.

Kiarostami thus presents us with a range of arguments on the issue of death, whilst he himself remains silent in the face of these theistic debates. In fact, when the truck driver asks him what sin the nation has committed to be punished by God in this way, he evades the question, saying instead, 'Give me way so that I can escape by the side road' implying his reluctance to engage in such theological reasoning. He is, perhaps, seeking a 'side road' in order to avoid the heavy traffic of the dominating religious debates. Kiarostami's search for an alternative way is not an attempt to avoid contemplating issues of death and suffering. Rather, it is a provocative proposal to re-evaluate our preconceived beliefs. In his opinion, 'Cinema and all other arts ought to be able to destroy the mind of their audience in order to reject the old values and make us susceptible to new values'.[46]

A Kiarostami film is constituted not only by what is said or shown on screen, but also, more often than not, by the unsaid and hidden, which is in fact of greater significance. To use his own words, Kiarostami wants to 'create the type of cinema that shows by not showing'.[47] It is his approach of 'showing by not showing', 'saying by not saying', that makes interesting parallels with Wittgenstein's philosophy. When Wittgenstein sent the manuscript of his *Tractatus* to Ludwig von Ficker to be considered for publication, he explained that his book consisted of two parts:

> I once wanted to give a few words in the foreword which now actually are not in it, which, however, I'll write to you now because they might be a key for you: I wanted to write that my work consists of two parts: of the one which is here, and of everything which I have *not* written. And precisely this second part is the important one. For the Ethical is delimited from within, as it were, by my book; and I'm convinced that, *strictly* speaking, it can ONLY be delimited in this way. In brief, I think: All of that which *many are babbling* today, I have defined in my book by remaining silent about it.[48]

Wittgenstein's silence to 'that of which many are babbling today' is echoed in Kiarostami's refusal to explicitly comment on specific religious views, such as death and suffering. In fact, through the medium of cinema he materialises Wittgenstein's great desire of showing that which the limits of language make impossible to talk about. In his *Tractatus*, Wittgenstein suggests that a particular way of looking at the world constitutes 'the mystical'.[49]

> 6.44 It is not *how* things are in the world that is mystical, but *that* it exists.

6.45 To view the world sub specie aeterni is to view it as a whole – a limited whole. Feeling the world as a limited whole – it is this that is mystical.

Like Wittgenstein, Kiarostami finds the world's existence itself to be the mystical. Unlike the usual dead bodies and mourning relatives which constitute the main *mise-en-scène* of earthquake films, as seen for example, in *Wake Up Arezu* (*Bidar sho Arezu*, Ayari, 2005) – a film based on the 2003 earthquake in Bam which was also filmed on location – in Kiarostami's films, the beauties of nature provide the backdrop for life that strives to continue in face of all adversity. We see people digging, not in search of bodies, or to bury the dead, but to find the means of living, be it digging for a kettle, a carpet, a pillow, a lamp, or indeed setting up television antennas to follow the World Cup. Kiarostami's camera does not avoid the destruction that the earthquake has left in its wake, rather he sees through it: the destroyed shells of windows and doors, standing empty in the rubble, frame a world of beauty. Instead of focusing his lens on death and suffering, Kiarostami redirects our gaze to man's struggle for life, and the existence of the world itself becomes the object of wonder and mystery. Commenting on *And Life Goes On,* Kiarostami remarks that what he needed to address was 'life, the continuity of life itself, not individuals and their fate, though that is the starting point for the larger lesson'.[50]

Death as Desire

In *Taste of Cherry,* death finds a new twist. It is turned on its head from being the cause of pain and suffering to being an object of desire. The film revolves around Badi'i, a middle-aged man who wants to commit suicide in a very particular way – by taking an overdose of sleeping pills at night and sleeping in a hole dug under a lone tree in the mountains outside Tehran. However, he wants someone to come and check on him the following morning in order to help him out of the hole if he is still alive, or bury him if he is dead. He drives around in his car looking for that one person. Death in *Taste of Cherry,* therefore, becomes an act sought by an individual, rather than a tragic incident inflicted upon masses as in the last two instalments of the Koker Trilogy. The conflicts of death and life are hence reversed such that Badi'i's actions become an attempt to claim death, rather than death claiming life.

As in the Koker Trilogy, in *Taste of Cherry* we are presented with various theological arguments. However, this time they are not employed to justify death and misery, but rather to preserve the sanctity of life itself. Badi'i gives lifts to the people he thinks may be potential helpers. One of them is an Afghan seminarian who listens attentively to Badi'i, then quotes from the Qur'an and hadith and employs the religious vocabulary of God, sin and punishment in order to dissuade Badii from wanting to kill himself. Badi'i, however, dismissively responds to him by stating: 'You can understand me, you can pity me, but you can't feel my pain ... the only thing I need from you right now is a pair of hands.'

Badi'i finally comes across Baqeri, a middle-aged taxidermist working at the Natural History Museum. Baqeri takes Badi'i on a new route, different from the desolate landscape in which he has been driving thus far. This route, Baqeri states, is longer, but more beautiful. He agrees to help Badi'i not only because of the money he needs for his sick child, but also as an act of friendship. Baqeri states that he would have preferred to save a life rather than help to take it away, but that he also wants to be a friend to Badi'i. As a friend, therefore, he would be there for him even during difficult times.

In discussing the ending of *Taste of Cherry*, Elena finds it bears 'some extraordinarily rich connotations. The storm that breaks just as Badi'i is getting into the grave and the specific image of the cloud crossing the moon refer to the imagery of the Day of Judgement in Islamic tradition',[51] quoting Qur'an 25:25 and 18:19 in support of this reading. Elena also goes on to say that Kiarostami's use of Louis Armstrong's trumpet in *St James Infirmary* reminds one of the trumpet of the angel of resurrection, Israfil, of the Persian Islamic tradition. Kiarostami himself, however, has another explanation for his use of this music in the film:

> This music, funeral music played over a dead body, interested me because of the sensuality of Louis Armstrong's trumpet-playing, particularly cheerful and optimistic in spite of everything, which expresses very well that idea of life that the film tries to convey. A piece of music that in this sense is I think very close to the poetry of Khayyam, where joy finally emerges from sorrow.[52]

Optimism and cheerfulness in the face of death and despair? Kiarostami certainly does not endorse a nihilistic approach to life, celebrating nothingness. However, Badi'i's encounter with the taxidermist, Baqeri, might well be the reason for this hopefulness. Baqeri offers him a different route – both literally and metaphorically – a longer but more beautiful route, a reference to a life which might be longer and perhaps, therefore, entail more difficulties, but nonetheless worth the beauty that one experiences along the way. More importantly, the hopefulness may also be the result of Baqeri's friendship. Instead of warning Badi'i of punishment and a God who despises the sinner, Baqeri empathises with him and agrees to carry out his wishes as a final act of friendship.

All along, perhaps, Badi'i's quest was not for someone to help him in his death, but instead a search for a friend, and for meaning. Thus, Badi'i's encounter with Baqeri is not significant only because the latter invites him to appreciate the beauties of nature and the joys of life despite its concomitant difficulties, which, to expand upon Kiarostami's point above, would constitute only half of a typical Khayyam quatrain. It is also significant because having a friend on this journey, painful and difficult as it might be, is what makes life bearable and meaningful. This theme – that the temporality and struggle of life is balanced by the good fortune of having a friend to share in this journey – is an enduring trope in Persian poetry. Badi'i's success in finding a friend, knowing that he would be there the following morning, can be seen as the 'joy' that 'finally emerges from sorrow'.

This may be the reason why Kiarostami decides to leave the outcome of Badi'i's suicide attempt ambiguous. For Badi'i's achievement is not dependent on the success or failure of his suicide, but rather on the journey he had begun. His very method of choice in committing suicide leaves him with two possibilities – death or life – as opposed to a definitive method of death. In other words, if the sleeping pills are ineffective, Badi'i wants to be able to come out of the hole, instead of, for example, taking more pills. He is even worried that Baqeri might bury him alive, mistaking him to be dead when he might have only fallen asleep. This leads one to believe that Badi'i does not intend to take complete control over ending his life, thus leaving room for an unseen power or grace to intervene. He gambles with fate like the knight in Bergman's *The Seventh Seal* (1957) who plays chess with Death. Both protagonists are in search of the meaning of life. Thus, if some form of divine intervention were to take place, a friend would pull Badi'i out. He would then be redeemed through the act of suicide and his life would have meaning and purpose.

Kiarostami also delves into the semiotics of Islamic theology in naming his protagonist. 'Badi'i' means 'unprecendented', 'unique', from the

Arabic root 'bada'a', which is also the root for 'bida'a', meaning 'heretical doctrine' or heresy or (undesirable) innovation. Historically in Islam, the term has been used to refer to Muslims who deviate from 'orthodox' practices. The semiotics of this name could be read in two different ways: the fact that Badi'i wants to commit suicide in this specific manner is likely to be without precedent. Moreover, the very specific manner in which he intends to be buried implies a doing-away with Islamic burial rites. Thus, he is not only a sinner for taking his life but also a heretic for creating new rituals that go against normative practice.

Suicide, one of the cardinal sins in Islam, becomes the protagonist's goal and desire in *Taste of Cherry*. The religious discourse of the Afghan seminarian clearly fails to respond meaningfully to certain life situations. The seminarian understands what Badi'i wants from him, but is bound by his belief system and instead employs his own trope of religious vocabulary to try to change Badi'i's mind. In discussing the character of the seminarian, Kiarostami remarks that 'the man of religion is the embodiment of a certain discourse and philosophy that imposes *a priori* the boundaries between Good and Evil. With this character I wanted to show, beyond religious dogmatism as such, all those social conventions that are imposed on us without any real justification'.[53]

As Wittgenstein states, however, notions of faith cannot be stated as fact, but rather only spoken of poetically. Baqeri, the very man who has agreed to be an accomplice to Badi'i's suicide, is the one who talks about life poetically. He invites Badi'i to view the intricate beauties of nature and appreciate the pleasures they convey. He does not engage in a religious discussion by referring to sin and punishment. In fact, he invokes God only once, and that, too, not as the One Who despises the sinner, but Whose compassion exceeds that of any mother. In Baqeri's view, the compassion is evident from all the beauty that He has offered man. He then asks Badi'i if he would no longer want to see the sunrise, the red and yellow of the sunset, the stars, the full moon in the sky and, more importantly, to experience the taste of a cherry. Kiarostami's use of this last experience as the title of the film emphasises the significance of this conversation and the message it implies. Baqeri poetically talks about the notions of life, death, and God and conveys the unutterable by showing these to him when he takes Badi'i on a different route. Kiarostami communicates without trying to restrict the inexpressible to words, in as much as 'Wittgenstein's ideal is to communicate the inexpressible by *not* attempting to express it'.[54]

Death as an Object of Scientific Study

So far, Kiarostami's dialogical films examined the various approaches to death. In all of these films, death was a matter of emotional import. In *The Wind Will Carry Us*, Behzad, the educated Tehrani, comes to the village with the sole purpose of documenting the rites and ceremonies surrounding death, an act that is devoid of any emotional involvement for him. His interest in death arises not out of passion or a quest for meaning. Instead, he eagerly awaits the old woman's death only because it will provide him with footage for his documentary. Her death would, therefore, be simply an object of scientific study.

This time, Kiarostami takes on the challenge of questioning the scientific approach to death and life. For all intents and purposes, Behzad is an anthropologist, albeit with a cold and unconcerned approach, interested in studying the rites and rituals of death in a social group different from his own. In fact, so reluctant is he to miss this opportunity that, to his mother's extreme displeasure, he refuses to leave the village and attend the funeral of a close relative. For him, death is solely a dispassionate object of study and nothing more. His obsession with death is symbolised by the leg-bone he keeps on top of his car dashboard. His impatient wait for the old woman's death is not a passionate pursuit of meaning or understanding. Instead, death is a commodity to be sought after, a scientific assignment to be completed.

Behzad's limited engagement with the local adults includes the schoolteacher and the doctor. Both, by virtue of their jobs, would have been trained in a modern educational system, thus presuming a closer affinity with Behzad. However, as Behzad finds out, their scientific training does not appear to have shaped their outlook on life in the way that it has formed his. The formal training of the doctor appears to be incidental to what he does, and unlike Behzad, he does not seem to be defined by it. When Behzad asks the doctor about the old woman's illness, he says it is very painful and that she is suffering a lot. However, death, he asserts, is worse than illness. 'It is the worst of everything'. In what seems to be an echo of Baqeri in *Taste of Cherry*, the doctor states that death is being deprived of the wonders of nature, its beauty and God's blessing and generosity. Once you have left this world, he states, there is no coming back and that is a great loss.

Both the doctor and Behzad are constantly on the move, Behzad looking for a subject to film or study and the doctor looking for patients wanting to undergo circumcision or ear-piercing. Behzad, however, moves in the enclosed space of his car, with its grimy windscreen, where he cannot see the world clearly. Behzad thus seems blind to all the life around him, focusing instead on death and impatiently awaiting its arrival, while the doctor travels on a motorbike, which allows him to take in all the visual beauty around him.

As Kiarostami reminds us, knowing poetry is different from having a poetic outlook. Both the doctor and Behzad are men of verse. We have already heard Behzad recite poetry to Farzad, the young boy who acts as his guide at the beginning of the film, and to Zaynab, the lover of the telecommunications digger. It is Behzad who recites Forugh Farrokhzad's famous poem on death and despair, and from which Kiarostami borrows the title of the film. This latter scene has been the subject of much analysis and criticism, which I will not, however, enter into here. What is important to note for the purposes of this chapter, is that Behzad's use of poetry betrays his sense of superiority over the locals. This is evident in his surprise at Farzad's knowledge of poetry, and the patronising tone with which he addresses Zaynab when asking her if she knows who Forugh is. For the doctor, however, Khayyam's poetry has something to say about life and death that equips him with a different understanding of the world. Behzad appears to be one of those people that Wittgenstein refers to as those who 'think that scientists exist to instruct them, poets, musicians, etc. to give them pleasure. The idea *that these have something to teach them* – that does not occur to them.'[55]

If indeed Kiarostami's films pose philosophical questions that resonate strikingly with those of Wittgenstein, his poetic discourse is deliberately and consciously rooted in Persian tradition. He speaks of taking refuge in poetry at times of conflict and anxiety, asserting that 'poetry is much more helpful in times of difficulty than in times of calm; it enables us to find a certain stability, an internal energy. When religion cannot fill this void, poetry can do so'.[56] Thus, we hear Sepehry's poetry echoing in Kiarostami's films: 'Let's not fear death... Let's not close the door on the living.' Kiarostami certainly invites us to 'float on the spell of the red rose' as Sepehry asks us to do, for 'It's not our job to know the mystery of the red rose'.[57]

Like many of Kiarostami's other films, *The Wind Will Carry Us* did not follow a tightly written script, but developed on location. Kiarostami's initial plan was to document the death of the old woman. However, the film turns into a questioning of such an approach itself. Once again, Kiarostami's film questions our pre-determined notions, and this time it is the superiority of science over arts. One of the foci of Wittgenstein's philosophy was also the impotency of science in addressing certain aspects of life. In his view,

> the subject matter, questions, problems and solutions of philosophy are fundamentally different from those of the natural sciences because they are not empirical in character. While the natural sciences aim to explain empirical phenomena, philosophy is concerned exclusively with something that antecedes and is separable from empirical inquiry: namely, questions of sense and meaning.[58]

Behzad's experience in the village, however, transforms him and he is no longer interested in documenting the death ceremonies. Alain Bergala reads the ending of the film, where Behzad throws the leg-bone into the river and washes his windscreen, as a shot that

> elegantly and brilliantly, brings to a close the most important discourse in this enigmatic film, which is the re-education of the gaze.... Now [Behzad] has found a new way of looking at the world, one that is free of all impure motivations and from any utilitarian mentality, open to whatever might happen unexpectedly on the uncontrollable fringes of vision, ready to accept the enigma of 'otherness'. The grimy windscreen, through which Kiarostami has refused to let his own vision as a film-maker focus, is now perfectly clean.[59]

Kiarostami leads us to look at the world in a different way. For this, his films take us on a journey that questions our convictions – whether religiously or scientifically biased – whilst gently offering an alternative way of looking. One of the main themes in Wittgenstein's later works is the 'importance of preserving the integrity of *non-scientific* forms of understanding, the kind of understanding characteristic of the arts'.[60] Behzad epitomises this scientific understanding, one that engulfs his perception of life in *The Wind Will Carry Us*. Moreover, Kiarostami leads us to look at the world in a different way. The 're-education' of the gaze subtly alluded to in the film is where Kiarostami, Wittgenstein and Sepehry converge. Wittgenstein emphasises not only 'on showing the reader things that cannot be said, but on getting the reader to see things afresh'.[61] And just as Sepehry first asks:

> I don't know why the good nature of horses
> and the beauty of the pigeons have won repute,
> why no vulture is kept as a pet.

And only then proceeds to propose that,

> We need to rinse our eyes and view
> Everything in a different light.
> We should cleanse our words
> To be both wind and rain.[62]

Conclusions

Depicting the sacred through the profane in a medium such as film is a challenge for any director wishing to address the metaphysical without falling into the trap of the dogmatic. Kiarostami is no exception and he counters this challenge with a unique approach. His films are poetic philosophies that contemplate man's existence and its meaning. They are, as Wittgenstein states, one of those 'artistic creation[s which] can mediate what is higher'.[63] Even though his films demonstrate certain theological or philosophical ideas, he does not attempt to prove the truth or untruth of any of these claims. Instead, his references to the mystical go beyond that of any religious or scientific debate. As Wittgenstein states, human language is incapable of explaining the mystical. The religious, however, are often tempted to make the mistake of explaining it. The moment an explanation is offered, the mystery and wonder of the mystical is destroyed. Kiarostami does not offer an explanation; he just points to another way of looking, allowing his audience to arrive at a certain understanding themselves. Both Kiarostami and Wittgenstein emphasise showing the viewer/reader a way to see things afresh.

The question of life and death is certainly one of Kiarostami's main philosophical deliberations, evident in his numerous films that deal with this issue. It, therefore, provides us with an interesting study of how his films are 'philosophy in action' and how they deliberate about religion. In all these films (*And Life Goes On, Through the Olive Trees, Taste of Cherry* and *The Wind Will Carry Us*) not a single dead body or dying person is actually shown. There are long shots of burial scenes but no close-ups. Like many of Kiarostami's hidden characters whom we never see but do get to know, death is also present but not staring us in the face. Instead, Kiarostami poetically thinks about the question of life, death and suffering.

This approach is not argued to the exclusion of any other understanding of death and suffering; rather, it finds significance through its contrasts. Many of the religious discourses articulated in relation to life and death seem to fail in responding meaningfully to those facing it. It becomes evident that articulations of death as God's wrath and punishment, or as a necessity arising out of the existence of evil for a better appreciation of good, or as a law of nature, lack, as Wittgenstein would argue, the pictorial relation to the world that is essential for the possession of meaning. In a culture that lays great emphasis on mourning rituals and ceremonies, Kiarostami invites us to rethink our approach to death and life. Like Wittgenstein's silence to 'that of which many are babbling today', Kiarostami, too, refuses to comment on any of the views that he introduces within the film. Instead, after he has presented us with the authoritarian accounts of the religious, the positivist, as well as the sceptic, he arrives at a poetic account of death and life. In line with Wittgenstein's thought, Kiarostami's references to the mystical are different from scientific and common-sense statements. His films, therefore, as seen through the example of the theme of life and death, demonstrate a poetic philosophy, an approach that clearly stands out in comparison to the other approaches to religion and spirituality in Iranian films.

CONCLUSION

In a gathering on 13 June 2006, Ayatollah Sayyid Ali Khamenei, the Supreme Leader of the Islamic Republic, received 16 of the country's cinema directors as well as the Minister of Culture and Islamic Guidance, Hossein Saffar-Harandi, and advised them on the crucial role they play in society. He said:

> The key to the country's progress lies to a considerable extent in the hands of cinematic artists. The reason is that, considering the influential role of this art, those who are involved in the lofty art of cinema are able to foster noble aspirations, eagerness to make progress, motivation, dynamism, self-confidence and adherence to Islamic and national values in society through their cinematic productions and thus play a great role in the country's progress and in the promotion of sublime values in society.[1]

Ayatollah Khamenei's address, just like Ayatollah Khomeini's reference to cinema as an educational tool in the early years of the Revolution, as discussed in Chapter 2, signifies the continuity of the regime's acknowledgment of the medium's power and significance.

In the context of the socio-political power of media, where images and representation play a significant role in perpetuating or reconstructing various social and political agendas, it is also important to examine the medium's inherent ability to allow for a polyvocality of discourses including those that challenge or debate views. As I discussed in the Introduction, depictions of Muslims and constructions of their 'Otherness' within Western media have stirred vehement debates and resulted in numerous studies. However, it is equally important to study the various articulations and constructions from within the Muslim context. But what are these Muslim discourses in religion?

During the in-conversation between Abbas Kiarostami, Ahmad Karimi-Hakkak and Geoff Andrew that followed Kiarostami's *ta'ziyeh* installation at the V&A in London in 2005, Karimi-Hakkak asked Kiarostami whether, as an Iranian, as an artist, he personally found the *ta'ziyeh* narrative a little too unsettling, or was it the likes of him, now living in the West, who had grown squeamish. He asked:

> Would you moderate the drama if you had the power to, if it were your choice, to spare the blood and gore or do you think there is something inherently dramatic about the explicit nature of this narrative that moves the crowd to tears? Is it the sight of the blood and the shroud and all that? I ask this because I'd like this genre to continue but I can't think [it appealing] to the new generation; and the reason this has been ghettoised in Iran in the villages and in the lower classes is that the more urban classes are finding it too explicit and not to their tastes.

Kiarostami responded:

> There is so much contradiction in Iran. It is difficult for me to speak here in front of the microphones; it usually causes misunderstanding. We live in a religious society and people often misunderstand me and accuse me of being in favour of religion, which is not at all the case... there are so many contradictions in our country, complex issues. If I say that religion is just superficial and an imposition on the youth, that isn't the case either. Some of my own son's friends, who are very young, are very serious about religion. They fast during Ramazan and observe the religious rituals. It is surprising and difficult to completely understand. It cannot be easily judged. Even if Shajarian [one of the most elite classical singers in Iran] had sung these [folkloric] verses it would have brought tears to people's eyes.
>
> If I turn the same question to Hakkak it would be a difficult question for him to answer. I noticed him tearing during the screening [of the *ta'ziyeh* installation]. Does that mean he is religious?

Karimi-Hakkak ignored this and turned to the audience to take further questions.

The exchange above is a brief reminder of the difficulties surrounding a definitive explanation of what constitutes religion, who is religious, which members of the social strata endorse a specific religious practice in Iran, and how much one is allowed, or even allows oneself, to publicly express one's views on these topics. As I explored in the early chapters of the book, there are different modalities of Shi'i interpretation in Iran, which make it a rich and complex context. These vary from legalistic and formalistic approaches to religion, to more popular discourses and personal interpretations. Each of these modalities are themselves not fixed but have, in fact, evolved over time and been expressed in various forms. Iranian films have engaged with these various interpretations and approaches.

Within the Iranian context, there are a range of views on what constitutes film's engagement with religion and spirituality. Authorities, academics, religious leaders and critics have all struggled to define the relationship of film with religion and spirituality. Ayatollah Moravveji's treatise (1999) on Islamic jurisprudence and cinema was an exercise in aligning traditional theocratic positions with state laws and contemporary social practices. Critics such as Maddadpur (1997) argued that the very medium of film is incompatible with Islamic religious values. The category of *ma'nagara* cinema introduced in 2005 resulted in heated debates encompassing a wide range of interpretations. As in the case of Western film studies, no one approach can do justice to the numerous possibilities of studying religion and spirituality in Iranian film. What is significant in the Iranian case, however, is that these debates reflect a general recognition of cinema's legitimate participation in discourses on religion and spirituality and, more importantly, film's ability to articulate its own discourse on these topics.

By synthesising and categorising the various approaches to the study of film's engagement with religion and spirituality, it became clear that the intersections between them make it impossible to define a distinct and independent approach. Aside from the fluidity of boundaries between these approaches, it also became clear that no single approach can be identified as the one best suited to the study of religion and spirituality in film. Rather, it is the nature of the particular film under study and the angle from which the scholar approaches it, that determines the most appropriate method or methods. This has allowed me to be flexible in my own approach, rather than restrict it to films that could be fitted within a particular method or approach.

In locating the films within the much larger socio-historical context of Iran, my analysis of the films demonstrated an important point: it established how film is a serious medium in the examination and understanding of current Shiʻi religious expressions within Iran that could be placed as part of a much older conventional discourse on religion and spirituality in this region.

The filmic discourses on the role of the clergy participate in debates that are critical of doctrines that empower them, without denying their relevance to the believer. Just as the clergy's political and religious authority have historically been contested, the films question and propose a more fluid relationship between people, the clergy and the Divine – one that is not restricted to the rigid boundaries of seminary debates. Both *The Lizard* (2004) and *Under the Moonlight* (2001) function as parables, depicting the world of the clergy in its current form within Iranian society as well as including a moral vision of how it ought to be.

The films of Majidi which were examined next reflected some core Sufi teachings, such as man's spiritual attainment and his proximity to God. Majidi's films provide an alternative view of expressions of Iranian Shiʻism, which are inspired by the works of great masters such as Rumi, ʻAttar and Jami. Studying Majidi's films also reveal how these literary and poetic forms inform this expression of Islam. Eschewing the debate on the legalistic approach, Majidi instead employs the medium of film to explore a few key mystical concepts such as love, suffering and annihilation, and their relevance to the modern-day lives of ordinary people. In all these films, spiritual attainment requires no special rank, distinction or an understanding or study of the traditional sources. The Sufi concepts embedded in the film allow viewers to share in the spiritual experiences of the characters. As demonstrated, these films succeed in producing a modern discourse that offers an alternative way of understanding religion and spirituality, but one that is rooted in medieval Iranian mystical interpretations of Islam.

Through their engagement with *taʻziyeh* in film, Beyzaie and Kiarostami have reinterpreted this older form of performing art. They have – even if inadvertently – reintroduced this dying art form to their audiences through a new medium. Thus, in the face of the increasing pressure on *taʻziyeh* as well as the evolving traditions of Muharram more generally, these films act not only as cultural reservoir for a threatened tradition, but also more importantly, endow it with new life.

Kiarostami's films are poetic philosophies that contemplate man's existence and its meaning. His approach to religion and spirituality is, in fact, a departure from the conventional approaches discussed above. Even though his films present us with authoritarian accounts of the religious, positivist and sceptic, Kiarostami does not set out to prove the truth or untruth of any of these accounts. Instead, he remains silent to these various articulations and arrives at a poetic way of understanding the mystical. He alludes to the mystical by pointing to another way of looking, allowing his audience to arrive at a certain understanding themselves. His films are 'thinking texts' that employ the lyrical language of Iranian poets but do not aim to demonstrate existing philosophies. Rather, they invite us to rethink our preconceptions and look afresh at life. Kiarostami's 'thinking' films are important in that they not only contemplate all these various approaches, but also go beyond them to provide a vision of an alternative discourse on religion and spirituality in Iran today.

NOTES

Introduction

1. Tapper, 2002: 8.
2. Fischer, 2001; Ridgeon, 2000 and 2008.
3. I had decided early on not to study Sacred Defence Cinema even though some of the Shi'i expressions of religion and spirituality that I examine, such as martyrdom, have been heavily employed in this genre. This was primarily because it had already been the subject of several studies (e.g. Reichmuth, 2001 and Varzi, 2006) and I did not wish to duplicate them. In the same vein, I have not examined the topic of propagandist films, despite their extensive use of religious discourse.
4. Quoted in Naficy, 2002b: 36.
5. Bennett and Dunbar, 2005.
6. Baugh, 1997: 9.
7. Martin and Ostwalt, 1995: 13–14.
8. Martin and Ostwalt, 1995: 14.
9. Grimes, 1995: 19–29.
10. Martin, 1995: 6.
11. Gordon, 1995: 78.
12. Gordon, 1995: 82.
13. Martin and Ostwalt, 1995: 69.
14. Nathanson, 2003: 90.
15. Nathanson, 2003: 95.
16. Plate, 2003 and Lyden, 2003.
17. Lyden, 2003: 17.
18. Plate, 2003: 2.
19. Ostwalt, 1995: 154.

20. May, 1982: 31.
21. May, 1982: 43.
22. Deacy, 2001: 18.
23. Deacy, 2001: 19.
24. Deacy, 2001: 20.
25. Deacy, 2001: 54.
26. Eliade, 1987: 12.
27. Bird, 1982: 14.
28. Bird, 1982: 13.
29. Bird, 1982: 14.
30. Bird, 1982: 17.

1 Shi'ism in Iran: An Historical Overview

1. Illustration of the *Mi'raj-nama*, Persian, fifteenth century, Bibliotheque Nationale, Paris.
2. Jafri, 1979: 49.
3. Daftary, 1998: 23.
4. Jafri, 1979: 50. Emphasis in original.
5. Daftary, 1998: 23.
6. Madelung, 1997: 17.
7. Madelung, 1997: 17.
8. Daftary, 1998: 24.
9. Daftary, 1998: 31. For a fuller discussion on the implications of clientship, see Lapidus, 2002, pp. 40–44 and 54.
10. Berkey, 2003: 133.
11. Berkey, 2003: 133–134.
12. Richard, 1995: 40–42; Halm, 2004: 33–37.
13. Lapidus, 2002: 76.
14. Mottahedeh, 1985: 156–157; Lapidus, 2002: 127.
15. Cahen, 2008.
16. Berkey, 2003: 115.
17. Berkey, 2003: 193.
18. Kennedy, 1986: 7.
19. Choksky, 2008.
20. Aslan, 2006: 174.
21. Gutas, 1998: 29.
22. Daftary, 2007: 316.
23. Berkey, 2003: 182.
24. Jamal, 2002: 85.

25. Jamal, 2002: 85.
26. Nasr, 2007: 64.
27. Jahanbakhsh, 2001: 123.
28. Keddie, 1995: 24.
29. Keddie, 1995: 24.
30. Algar, 1980: 35. There is considerable debate about whether Astarabadi was the founder or propagator of the Akhbari school. See R. Gleave, 'Akhbariyya and Usuliyya', *Encyclopaedia of Islam,* 3rd ed. Edited by: Gudrun Krämer, Denis Matringe, John Nawas and Everett Rowson. Brill, 2010. Brill Online. Institute Of Ismaili Studies Ltd. 25 April 2010 http://www.brillonline.nl/subscriber/entry?entry=ei3_COM-0029.
31. Algar, 1980: 34.
32. Keddie, 1995: 97.
33. Algar, 1980: 35.
34. Keddie, 1995: 97–98.
35. Mir-Hosseini and Tapper, 2006: 10.
36. Keddie, 1995: 22.
37. Keddie, 1995: 92.
38. Keddie, 1995: 93
39. Keddie reports that the French Huguenot watchmaker, Chardin, 'who spent years in Iran, tells us that one group of mujtahids claimed that they were more qualified to rule than were the wine-bibbing impious shahs' (1995: 165).
40. Mir-Hosseini and Tapper, 2006: 19.
41. Brumberg, 2001: 118.
42. For a detailed account of the events that led to the success of the IRP over Bani-Sadr, which reflected the defeat of the moderates and the left-wing political group, see Bakhash, 1985: 92–165.
43. Brumberg, 2001: 118.
44. Brumberg, 2001: 88.
45. Brumberg, 2001: 129.
46. Mottahedeh, 1985: 89.
47. Pedersen, et al. 2007.
48. Halm, 2004: 58–59.
49. Berkey, 2003: 45.
50. Farmanian, 2002: 453. Some have argued that the Nizamiyyas were taken from the Fatimid al-Azhar model, where the Ismaili Shi'i *da'i*s taught the faith (Farmanian, 2002: 453).
51. Pedersen et al, 2007.
52. Halm, 2004: 58.
53. Nanji, 2006: 84.

54. Pedersen et al, 2007.
55. Pedersen et al, 2007.
56. Mottahedeh, 1985: 89.
57. Zubaida, 2003: 183.
58. Mottahedeh, 1985: 105.
59. Zubaida, 2003: 183–184.
60. Mottahedeh, 1985: 52.
61. Zubaida, 2003: 188.
62. Zubaida, 2003: 188.
63. Zubaida, 2003: 190–191.
64. Zubaida, 2003: 193.

2 Contemporary Iranian Discourses on Religion and Spirituality in Cinema

1. The only exception was in 2006, when the Festival was brought forward because the Fajr celebrations coincided with the 10-day mourning period of the month of Muharram.
2. The Farabi Cinema Foundation was established in 1983 as the Executive Assistant Department of the Ministry of Islamic Guidance. According to their official website it 'started its activities based on the executive policies and methods of the IRI [Islamic Republic of Iran] cinema and continued the supportive programs in respect to the production and screening of feature films with the aims of supporting the Iranian cinema industry, giving qualitative and quantitative aids and reinforcing the cinematic activities.' (http://www.fcf.ir/english/home.asp?) dbname=profile, visited 4 July 2006).
3. On my first field trip to Iran in 2003/2004, I found only a handful of books that attempted to discuss religion and cinema. In fact, when I interviewed some of the authorities in Iran, including those within Farabi, they were almost without exception intrigued by my research. By the following year, however, the new category of 'Spiritual Cinema' was included in FIFF. By 2006, Farabi had published over a dozen books on this topic, including articles by Iranian authors as well as translations of Western scholarship deemed relevant to the project. With the coining of this new term both the authorities and authors struggled to articulate a definition for 'Spiritual Cinema' and for that matter, what qualified a film as 'spiritual' or 'religious'.
4. *Jashnvareh*, 31 January, 2005: 24.
5. *Jashnvareh*, 31 January 2005: 9.
6. Mir-Hosseini, 2001: 27

7. Issari, 1989: 60.
8. Issari, 1989: 60.
9. Naficy, 2002a: 256.
10. Issari, 1989: 71.
11. In painting, Kamal al-Mulk (d.1940) introduced the Western realist style, which marks the beginning of modernism in Iranian painting. However, his students from the Faculty of Fine Arts, University of Tehran, brought about a new style of painting as a kind of resistance to what was considered foreign art. Zendeh Roudi, Karim Imami and Parviz Tanavoli are some of the painters who sought to establish nativism in their works. This style, later on referred to as the *saqa khaneh* style, was inspired not by high art but by local, and thus, religious forms. This was to create a distinct form of Iranian painting, which bore what was assumed to be significant Iranian structures and styles. For details, see Keshmershekan, 2004.
12. Khomeini, 1981: 258.
13. All quotations from Moravveji are my own translations from the Persian.
14. Jabbaran, 1999: 13.
15. Jabbaran, 1999: 13.
16. Moravveji, 1999: 9.
17. Mir-Hosseini, 2000: 67.
18. Quoted in Mir-Hosseini, 2000: 68.
19. Mulvey, 1999: 62.
20. Moravveji, 1999: 156.
21. Mir-Hosseini, 2000: 78.
22. Boroujerdi, 1996: 63.
23. Vahdat, 2002: 114.
24. Boroujerdi, 1996: 176.
25. Boroujerdi, 1996: 179.
26. All quotations from Maddadpur are my own translations from the Persian.
27. Maddadpur, 1997: 22.
28. Maddadpur, 1997: 31–32.
29. Maddadpur, 1997: 56.
30. Maddadpur, 1997: 24.
31. Heidegger, 1993: 318–319.
32. Heidegger, 1993: 319
33. Maddadpur, 1997: 61.
34. Maddadpur, 1997: 76.
35. American media theorist and cultural critic.
36. Maddadpur, 1997: 76.
37. Maddadpur, 1997: 134.
38. Maddadpur, 1997: 137.

39. Maddadpur, 1997: 133.
40. This is a reference to Sohravardi's School of Illumination.
41. Maddadpur, 1997: 109.
42. Zimmerman, 1990: 232.
43. Dabashi, 2002: 117.
44. Dabashi, 2002: 118–119.
45. Dabashi is, of course, aware that Iran was never officially colonised. For a detailed account of how he uses the terms 'colonial' and 'post/colonial' see Dabashi, 2002: 152.
46. Dabashi, 2002: 122.
47. Dabashi, 2002: 122.
48. Makhmalbaf was about 22 years old at the time of the Revolution.
49. Dabashi, 2002: 122.
50. Dabashi, 2002: 123.
51. Dabashi, 2002: 133.
52. Heidegger, 1993: 341. Heidegger himself had taken this notion from the poet Freidrich Holderlin: *'But where danger is, also grows the saving power'*.
53. Dabashi, 2002: 135
54. Dabashi, 2002: 133–135
55. Dabashi, 2002: 135.
56. All quotations from Mir-Ehsan are my own translations from the Persian.
57. Mir-Ehsan, 2005: 23.
58. Mir-Ehsan, 2005: 31–32.
59. Mir-Ehsan, 2005: 33.
60. Unless otherwise stated, all of the sources referred to in this section are my own translations from Persian.
61. http://www.fcf.ir/english/cultural_maanagara.htm, visited 5 July 2006.
62. Bolkhari teaches philosophy of art at al-Zahra and Tabataba'i Universities in Tehran and has held various posts including Council Member of the Islamic Republic of Iran Broadcasting. His analysis in February 2006 on Iranian television of the children's cartoon series *Tom and Jerry* made news nationally and abroad when he stated that the cartoon was a project to change Europe's views of mice and, by association, of Jews, from being dirty and sly to cute and clever creatures. With his craftiness and cunning abilities, Jerry the mouse causes much pain and misery for Tom. However, despite all the suffering inflicted on Tom, Bolkhari said, the viewer does not hate Jerry for his acts. Instead, the film depicts Jerry as a clever and adorable character. It is in the same vein, Bolkhari asserted, that the cunning and worldly Jews are not to be hated for the havoc they play on Palestine.
63. Bolkhari, 2006: 4.
64. Esfandiyari, 2006: 35.

65. Esfandiyari, 2006: 37.
66. Esfandiyari, 2006: 51.
67. Bolkhari 2006: 1.
68. Bolkhari, 2006: 1–3.
69. Bolkhari, 2006: 6–7.
70. Esfandiyari, 2006: 37–38.
71. Bolkhari, 2006: 4–5.
72. Esfandiyari, 2006: 40.
73. Esfandiyari, 2006: 40–47.
74. Mir-Ehsan, 2006: 11.
75. Mir-Ehsan, 2006: 10–12.
76. Horri, 2006: 57.
77. Horri, 2006: 58.
78. Yathribi, 2006: 79. Bolkhari, Horri and Yathribi's emphasis on the role of the audience can be paralleled to Lyden's study of 'film as religion', discussed in the Introduction.
79. Yathribi, 2006: 71.
80. See Esfandiyari's concern that *ma'nagara* films would be referred to as 'religious' films (2006: 35) discussed above.
81. Yathribi, 2006: 67–71.
82. Yathribi, 2006: 69.
83. Bird, 1982.
84. Farokh Ansari-Basir, 2006: 86.
85. Qur'an 2:164. All Qur'anic translations are from Yusuf 'Ali, 1999.
86. Ansari-Basir, 2006: 87–88.
87. Ansari-Basir, 2006: 93–98.
88. Ansari-Basir, 2006: 99.
89. Alireza Rezadad, the director of the Farabi Cinema Foundation, expressed great interest in my PhD thesis and graciously offered to translate it into Persian once it was completed.
90. Shamaqdari, 2006.
91. Shamaqdari, 2006.
92. Bakideh, 2006.

3 Filmic Discourses on the Role of the Clergy in Iran

*An earlier version of this chapter appeared as 'Filmic Discourses on the Role of the Clergy in Iran', *British Journal of Middle Eastern Studies: A Special Issue on Modern Iranian Intellectuals*. Taylor & Francis Ltd. Dec 2007, which was subsequently also published in *Iranian Intellectuals, 1997–2007*, ed. Lloyd Ridgeon. London: Routledge, 2008. I am grateful for permission to use this material here.

1. Bosworth, 2008.
2. Naficy, 2002b: 36.
3. Talebi-Nejad, 2006.
4. http://www.bbc.co.uk/persian/iran/2010/01/100122_l06_fajr_festival.shtml, visited 21 February 2010.
5. Zubaida, 2003: 184.
6. Keddie, 1995: 164.
7. Mir-Hosseini and Tapper, 2006: 119.
8. Mir-Hosseini and Tapper, 2006: 20–21.
9. Jahanbakhsh, 2001: 140.
10. Mir-Hosseini and Tapper, 2006: 27.
11. For a detailed list of Soroush's speeches and articles in both Persian and English see his website www.drsoroush.com.
12. Soroush, 2000: 174.
13. Soroush, 2000: 174–175.
14. Mir-Hosseini and Tapper, 2006: 38.
15. Mir-Hosseini and Tapper, 2006: 37.
16. Mir-Hosseini and Tapper, 2006: 115.
17. Mir-Hosseini and Tapper, 2006: 111–119.
18. Arjomand, 2000: 288.
19. Shahidi, 2006: 24.
20. Soroush, 2000: 19.
21. Quoted in Vakili, 1997: 17.
22. Adelkhah, 1999: 30.
23. For a comprehensive account of the economic situation during the early years of the Revolution, see Ehteshami (1995: 88–99).
24. Menashri (2001: 13–41) discusses the debates over *marja'iyat*, particularly the opposition of clerical and lay intellectuals that followed Khamenei's appointment as supreme leader after Khomeini.
25. Quoted in Mir-Hosseini and Tapper, 2006: 105.
26. Kadivar (1998, 1999a and 1999b). Also see Vahdat (2005). For a detailed list of Kadivar's speeches and summary of articles in Persian visit www. Kadivar.com.
27. Quoted in Mir-Hosseini and Tapper, 2006: 109.
28. Kadivar, 2002.
29. Butler, 1969: 181.
30. The BBC reported that by the time *The Lizard* opened in America, it had already made $1 million in Iran, with cinemas being forced to schedule extra screenings to meet the huge demand. See 'Lizard Director Stays with Religion' at http://news.bbc.co.uk/go/pr/fr/-/2/hi/entertainment/3786905. stm, visited 9 June 2004.

31. For a list of the awards of the 22nd Fajr International Film Festival, see its official website: http://www.fajrfestival.ir/english/fajr/asp/awards.asp?f_number=22.
32. This included The Times BFI 48th London Film Festival (2004). Parviz Parastooyi, the protagonist of the film, was the fourth runner-up for best actor in the Seattle International Film Festival (19 May–12 June 2005), the biggest international film festival in the US (see http://www.seattlefilm.org/festival/film/detail.aspx?id=5222&fid=5). The film was also screened in the Asia 2004 Fukuoka International Film Festival (10–20 September 2004), for which see http://www.focus-on-asia.com/e/report/2004/The-Lizard.html.
33. This was in conversation with several non-Iranian members of the audience after the screening of the film at the London Film Festival.
34. The BBC reported that "It has now become the most successful Iranian film ever following its release in the US." See http://news.bbc.co.uk/go/pr/fr/-/2/hi/entertainment/3786905.stm, visited 9 June 2004.
35. Interview with the author in Iran in February 2005.
36. King, 2002: 2.
37. Mir-Hosseini and Tapper, 2006: 165.
38. Verses 1727–1791.
39. Soroush, 2000: 174.
40. Soroush, 2000: 175.

4 Sight, Sound and Sufism: Mystical Islam in Majidi's Films

1. Sells, 1996: 217.
2. Majidi, 'Thoughts on Culture and Europe', May 2003, http://www.cinemajidi.com.
3. Kynsh, 2000: 326.
4. Makris, 2007.
5. Knysh, 2000: 326.
6. Nasr, 1972: 105.
7. Schimmel, 1975: 3.
8. Chittick, 2000: 2.
9. Chittick, 1983: 10.
10. Smith, 1995: 4.
11. Schimmel, 1975: 4.
12. Schimmel, 1975: 4.
13. Sells, 2007: 45.
14. Smith, 1995: 3–6.
15. Knysh, 2000: 8.

16. For a comparison of the various religious attitudes and devotional styles see Knysh (2000: 18–26) on Ibrahim b. Adham, Ibn al-Mubarak and Fudayl Ibn 'Iyad.
17. Mottahedeh, 1985: 146.
18. Lings, 1993.
19. Lings, 1993: 16.
20. Lings, 1993: 15.
21. Singular *'arif.*
22. Nasr and Matini, 1991: 332.
23. Lewisohn, 1995: 19.
24. Kynsh, 2000: 150.
25. Knysh, 2000: 150–151. From the tenth century, the focus of cultural life within the Islamic world began to move eastwards. Kynsh suggests the 'transition, in the eastern areas of Islamdom, from Arabic to Persian as the principle vehicle of ascetic and mystical ideas underline this momentous change in cultural orientation' (2000: 139). Notably, this transition also coincides with the revival of literary Persian in Iran after almost two centuries of silence following the Arab conquest. In fact, Nasr suggests that Persia is not only one of the main arenas of Sufism with some of the greatest Sufi saints and sages hailing from there, but also that it was their poetic creations 'which transformed the religious and spiritual life of much of Asia' (Nasr, 1991: 206).
26. Chittick, 1983: 3.
27. Hodgson, 1974: 305.
28. Knysh, 2000: 161.
29. Yarshater, 1962: 70.
30. Saeed-Vafa, 2003: 58.
31. For example, Knysh (2009) explains how the Sufi exegete, Samnani, spoke of the four hierarchical levels of human understanding of the Qur'an. These understandings in ascending order are through hearing, divine inspiration, righteous acts and direct witness. The fact that the Qur'an itself was and remains an aural experience amongst Muslims is also very significant. In fact Graham (2009) provides a recent example of this through the modern Iranian scholar, Muhammad Taqi Shari'ati-Mazinani: 'The Qur'an was a light that extended through the opening of the ears into the soul; it transformed this soul and as a consequence of that, the world'.
32. Bukhari, 2007–2008.
33. *Mathnawi*, III 4163–4164, translated in Chittick, 1983: 80.
34. *Mathnawi* IV 2915–2916 translated in Chittick, 1983: 115.
35. *Mathnawi* VI 1756–1757, translated in Chittick, 1983: 58.
36. Chittick, 1983: 237.
37. Chittick, 1983: 238.

38. Rumi, *Divan* 123, translated in Chittick, 1983: 297.
39. On his official website Majidi narrates how he came across someone a few years before who had lost and then regained his sight, and that this encounter was the inspiration for *The Willow Tree*. Some Iranian media have reported that Majidi met this man when he was researching *The Colour of Paradise*, but abused his trust and his story. The man, Yaqub Abdipoor from Tehran, was blinded in an explosion when he was six and later regained his sight. However, Abdipoor claims that the film has no similarity to his life and states that he regrets having shared his story with Majidi. The media have also criticised Majidi for not crediting Abdipoor in the film (see for example, http://www.aftab.ir/news/2005/sep/21/c5c1127318899_art_culture_cinema_majid_majidi.php, visited 12 June 2007). The film's departure from the real story might in fact explain Majidi's decision to remove the credit to Abdipoor.
40. Boutilier, 2005.
41. Interview with Boutilier, 2005.
42. Lewisohn et al., 2007.
43. Nasr, 1972: 112.
44. Quoted in Lewisohn, 2001: 178.
45. Smith, 1995: 203.
46. Chittick, 1983: 11–12.
47. Nasr and Matini, 1991: 344.
48. Quoted in Smith, 1995: 210.
49. Smith, 1995: 211.
50. Nasr, 1972: 112.
51. Chittick, 1983: 11.
52. Chittick, 1983: 12.
53. Abu'l-Khayr, *Asrar al-tawhid* p. 229 quoted in Nurbaksh, 1982–1988: 8.
54. Chittick, 1983: 179.
55. Quoted in Nurbakhsh, 1982: 64.
56. Chittick, 1983: 187.
57. Chittick, 1983: 232.
58. Smith, 1995: 207.
59. Qur'an 28: 24.
60. I am grateful to Reza Shah-Kazemi for bringing this Qur'anic reference to my attention.
61. Chittick, 1983: 12.
62. Smith, 1995: 209.
63. I would like to thank Reza Shah-Kazemi for directing me to this Qur'anic reference and drawing my attention to Rumi's use of the term.
64. Chittick, 1983: 194.

5 Cinema as a Reservoir for Cultural Memory

1. Tohi, 2007.
2. Unless otherwise stated, all translations of Persian material in this chapter are mine.
3. www.youtube.com/watch?v=aKf4txnbCKM
4. www.youtube.com/watch?v=W7gYkOdBLA
5. This is not to say that these practices did not exist amongst Sunnis. For example, there are numerous Ottoman manuscripts that include depictions of the prophets.
6. http://www.youtube.com/watch?v=uZ950_60684
7. Canby, 2009: 245.
8. Vaglieri, 2009.
9. Daftary, 1998: 25–26.
10. Cook, 2007: 1–2.
11. Cook, 2007: 2.
12. Cook, 2007: 3.
13. Cook, 2007: 58.
14. Lapidus, 2002: 483.
15. Aslan, 2006: 178.
16. Aslan, 2006: 178.
17. Nasr, 2007: 40.
18. Lapidus, 2002: 76.
19. Nasr, 2007: 108.
20. Browne, 1956: 31.
21. Chelkowski, 2009.
22. Chelkowski, 1991: 771.
23. Chelkowski, 1979: 2.
24. Beyzaie, 2001; Homayuni, 2001; and Malekpour, 2004.
25. Beyzaie, 2001: 31–32.
26. Homayuni, 2001: 61.
27. Baktash, 1979: 107.
28. Tapper, 2002: 6.
29. Pelly, 1879.
30. Beyzaie, 2001: 137–141.
31. Beyzaie, 2001: 128.
32. Beyzaie, 2001: 121.
33. Homayuni, 2001: 82–83.
34. Homayuni, 2001: 94.
35. Homayuni, 2001: 92.
36. Beyzaie, 2001: 143.

37. Chelkowski, 1979: 10.
38. Beyzaie, 2001: 84.
39. Beyzaie, 2001: 81–82.
40. The results are based on a search made on www.amazon.com and www.IMDb.com on 20 June 2007.
41. IMDb.com, 19 April 2007.
42. IMDb.com, 23 December 2003.
43. Khalili Mahani, 2003.
44. Maddadpur, 1997: 143.
45. Dabashi, 2002: 135.
46. Quoted in Bordwell, 1997: 107.
47. Bordwell, 1997: 108.
48. Bordwell, 1997: 107.
49. Bordwell, 1997: 13.
50. Bordwell, 1997: 86.
51. Farahmand, 2002: 97–98.
52. Rezadad, 2004: 16.
53. This in itself has been argued to have derived from older forms of performing art (*Kuseh-bar neshin* and *Mir-e nowruzi*) in which people would have an opportunity to criticise the landlords or those under whom they were generally suffering.
54. Beyzaie, 2001: 132–133.
55. Kennedy, 1986: 48.
56. Kennedy, 1986: 45.
57. Adelkhah, 1999: 30.
58. Adelkhah, 1999: 33.
59. Adelkhah, 1999: 33.
60. Imam 'Ali, the first Shi'i imam, who is also Imam Husayn's father, was murdered in the mosque of Kufa by a dissident. "Ali' in this slogan is also a rhetorical reference to the supreme leader of the Islamic Republic, currently Ali Khamenei.
61. Some Western productions have used similar modes such as the BBC drama series of Anthony Trollope's *He Knew He was Right*, broadcast between mid April and early May 2004. In this drama, too, some actors would look at the camera and speak about their innermost feelings and thoughts as well as the courses of actions they were about to take. However, they did not give away the whole story and thus maintained its suspense amongst viewers.
62. Beyzaie, 2001: 140–141.
63. Karimi-Hakkak is a Persian Studies scholar based in the United States; Geoff Andrew is a film critic in Britain.

64. In my own translations here, I have tried to retain the original humour as much as possible.
65. Kiarostami must have meant Shimr, for Yazid the caliph was not present in Karbala, and the battle scenes of *ta'ziyeh* depict Shimr as the commander of the opposing forces.
66. Quoted in 'Abbas Kiarostami "In-Conversation" with Ahmed Karimi-Hakak and Geoff Andrew plus Kiarostami's *Ta'ziyeh*', Iran Heritage Foundation, 2005 at www.iranheritage.org/kiarostamikarimi, visited 4 July 2007.

6 Thinking Films: Kiarostami, a Poetic Philosopher

1. According to the programme booklet, the festival aimed to 'celebrate the achievements of this artist and his impact on contemporary culture and society both inside and outside Iran'. These events were organised by the Iran Heritage Foundation in collaboration with some of the UK's leading national institutions including the Victoria and Albert Museum (V&A), the National Film Theatre (NFT), Channel 4, the London Film School, the French Institute and the British Film Institute (BFI). The events included installations, photographic exhibitions, a Kiarostami film retrospective, film workshop and conference, as well as publications, DVDs, various interviews and in-conversations.
2. Saeed-Vafa and Rosenbaum, 2003; Andrew, 2005.
3. See Chapter 1 for a discussion of these approaches.
4. Jeffries, 2005.
5. Bird, 1982.
6. Falzon, 2002: 6.
7. Kant, 1987.
8. Falzon, 2002: 87.
9. Goodenough, 2005: 1–25.
10. Mulhall, 2002.
11. Goodenough, 2005: 21.
12. Goodenough, 2005: 21–23.
13. Litch, 2002: 2.
14. Goodenough, 2005: 14.
15. Farahmand, 2002; Dabashi, 2001.
16. Sylvie Rollet, quoted in Elena, 2005: 187.
17. Mir-Ehsan, 2005.
18. Farahmand, 2002: 100.
19. Quoted in Elena, 2005: 104.
20. Maddadpur, 1997: 56.

21. Maddadpur, 1997: 143.
22. Rapfogel, 2001.
23. Rapfogel, 2001.
24. Read, 2005: 31.
25. Mulhall, 2002: 2.
26. Ayer, 1950: 116.
27. Jasper, 2003: 291.
28. I would like to thank Aziz Esmail of The Institute of Ismaili Studies for his illuminating lectures on Wittgenstein, which have informed much of my thinking and understanding of this philosopher's ideas and thoughts.
29. Wittgenstein, 2001: 44.
30. Wittgenstein, 2001: 7.
31. Wittgenstein, 2001.
32. Clack, 1999: 28.
33. Barrett, 1991: 74.
34. Monk, 2005: 21.
35. Clack, 1999: 32.
36. Vasiliou, 2001: 39.
37. Walsh, 2000.
38. See Litch, 2002: 165–183 for a discussion on the Christian variant of the problem of evil, and the examples of *The Seventh Seal* (1957) as well as *The Rapture* (1991) as engagements of film with this problem.
39. Qur'an, 7: 96–97.
40. Qur'an, 7: 60–64.
41. Qur'an, 7: 65–72.
42. Qur'an, 7: 73–78.
43. Qur'an, 7: 80–84.
44. Qur'an, 7: 85–93 (and also 29: 36–37).
45. Qur'an, 7: 103–155.
46. Quoted in Elena, 2005: 192.
47. Quoted in Elena, 2005: 154.
48. Wittgenstein, 1979: 94–95.
49. Wittgenstein, 2001: 88.
50. Quoted in Nichols, 1994: 25.
51. Elena, 2005: 141.
52. Quoted in Elena, 2005: 142.
53. Quoted in Elena, 2005: 135.
54. Monk, 2005: 25.
55. Quoted in Monk, 2005: 102.
56. Quoted in Elena, 2005: 189.
57. Sepehry, 1988: 163–181.

58. Allen and Turvey, 2001: 4.
59. Quoted in Elena, 2005: 158–159.
60. Monk, 2005: 101.
61. Monk, 2005: 65.
62. Sepehry, 1995. My translation.
63. Quoted in Clack, 1999: 46.

Conclusion

1. Quoted in *Awareness Times*, 2006. Available at http://news.sl./drwebsite/exec/view.cgi?archive=3&num=2912

SELECT BIBLIOGRAPHY

Abbas Kiarostami: Visions of the Artist. 27 April–19 June 2005. London, UK.
Adelkhah, Fariba. 1999. *Being Modern in Iran*, trans. Jonathan Derrick. London: Hurst and Company in association with Centre d'Etudes et de Recherches Internationales Paris.
Algar, Hamid. 1980. *Religion and State in Iran: The Role of the Ulama in the Qajar Period, 1785–1906*. Berkeley, Los Angeles and London: University of California Press.
Allen, Richard and Malcolm Turvey. 2001. *Wittgenstein, Theory and the Arts*. London: Routledge.
Andrew, Geoff. 2005. *Ten*. London: BFI Publishing.
Ansari-Basir, Farokh. 2006. Neshane shenasi sinama-ye ma'nagara. In *Nameha-ye ma'nawi: majmu'e maghalat-e nevisandegan-e mokhtalef darbare-ye sinama-ye ma'nagara*, ed. Howzeh sinama-ye ma'nagara (Spiritual Cinema Centre), pp. 81–124. Tehran: Bonyad-e sinama-ye Farabi (Farabi Cinema Foundation).
Arjomand, Said Amir. 2000. Civil Society and the Rule of Law in the Constitutional Politics of Iran under Khatami. In *Social Research*, 67 (2), pp. 283–301.
Armstrong, Louis. 1928. St James Infirmary.
Arrington, Robert L. and Mark Addis. 2001. *Wittgenstein and the Philosophy of Religion*. London: Routledge.
Aslan, Reza. 2006. *No God but God: The Origins, Evolution, and Future of Islam*. New York: Random House.
'Attar, Farid al-Din. 1963. *Mantiq al-tayr*, ed. Seyyed Sadeq Gowharin. Tehran: Sherkat-e entesherat-e elmi va farhangi.
Awareness Times. 2006. Leader of the Islamic Republic of Iran Receives Cinema Directors. Freetown, Sierra Leone. 30 June.
Ayer, A. J. 1950. *Language, Truth and Logic*. n.c.: n.p.

Bakhash, Shaul. 1985. *The Reign of the Ayatollahs: Iran and the Islamic Revolution*. London and New York: I.B.Tauris.

Bakideh, Nasir. 2006. Sinama-ye ma'nagara-3, Nasir Bakideh mo'taqed ast ke sinama-ye ma'nagara vujud-e dakheli nadarad! (22/6/1385). At http://persiancinema.persianblog.com/1385_6_18_persiancinema _archive.html, visited 19 January 2007). Now moved to http://persiancinema. persianblog.ir/1385/6/18/.

Baktash, M. 1979. Ta'ziyeh and its Philosophy. In *Ta'ziyeh: Ritual and Drama in Iran*, ed. Peter Chelkowski, pp. 95–120. New York: New York University Press.

Barrett, Cyril. 1991. *Wittgenstein on Ethics and Religious Belief*. Oxford: Basil Blackwell.

Barsotti, Catherine and Robert K. Johnston. 2004. *Finding God in the Movies: 33 Films of Reel Faith*. Grand Rapids, MI: Baker Books.

Baugh, Lloyd. 1997. *Imaging the Divine: Jesus and Christ-Figures in Film*. Kansas City, MO: Sheed and Ward.

Bennet, Richard and Virgil Dunbar. 2005. *The Passion of Christ*: Mel Gibson's Vivid Deception. At www.bereanbeacon.org/articles/mel_gibsons_vivid _deception.htm, visited 11 December 2005.

Berkey, Jonathan P. 2003. *The Formation of Islam: Religion and Society in the Near East, 600–1800*. Cambridge: Cambridge University Press.

Beyzaie, Bahram. 1984. *Ruz-e vaqe'eh*. Screenplay.

——. 2001. *Nameyesh dar Iran*. Tehran: Intesharat-e roshangeran va mutale'at-e zanan.

Bird, Michael. 1982. Film as Hierophany. In *Religion in Film*, ed. John R. May and Michael Bird, pp. 3–22. Knoxville: University of Tennessee Press.

Bolkhari, Hasan. 2006. Ma'na va mafhum-e 'ma'na' dar honar va sinama-ye ma'nagara. In *Nameha-ye ma'nawi: majmu'e maghalat-e nevisandegan-e mokhtalef darbare-ye sinama-ye ma'nagara*, ed. Howzeh sinama-ye ma'nagara (Spiritual Cinema Centre), pp. 1–8. Tehran: Bonyad-e sinama-ye Farabi (Farabi Cinema Foundation).

Bordwell, D. 1997. *On the History of Film Style*. Cambridge, MA: Harvard University Press.

Boroujerdi, M. 1996. *Iranian Intellectuals and the West: The Tormented Triumph of Nativism*. Syracuse: Syracuse University Press.

Bosworth, C.E. 2008. Muhallil. In *Encyclopaedia of Islam*, ed. P. Bearman, Th. Bianquis, C.E. Bosworth, E. van Donzel and W.P. Heinrichs. Brill Online, SOAS, http://www.brillonline.nl/subscriber/entry?entry=islam_SIM-883, visited 23 July 2008.

Boutilier, Corey. 2005. Toronto Film Festival. '*The Willow Tree*' by Majid Majidi: Exclusive Interview with Iranian Film-maker Majid Majidi and film co-writer Fouad Nahas, 29 September. At http://www.independentfilm.com/films /toronto-the-willow-tree-majid-majadi.shtml, visited 29 January 2007.

Browne, Edward G. 1956. *A Literary History of Persia*. Cambridge: Cambridge University Press.
Brumberg, Daniel. 2001. *Reinventing Khomeini: The Struggle for Reform in Iran*. Chicago: The University of Chicago Press.
Bukhari, Muhammad ibn Ismail. 2007–2008. *Sahih Bukhari*, Vol. 1, Book 1, no. 2. Center for Muslim-Jewish Engagement and the University of Southern California. At http://www.usc.edu/schools/college/crcc/engagement/resources/texts/muslim/hadith/bukhari/001.sbt.html
Butler, Ivan. 1969. *Religion in the Cinema*. New York and London: Zwemmer.
Cahen, Cl. 2008. Buwayhids or Buyids. In *Encyclopaedia of Islam*, ed. P. Bearman, Th. Bianquis, C.E. Bosworth, E. van Donzel and W.P. Heinrichs. Brill Online, SOAS, http://www.brillonline.nl/subscriber/entry?entry=islam_SIM-1569, visited 8 February 2008.
Canby, Sheila R. 2009. *Shah 'Abbas: The Remaking of Iran*. London: The British Museum Press.
Campbell, Joseph. 1949. *The Hero with a Thousand Faces*. Princeton: Princeton University Press.
Chelkowski, Peter. ed. 1979. *Ta'ziyeh: Ritual and Drama in Iran*. New York: New York University Press.
———. 1979. *Ta'ziyeh*: Indigenous Avant-Garde Theatre of Iran. In *Ta'ziyeh: Ritual and Drama in Iran*, ed. Peter Chelkowski, pp. 1–11. New York: New York University Press.
———. 1991. Popular Entertainment, Media and Social Change in Twentieth Century Iran. In *Cambridge History of Iran, Vol. 7: From Nadir Shah to the Islamic Republic, 765–814*, ed. Peter Avery et al. Cambridge: Cambridge University Press.
———. 2009. Rawda-khwani. In *Encyclopaedia of Islam*, 2nd edition, ed. P. Bearman, Th. Bianquis, C.E. Bosworth, E. van Donzel and W.P. Heinrichs. Brill Online, Inst. of Ismaili Studies Ltd. http://www.brillonline.nl/subscriber/entry?entry=islam_SIM-6256, visited 7 February 2009.
Chittick, William. 1983. *The Sufi Path of Love: The Spiritual Teachings of Rumi*. Albany: State University of New York Press.
———. 2000. *Sufism: A Short Introduction*. Oxford: Oneworld Publications.
Choksky, Jamsheed K. n.d. Sacral Kingship in Sasanian Iran. At www.cais-soas.com/CAIS/History/Sasanian/sacral_kingship.htm, visited 8 February 2008.
Clack, Brian R. 1999. *An Introduction to Wittgenstein's Philosophy of Religion*. Edinburgh: Edinburgh University Press.
Cook, David. 2007. *Martyrdom in Islam*. Cambridge: Cambridge University Press.
Cunneen, Joseph. 2003. *Robert Bresson: A Spiritual Style in Film*. New York: Continuum.
Dabashi, Hamid. 2001. *Close Up: Iranian Cinema, Past, Present and Future*. London and New York: Verso.

———. 2002. Dead Certainties. In *The New Iranian Cinema: Politics, Representation and Identity*, ed. Richard Tapper, pp. 117–153. London: I.B.Tauris.

Daftary, Farhad. 1988. *A Short History of the Ismailis: Traditions of a Muslim Community*. Edinburgh: Edinburgh University Press.

———. 2007. *The Ismailis: Their History and Doctrines*, 2nd ed., Cambridge: Cambridge University Press.

Deacy, C. 2001. *Screen Christologies: Redemption and the Medium of Film*. Cardiff: University of Wales Press.

Ehteshami, Anoushiravan. 1995. *After Khomeini: The Iranian Second Republic*. London and New York: Routledge.

Elena, Alberto. 2005. *The Cinema of Abbas Kiarostami*, trans. Belinda Coombes. London: Saqi in association with Iran Heritage Foundation.

Eliade, Mircea. 1987. *The Sacred and the Profane: The Nature of Religion*, trans. William Trask. Orlando, FL: Harcourt Inc.

Esfandiyari, Abdollah. 2006. Sinama-ye ma'nagara chist? In *Nameha-ye Ma'nawi: Majmu'e maghalat-e nevisandegan-e mokhtalef darbare-ye sinama-ye ma'nagara*, ed. Howzeh sinama-ye ma'nagara (Spiritual Cinema Centre), pp. 35–38. Tehran: Bonyad-e sinama-ye Farabi (Farabi Cinema Foundation).

Estess, Ted L. 1995. Angels in the Primum Mobile: Dimensions of the Sacred in William Kennedy's *Ironweed*, Novel and Film. In *Screening the Sacred: Religion, Myth, and Ideology in Popular American Film*, ed. Joel W. Martin and Conrad E. Ostwalt Jr., pp. 30–43. Boulder, Colorado: Westview Press.

Falzon, Christopher. 2002. *Philosophy Goes to the Movies: An Introduction to Philosophy*. London: Routledge.

Farabi Cinema Foundation. www.fcf.ir.

———. 2006. Spiritual Cinema. At www.fcf.ir/english/cultural_maanagara.htm, visited 5 July 2006.

———. 2007. Dar bisto nohomin neshast-e kanun-e film-e ma'nagara 'onvan shod: sinama-ye ma'nagara mitavanad be jaryan-e hamegani tabdil shavad, (14/5/1385). At http://www.fcf.ir/farsi/newsdetail.asp?newsid=131, visited 11 January 2007.

Farahmand, Azadeh. 2002. Perspectives on Recent (International Acclaim for) Iranian Cinema. In *The New Iranian Cinema: Politics, Representation and Identity*, ed. Richard Tapper, pp. 77–85. London: I.B.Tauris.

Farmanian, Mehdi. 2002. Shahrestani; Sonni-ye Ash'ari ya Shi'e-ye Bateni? In *Isma'iliye: majmu'-e maqalat*, ed. Goruh-e mazaheb-e Eslami. Qom: The Centre for Religious Studies (C.R.S).

Farrokhzad, Forugh. 1982. *Bargozide-ye ash'ar-e Forugh Farrokhzad*, trans. Jascha Kessler and Amin Banini. Delmar, NY: Caravan Books.

Ferdowsi, Abu'l-Qasim. 1997. *Shahnameh*, ed. Jalal Khaliqi Mutlaq. California and New York: Mazda ba hamkari-ye bonyad-e miras-e Iran.

Fischer, Michael M. 1980. *Iran: From Religious Dispute to Revolution*. Cambridge, MA: Harvard University Press.

———. 2001. Filmic Judgement and Cultural Critique: The Work of Art, Ethics, and Religion in Iranian Cinema. In *Religion and Media*, ed. Hent de Vries and Samuel Weber, pp. 456–486. Stanford, CA: Stanford University Press.

Goodenough, Jerry. 2005. Introduction 1: A Philosopher Goes to the Cinema. In *Film as Philosophy: Essays on Cinema after Wittgenstein and Cavell*, ed. Rupert Read and Jerry Goodenough, pp. 1–28. Houndmills, Basingstoke: Palgrave Macmillan.

Gordon, Andrew. 1995. *Star Wars*: A Myth for Our Time. In *Screening the Sacred: Religion, Myth, and Ideology in Popular American Film*, ed. Joel W. Martin and Conrad E. Ostwalt Jr., pp. 73–82. Boulder, Colorado: Westview Press.

Graham, William A. 2009. Orality. In *Encyclopaedia of the Qur'an*, ed. Jane Dammen McAuliffe. Brill Online. Inst. Of Ismaili Studies Ltd. http://www.brillonline.nl/subscriber/entry?entry=q3_SIM-00310, visited 24 August 2009.

Grimes, Larry E. 1995. Shall These Bones Live? The Problem of Bodies in Alfred Hitchcock's *Psycho* and Joel Coen's *Blood Simple*. In *Screening the Sacred: Religion, Myth, and Ideology in Popular American Film*, ed. Joel W. Martin and Conrad E. Ostwalt Jr., pp. 19–29. Boulder, Colorado: Westview Press.

Gutas, Dimitri. 1998. *Greek Thought, Arabic Culture: The Graeco-Arabic Translation Movement in Baghdad and Early 'Abbasid Society (2nd – 4th / 8th – 10th centuries)* London and New York: Routledge.

Halm, Heinz. 2004. *Shi'ism*, 2nd ed., trans. Janet Watson and Marian Hill. Edinburgh: Edinburgh University Press.

Heidegger, M. 1993. *Basic Writings from 'Being and Time' (1927) to 'The Task of Thinking' (1964)*, ed. David Farrell Krell. London: Routledge.

Hodgson, Marshall G. S. 1974. *The Venture of Islam: Conscience and History in a World Civilization*, vol. 2. Chicago: University of Chicago Press.

Homayuni, Sadeq. 2001. *Ta'ziyeh dar Iran*. Shiraz, Iran: Navid Publications.

Horri, Abolfazl. 2006. Naqsh-e mokhatab dar sinama-ye ma'navi. In *Nameha-ye ma'nawi: majmu'e maghalat-e nevisandegan-e mokhtalef darbare-ye sinama-ye ma'nagara*, ed. Howzeh sinama-ye ma'nagara (Spiritual Cinema Centre), pp. 55–64. Tehran: Bonyad-e sinama-ye Farabi (Farabi Cinema Foundation).

Hume, David. 2007. *Dialogues Concerning Natural Religion*, ed. Dorothy Coleman. Cambridge: Cambridge University Press.

Internet Movie Database. www.imdb.com

Iran Heritage Foundation. 2005. Abbas Kiarostami 'In-Conversation' with Ahmad Karimi-Hakkak and Geoff Andrew plus Kiarostami's *Ta'ziyeh*. At http://www.iranheritage.org/kiarostamikarimi, visited 4 July 2007.

Issari, M. A. 1989. *Cinema in Iran, 1900–1979*. Metuchen, NJ: Scarecrow Press.

Jabbaran, Mohammad Reza. 1999. Introduction. In *Sinama dar ayine-ye fiqh* (Cinema in the Mirror of *Fiqh*. Tehran: Pazhuhishgah-e farhang va honar-e Islami.

Jafri, S. Husain M. 1979. *Origins and Early Development of Shi'a Islam*. London: Longman.

Jahanbakhsh, Forough. 2001. *Islam, Democracy and Religious Modernism in Iran (1953–2000): From Bazargan to Soroush.* Leiden: Brill.

Jamal, Nadia E. 2002. *Surviving the Mongols: Nizari Quhistani and the Continuity of Ismaili Tradition in Persia.* London: I.B.Tauris and The Institute of Ismaili Studies.

Jashnvareh: Daily Bulletin of 23rd Fajr International Film Festival. 31 January 2005.

Jasper, David. 2003. From Modernism to Post Modernism. In *Major World Religions: From Their Origins to the Present*, ed. Lloyd Ridgeon, pp. 289–323. London: Routledge Curzon.

Jeffries, Stuart. 2005. Abbas Kiarostami: Not a Martyr. In *The Guardian*, 26 April 2005.

Kadivar, Mohsen. www.kadivar.com

———. 1998. *Andishe-ye siyasi dar Eslam*; Vol. 1: *Nazariye-ye dowlat dar feqh-e Shi'eh* (Theories of the State in Shia Jurisprudence); Vol 2: *Hokumat-e vela'i* (Government by Mandate). Tehran: Nashr-e ney.

———. 1999a. Negahi be karname-ye bist-sale-ye jomhuri-ye Eslami (A Look at the Twenty-year Balance Sheet of the Islamic Republic), *Khordad*, pp. 25–27, Bahman 1377 Sh./13–14 February.

———. 1999b. *Baha-ye azadi: defa'iyat-e Mohsen Kadivar dar dadgah-e vizhe-ye rowhaniyat* (The Price of Freedom: Mohsen Kadivar's Defence in the Special Clergy Court), ed. Zahra Rudi-Kadivar. Tehran: Nashr-e ney, 1378 Sh.

———. 2002. Velayat-e faqih va mardom salari (*Velayat-e faqih* and Democracy). At http://www.kadivar.com/Index.asp?DocId=591&AC=1&AF=1&ASB=1&AGM=1&AL=1&DT=dtv, visited 26 November 2006.

Kant, Immanuel. 1987. *Fundamental Principles of the Metaphysics of Morals*, trans. Thomas Abbot. Prometheus Books: New York.

Kashefi, Husayn Va'iz. 1962. *Rowzat al-shuhada'* (Paradise of Martyrs). Tehran: n.p. 1341Sh.

Keddie, Nikki R. 1995. *Iran and the Muslim World: Resistance and Revolution.* Hampshire and London: Macmillan Press Ltd.

——— and Rudi Matthee. eds. 2002. *Iran and the Surrounding World: Interactions in Culture and Cultural Politics.* Seattle: University of Washington Press.

Kennedy, Hugh. 1986. *The Prophet and the Age of the Caliphates: The Islamic Near East from the Sixth to the Eleventh Century.* London and New York: Longman.

Keshmershekan, Abdolhamid. 2004. Contemporary Iranian Painting: Neo-traditionalism during the 1960s to 1990s. PhD thesis, London: School of Oriental and African Studies.

Khalili Mahani, Najmeh. 2003. Bahram Baizai, Iranian Cinema, Feminism, Art Cinema. In *OffScreen.com*. At http://www.horschamp.qc.ca/new_offscreen/baizai.html, visited 20 June 2007.

Khomeini, Ruhollah. 1981. *Islam and Revolution: Writings and Declarations of Imam Khomeini*, trans. Hamid Algar. Berkeley: Mizan Press.

Kiarostami, Abbas. 2005. In-Conversation (with Ahmad Karimi-Hakak and Geoff Andrews) at the Victoria and Albert Museum, London. 1 May.
———. 2005. *A Look to Tazieh*. Installation at the Victoria and Albert Museum, London. 1 May.
King, Geoff. 2002. *Film Comedy*. London and New York: Wallflower Press.
Knysh, Alexander D. 2000. *Islamic Mysticism: A Short History*. Leiden: Brill.
———. 2009. Sufism and the Qur'an. In *Encyclopaedia of the Qur'an*, ed. Jane Dammen McAuliffe. Brill Online. Inst. Of Ismaili Studies Ltd. http://www.brillonline.nl/subscriber/entry?entry=q3_COM-00196, visited 24 August 2009.
Kulayni, Abu Ja'far Muhammad b. Ya'qub. 1968. *al-Usul min al-kafi*, ed. 'Ali Akbar Ghafari, 3rd ed. Tehran.
Lapidus, Ira M. 2002. *A History of Islamic Societies*, 2nd ed. Cambridge: Cambridge University Press.
Lewisohn, Leonard. 1995. *Beyond Faith and Infidelity: The Sufi Poetry and Teachings of Mahmud Shabistari*. Richmond, Surrey: Curzon Press.
———. 2001. *The Wisdom of Sufism*. Oxford: Oneworld.
———, Th. Zarcone, J. O. Hunwick, C. Ernst, F. de Jong, L. Massignon, Françoise Aubin. 2007. Tasawwuf. In *Encyclopaedia of Islam*, ed. P. Bearman, Th. Bianquis, C. E. Bosworth, E. van Donzel and W. P. Heinrichs. Brill Online. SOAS, http://www.brillonline.nl/subscriber/entry?entry=islam_COM-1188, visited 6 May 2007.
Lings, Martin. 1993. *What is Sufism?* Cambridge: Islamic Texts Society.
Litch, Mary M. 2002. *Philosophy through Film*. New York: Routledge.
Luckhardt, C. G. ed. 1979. *Wittgenstein: Sources and Perspectives*. Hassocks: Harvester Press.
Lyden, John C. 2003. *Film as Religion: Myths, Morals and Rituals*. New York: New York University Press.
Maddadpur, Mohammad. 1997. *Seyr va suluk-e sinamayi* (Cinematic Spiritual Journey). Tehran: Entesharat-e barg.
Madelung, Wilferd. 1997. *The Succession to Muhammad: A Study of the Early Caliphate*. Cambridge: Cambridge University Press.
Majidi, Majid. 2003. http://www.cinemajidi.com.
Makris, G. P. 2007. *Islam in the Middle East: A Living Tradition*. Malden, MA: Blackwell Publishing.
Malekpour, Jamshid. 2004. *The Islamic Drama*. London: Frank Class.
Martin, Joel W. 1995. Introduction: Seeing the Sacred on the Screen. In *Screening the Sacred: Religion, Myth, and Ideology in Popular American Film*, ed. Joel W. Martin and Conrad E. Ostwalt Jr., pp. 1–12. Boulder, Colorado: Westview Press.
———. 1995. Redeeming America: Rocky as Ritual Racial Drama. In *Screening the Sacred: Religion, Myth, and Ideology in Popular American Film*, ed. Joel W. Martin and Conrad E. Ostwalt Jr., pp. 125–133. Boulder, Colorado: Westview Press.

Martin, Joel W and Conrad E. Ostwalt Jr. eds. 1995. *Screening the Sacred: Religion, Myth, and Ideology in Popular American Film*. Boulder, Colorado: Westview Press.

——. 1995. Mythological Criticism. In *Screening the Sacred: Religion, Myth, and Ideology in Popular American Film*, ed. Joel W. Martin and Conrad E. Ostwalt Jr., pp. 65–71. Boulder, Colorado: Westview Press.

May, John R. 1982. Visual Story and the Religious Interpretation of Film. In *Religion in Film*, ed. John R. May and Michael Bird, pp. 23–43. Knoxville: University of Tennessee Press.

—— and Michael Bird. eds. 1982. *Religion in Film*, Knoxville: University of Tennessee Press.

Menashri, David. 2001. *Post-Revolutionary Politics in Iran: Religion, Society and Power*. London: Frank Cass.

Miles, Margaret R. 1996. *Seeing and Believing: Religion and Values in the Movies*, Massachusetts: Beacon Press.

Mir-Ehsan, Mir Ahmad. 2005. *Padidar va ma'na dar sinama-ye Iran* (Phenomenon and Meaning in Iranian Cinema). Tehran: Bonyad-e sinama-ye Farabi (Farabi Cinema Foundation).

——. 2006. Ma'nagara-yi dar sinama-ye Iran. In *Nameha-ye Ma'nawi: Majmu'e maghalat-e nevisandegan-e mokhtalef darbare-ye sinama-ye ma'nagara*, ed. Howzeh sinama-ye ma'nagara (Spiritual Cinema Centre), pp. 9–24. Tehran: Bonyad-e sinama-ye Farabi (Farabi Cinema Foundation).

Mir-Hosseini, Ziba. 2000. *Islam and Gender: The Religious Debate in Contemporary Iran*. London: I.B.Tauris.

——. 2001. Iranian Cinema: Art, Society and the State. In *Middle East Report*, 219, pp. 26–29.

—— and Richard Tapper. 2006. *Islam and Democracy in Iran: Eshkevari and the Quest for Reform*. London and New York: I.B.Tauris.

Monk, Ray. 2005. *How to Read Wittgenstein*. London: Granta.

Moravveji, A. A. 1999. *Sinama dar ayine-ye fiqh* (Cinema in the Mirror of *Fiqh*). Tehran: Pazhuhishgah-e farhang va honar-e Islami.

Mottahedeh, Roy. 1985. *The Mantle of the Prophet: Religion and Politics in Iran*. Pantheon Books: New York.

Mulhall, S. 2002. *On Film*. London: Routledge.

Mulvey, L. 1999. Visual Pleasure and Narrative Cinema. In *Feminist Film Theory*, ed. Sue Thornham, pp. 58–69. New York: New York University Press.

Naficy, H. 2002a. Cinematic Exchange Relations: Iran and the West. In *Iran and the Surrounding World: Interactions in Culture and Cultural Politics*, ed. Nikkie R. Keddie and Rudi Matthee, pp. 254–280. Seattle: University of Washington Press.

——. 2002b. Islamizing Film Culture in Iran: A Post-Khatami Update. In *The New Iranian Cinema: Politics, Representation and Identity*, ed. Richard Tapper, pp. 26–55. London: I.B.Tauris.

Nanji, Azim. 2006. al-Azhar. In *Medieval Islamic Civilization: An Encyclopaedia*, ed. Josef W. Meri, Vol. 1, pp. 84–85. New York: Routledge.

Nasr, Seyyed Hossein. 1972. Shi'ism and Sufism: Their Relationship in Essence and in History. In *Sufi Essays*, ed. S. H. Nasr, pp. 104–120. London: George Allen and Unwin.

——. ed. 1991. *Islamic Spirituality II: Manifestations*. New York: Crossroad.

——. 1991. Sufism and Spirituality in Persia. In *Islamic Spirituality II: Manifestations*, ed. Seyyed Hossein Nasr, pp. 206–222. New York: Crossroad.

—— and J. Matini. 1991. Persian Literature. In *Islamic Spirituality II: Manifestations*, ed. Seyyed Hossein Nasr, pp. 328–349. New York: Crossroad.

Nasr, Vali. 2007. *The Shia Revival: How Conflicts within Islam will Shape the Future*. New York and London: Norton.

Nathanson, Paul. 2003. Between Time and Eternity: Theological Notes on *Shadows and Fog*. In *Representing Religion in World Cinema: Filmmaking, Mythmaking, Culture Making*, ed. S. Brent Plate, pp. 89–104. New York: Palgrave Macmillan.

Nichols, Bill. 1994. Discovering Form, Inferring Meaning: New Cinemas and the Film Festival Circuit. In *Film Quarterly*, 47 (3), pp. 16–30. University of California Press. Also available at: http://www.jstor.org/stable/1212956.

Nurbakhsh, Javad. 1982–1988. *Farhang-e Nurbaksh: Estelahat-e tasavvof (The Nurbakhsh Treasury of Sufi Terms: A Compendium of the Mystical Terminology of the Sufis)*. London: Khaniqah-i Ni'mat Allahi Publications.

Omar Khayyam. 1998. *Ruba'iyat Omar Khayyam*. Tehran: Entisharat-e ateli-ye honar.

Ostwalt Jr., Conrad E. 1995. Hollywood and Armageddon: Apocalyptic Themes in Recent Cinematic Presentation. In *Screening the Sacred: Religion, Myth, and Ideology in Popular American Film*, ed. Joel W. Martin and Conrad E. Ostwalt Jr., pp. 55–63. Boulder, Colorado: Westview Press.

——. 1995. Conclusion: Religion, Film and Cultural Analysis. In *Screening the Sacred: Religion, Myth, and Ideology in Popular American Film*, ed. Joel W. Martin and Conrad E. Ostwalt Jr., pp. 152–159. Boulder, Colorado: Westview Press.

Pedersen, J., Munibur Rahman and Robert Hillenbrand. 2007. Madrasa. In *Encyclopaedia of Islam*, 2nd ed., P. Bearman, Th. Bianquis, C. E. Bosworth, E. van Donzel and W. P. Heinrichs. Brill Online. SOAS, http://www.brillonline.nl/subscriber/entry?entry=islam_COM-0610, visited 6 November 2007.

Pelly, Colonel Sir Lewis. 1879. *The Miracle Play of Hasan and Husain, Collected from Oral Tradition*. London: W.H. Allen.

Plate, S. Brent. ed. 2003. *Representing Religion in World Cinema: Filmmaking, Mythmaking, Culture Making*. New York: Palgrave Macmillan.

Rapfogel, Jared. 2001. Don't Look at the Camera: Becoming a Woman in Jafar Panahi's Iran. At http://www.sensesofcinema.com/contents/01/15/panahi_jared.html, visited 5 November 2005 and 20 June 2008)

Read, Rupert. 2005. Introduction II: What Theory of Film do Wittgenstein and Cavell Have? In *Film as Philosophy: Essays on Cinema after Wittgenstein and*

Cavell, ed. Rupert Read and Jerry Goodenough. Houndmills, Basingstoke: Palgrave Macmillan.

—— and Jerry Goodenough. eds. 2005. *Film as Philosophy: Essays on Cinema after Wittgenstein and Cavell*. Houndmills, Basingstoke: Palgrave Macmillan.

Reichmuth, Yvonne. 2001. Iranian Postrevolutionary Cinema as an Example of Islamic Cinema. MPhil thesis, Berlin: der Freien Universitat Berlin.

Rezadad, Alireza. 2004. *Jashnvareh, 22nd Fajr International Film Festival Bulletin*, 1 February. Tehran: Bonyad-e sinama-ye Farabi (Farabi Cinema Foundation).

Richard, Yann. 1995. *Shi'ite Islam: Polity, Ideology, and Creed*, trans. Antonia Nevill. Oxford: Blackwell.

Ridgeon, Lloyd. 2000. *Makhmalbaf's Broken Mirror: The Socio-Political Significance of Modern Iranian Cinema*. Durham Middle East Papers Series, ed. Neil Quilliam. Durham: Centre for Middle Eastern and Islamic Studies, University of Durham.

——. ed. 2003a. *Major World Religions: From Their Origins to the Present*. London: Routledge Curzon.

——. 2003b. The Islamic Apocalypse: Mohsen Makhmalbaf's Moment of Innocence. In *Representing Religion in World Cinema*, ed. S. Brent Plate, pp. 145–158. New York: Palgrave Macmillan.

——. 2008. Listening for an 'authentic' Iran: Mohsen Makhmalbaf's Film 'The Silence' (Sokut), in *Iranian Intellectuals 1997 – 2007*, ed. Lloyd Ridgeon, pp. 139–153. London and New York: Routledge.

Rumi, Jalal al-Din. 1998. *Koliyat-e mathnawi ma'navi Mowlavi*, Based on R.A. Nicholson's edition, with an introduction by Badi' al-Zaman Foruzanfar. Tehran: Chapkhane-ye Rostami.

Ruz-e haftom, *BBC Persian Radio*. At www.bbc.co.uk/persian.

Saeed-Vafa, Mehrnaz. 2002. Location (Physical Space) and Cultural Identity in Iranian Films. In *The New Iranian Cinema: Politics, Representation and Identity*, ed. Richard Tapper, pp. 200–214. London: I.B.Tauris.

—— and Jonathan Rosenbaum. 2003. *Abbas Kiarostami*. Urbana and Chicago: University of Illinois Press.

de Saint-Exupery, Antoine. 1995. *The Little Prince*, trans. Irene Testot Ferry. Ware, Hertfordshire: Wordsworth Press.

Schimmel, Annemarie. 1975. *Mystical Dimensions of Islam*. Chapel Hill, NC: University of North Carolina Press.

Sells, Michael A. 1996. Early Muslim Spirituality and Mysticism. In *The Muslim Almanac: A Reference Work on the History, Faith, Culture, and Peoples of Islam*, ed. Azim Nanji, pp. 215–221. New York: Gale Research Inc.

——. 2007. *Approaching the Qur'an: The Early Revelations*, 2nd ed. Oregon: White Cloud Press.

Sepehry, Sohrab. 1995. *Sohrab Sepehry: She'r-e Sepehry az aghaz ta emruz: she'rha-ye barguzideh – tafsir va tahlil-e muvaffaqtarin she'rha*, ed. Mohammad Hoquqi. Tehran: Nashr-e Suhayl.

———. 1988. *The Expanse of Green: Poems of Sohrab Sepehry*, trans. David L. Martin. Los Angeles: Kalimer Press/UNESCO.

Shahidi, Hossein. 2006. From Mission to Profession: Journalism in Iran, 1979–2004. In *Iranian Studies*, 39 (1), pp. 1–28.

Shakeri, Ali. 23 March 2007. Hossein Tohi Ravi vaqe'iyatha-ye talkh amma khandedar: Goftegu-ye Nowruzi ba haft chehre-ye musiqi-ye zirzamini-ye Iran (qesmat-e dovom). At http://www.zigzagmag.com/article/default.aspx/115, visited 15 June 2007.

Shamaqdari, Javad. 2006. Interview with Mehr News. Jahatgiri-ye barkhi filmha-ye jashnavare khastgah-e dakheli nadasht: dalili bara-ye jaygozini-ye sinama-ye ma'nagara be ja-ye sinama-ye dini nabud (1386-11-29 Sh./18 February 2006). http://www.mehrnews.com/fa/NewsDetail.aspx?NewsID=291358, visited 11 January 2007.

Smith, Margaret. 1995. *Early Mysticism in the Near and Middle East*. Oxford: Oneworld.

Soroush, Abdolkarim. www.drsoroush.com

———. 1995. Horriyat va rowhaniyat (Freedom and the Clerical Establishment). In *Kiyan* 4 (24).

———. 2000. *Reason, Freedom, & Democracy in Islam: Essential Writings of AbdolKarim Soroush*, trans. Mahmoud Sadri and Ahmad Sadri. Oxford: Oxford University Press.

———. 2006. Religious Pluralism: A Sufficient Condition for Religious Democracy. Lecture at the Centre for the Study of Democracy (CDS), University of Westminster. November 2006.

Talebi-Nejad, Ahmad. 2006. Naqd-e shafahi-ye film: *Yek Tekkeh Nan* tobename-ye sakht-e *Marmulak* ast, 1385/01/20 (Oral Critique of the Film: *One Piece of Bread* is a repentance-letter to the making of *The Lizard*). Mehr News Agency, 9 April 2006.

Tapper, Richard. 2002. Introduction. In *The New Iranian Cinema: Politics, Representation and Identity*, ed. Richard Tapper, pp. 1–25. London: I.B.Tauris.

Tatum, W. Barnes. 1997. *Jesus at the Movies: A Guide to the First Hundred Years*. Santa Rosa, California: Polebridge Press.

Tohi, Hossein. 2007. *BBC Persian Podcast*. 2 February 2007, downloaded 6 March 2007.

Tillich, Paul. 1959. *Theology of Culture*. Oxford: Oxford University Press.

Trollope, Anthony. 2004. *He Knew He Was Right*. BBC Drama Series.

Vaglieri, Veccia L. 2009. (al-) Husayn b. 'Ali b. Abi Talib. In *Encyclopaedia of Islam*, 2nd ed., P. Bearman, Th. Bianquis, C. E. Bosworth, E. van Donzel and W. P. Heinrichs. Brill Online, Inst. Of Ismaili Studies Ltd., http://www.brillonline.nl/subscriber/entry?entry=islam_COM-0304, visited 6 February 2009.

Vahdat, Farzin. 2002. *God and Juggernaut: Iran's Intellectual Encounter with Modernity*. Syracuse: Syracuse University Press.

———. 2005. Religious modernity in Iran: Dilemmas of Islamic Democracy in the Discourse of Mohammad Khatami. In *Comparative Studies of South Asia, Africa and the Middle East*, 25 (3), pp. 650–664.

Vakili, Valla. 1997. *Debating Religion and Politics in Iran: The Political Thought of Abdolkarim Soroush*. Studies Department Occasional Paper Series, no. 2. Council on Foreign Relations.

Varzi, Roxanne. 2006. *Warring Souls: Youth, Media and Martyrdom in Post-Revolution Iran*. Durham: Duke University Press.

Vasiliou, Jakovos. 2001. Wittgenstein, Religious Belief and On Certainty. In *Wittgenstein and the Philosophy of Religion*, ed. Robert L. Arrington and Mark Addis, pp. 29–50. London: Routledge.

Walsh, David. 2000. The Compassionate Gaze: Iranian Film-maker Abbas Kiarostami at the San Francisco Film Festival, World Socialist Website, 12 June 2000. At http://www.wsws.org/articles/2000/jun2000/sff8-j12.shtml, visited 4 February 2007.

Wittgenstein, Ludwig. 1979. *Letters to Ludwig von Ficker*, ed. Allan Janik, trans. Bruce Gillette. In *Wittgenstein: Sources and Perspectives*, ed. C. G. Luckhardt, pp. 82–98. Hassocks: Harvester Press.

———. 1980. *Culture and Value*, ed. G. H. von Wright in collaboration with Heikki Nyman, trans. Peter Winch. Oxford: Blackwell.

———. 2001. *Tractatus Logico-Philosophicus*, 2nd ed. London: Routledge.

Yarshater, E. 1962. Some Common Characteristics of Persian Poetry and Art. In *Studia Islamica*, no. 16. pp. 61–71.

Yathribi, Chista. 2006. Nokhost negah konim, sepas bebinim. In *Nameha-ye Ma'nawi: Majmu'e maghalat-e nevisandegan-e mokhtalef darbare-ye sinama-ye ma'nagara*, ed. Howzeh sinama-ye ma'nagara (Spiritual Cinema Centre), pp. 77–80. Tehran: Bonyad-e sinama-ye Farabi (Farabi Cinema Foundation).

Yusuf 'Ali, 'Abdullah. 1999. *The Meaning of the Holy Qur'an: New Edition with Qur'anic Text (Arabic), Revised Translation, Commentary and Newly Compiled Comprehensive Index*. Beltsville, Maryland: Amana Publications.

Zubaida, Sami. 2003. *Law and Power in the Islamic World*. I.B.Tauris: London.

Zimmerman, M. E. 1990. *Heidegger's Confrontation with Modernity: Technology, Politcs, Art*. Bloomington: Indiana University Press.

FILMOGRAPHY

2001: A Space Odyssey. 1968. Stanley Kubrick.
Abi and Rabi (Abi va Rabi). 1930. Ovanes Ohanian.
And Life Goes On (Zendegi va digar hich). 1992. Abbas Kiarostami.
Alien. 1979. Ridley Scott.
Baduk. 1992. Majid Majidi.
Ballad of Tara (Cherike-ye Tara). 1979. Bahram Beyzaie.
Baran. 2001. Majid Majidi.
The Boy and the Soldier. (Kudak va sarbaz). 2000. Reza Mirkarimi
A Beautiful Mind. 2001. Ron Howard.
Ben-Hur. 1959. William Wyler.
Blade Runner. 1982. Ridley Scott.
Boycott (Baycot). 1986. Mohsen Makhmalbaf.
O Brother, Where Art Thou? 2000. Joel and (Ethan) Coen.
Carrie. 2002. David Carson.
Children of Heaven (Bacheha-ye aseman). 1997. Majid Majidi.
The Colour of Paradise (Rang-e Khoda). 1999. Majid Majidi.
Crimes and Misdemeanors. 1989. Woody Allen.
The Day of Incident (Ruz-e vaqe'eh). 1994. Shahram Asadi.
Death of Yazdgerd (Marg-e Yazdgerd). 1982. Bahram Beyzaie.
The Diary of a Country Priest. 1951. Robert Bresson.
Downpour (Ragbar). 1971. Bahram Beyzaie.
Dragonfly. 2002. Tom Shadyac.
The Exorcist. 1973. William Friedkin.
Father (Pedar). 1996. Majid Majidi
Final Destination. 2000. James Wong.
Flatliners. 1990. Joel Schumacher.
Fleeing from Evil to God (Este'azeh). 1984. Mohsen Makhmalbaf.
Ghost. 1990. Jerry Zucker.
Haji Aqa, the Cinema Actor (Haji Aqa, actor-e sinama). 1932. Ovanes Ohanian.

The Hortiz Passion Play. 1897. Walter Freeman.
Indigo. 2003. Stephen Simon.
Intolerance. 1916. D. W. Griffith.
Ironweed. 1987. Hector Babenco.
Jesus of Montreal. 1990. Denys Arcand.
Justification (Towjih). 1981. Manouchehr Haqani.
The Last Temptation of Christ. 1988. Martin Scorsese.
Leyli is with Me (Leyli ba man ast). 1995. Kamal Tabrizi.
The Lizard (Marmulak). 2004. Kamal Tabrizi.
Maybe Another Time (Shayad vaqti digar). 1988. Bahram Beyzaie.
The Matrix trilogy. 1999–2003. Andy Wachowski and Larry Wachowski.
Mohallel (The Legaliser). 1971. Nosratollah Karimi.
Moses the Lawgiver. 1974. Gianfranco de Bosio.
The Moment of Innocence (Nun va goldun). 1995. Mohsen Makhmalbaf.
Not Without My Daughter. 1991. Brian Gilbert.
One Piece of Bread (Yek tekkeh nan). 2005. Kamal Tabrizi.
The Original Oberammergau Passion Play. 1898. Henry Vincent.
Others. 2001. Alejandro Amenábar.
The Passage ('Obur). 1989. Kamal Tabrizi.
The Passion of Christ (Léar Passion). 1897. Société Léar.
The Passion of the Christ. 2004. Mel Gibson.
The Pilgrim. 1923. Charlie Chaplin.
Pinocchio. 2002. Roberto Benigni.
Psycho. 1960. Alfred Hitchcock.
Rabid Killing (Sagkoshi). 2001. Bahram Beyzaie.
The Rapture. 1991. Michael Tolkin.
Reward (Padash). 2010. Kamal Tabrizi.
Rocky. 1976. John G. Avildsen.
The Seventh Seal. 1957. Ingmar Bergman.
The Seventh Sign. 1988. Carl Schultz.
Shadows and Fog. 1992. Woody Allen.
The Sixth Sense. 1999. M. Night Shyamalan.
So Far, So Close (Kheyli dur, kheyli nazdik). 2005. Reza Mirkarimi.
The Song of Sparrows (Avaz-e gonjeshkha). 2008. Majidi Majidi.
Star Wars. 1977. George Lucas.
Tales of Kish (Qeseha-ye Kish). 1999. Mohsen Makhmalbaf, Abolfazl Jalili and Naser Taqavi.
Taste of Cherry (Ta'm-e gilas). 1997. Abbas Kiarostami.
The Ten Commandments. 1956. Cecil B. DeMille.
Through the Olive Trees (Zir-e derakhtan-e zeytun). 1994. Abbas Kiarostami.
A Time to Love (Nowbat-e 'asheqi). 1990. Mohsen Makhmalbaf.
The Travellers (Mosaferan). 1992. Bahram Beyzaie.
Two Blind Eyes (Do chesm-e bisu). 1984. Mohsen Makhmalbaf.
Uncle Moustache (Amu Sibilu). 1969. Bahram Beyzaie.

Under the Moonlight (Zir-e nur-e mah). 2001. Reza Mirkarimi.
Wake Up Arezu (Bidar sho Arezu). 2005. Kianoush Ayari.
What Dreams May Come. 1998. Vincent Ward.
Where is the Friend's House? (Khane-ye dust kojast?). 1987. Abbas Kiarostami.
White Noise. 2006. Geoffrey Sax.
The Willow Tree (Bid-e majnun). 2005. Majid Majidi.
The Wind Will Carry Us (Bad ma ra khahad bord). 1999. Abbas Kiarostami.
Wings of Desire (Der Himmel über Berlin). 1987. Wim Wenders.
Wittgenstein. 1993. Derek Jarman.

INDEX

2001: A Space Odyssey 61
Abbasid(s) 18, 19, 20, 22, 25, 133
Abi and Rabi (*Abi va Rabi*) 49
Abu Bakr 17
Afrasiyab 135
ahl al-bayt 18, 22, 132
Ahmad Shah Qajar 143
Ahmadinejad, Mahmoud 63, 69, 70
Ahura Mazda 21
ahwal see Sufi states
'Aisha *see* Ayesheh
akhbar see hadith
Akhbari (*see also* Usuli) 25, 71, 74, 201(fn)
akhund see also mullah 40
Alamut 21, 22
aletheia 50, 53
'Ali b. Abi Talib (Shi'i imam) 17, 18, 21, 24, 83, 129, 130, 133, *139*, *154*, 211(fn)
'Ali al-Rida (Twelver imam) 19
Alien 7
Allama Hilli 23, 25
Allen, Woody 7, 170, 171
Amenábar, Alejandro 61
And Life Goes On (*Zendegi va digar hich*) 176, 180, 181, 182, 184, 191
Ansari, Khwaja 'Abd Allah 20

Antonioni, Michelangelo 147
'aql, exertion of reason 25
Arab 22, 23, 86, 96, 127, 132, 133, 150, 152, 153
 conquest 18, 152, 153, 208(fn)
Arabisation 18, 20, 152
architecture 47, 65, 101
Ardabili, Shaykh Safi al-Din 24
art 5, 47, 48, 49, 57, 59, 63, 65, 100, 101, 136, 144, 145, 146, 147, 172, 180, 183, 190, 193, 203(fn), 204(fn)
 and cinema 46, 48, 52
 film 57
 film as 8, 9, 10
 Islamic 50, 51
 performing (*see also* ta 'ziyeh) 94, 136, 141, 145, 146, 147, 150, 153, 156, 158, 162, 163, 164, 196, 211
Art Centre of the Islamic Development (Propaganda) Organisation (*Howzeh honari sazman-e tablighat-e Islami*) 94
Art University, Tehran 68
Asadi, Shahram 149, *149*, *151*
Ash'ari 28
'Ashura 32, 123, 130, 143
Astarabadi, Shaykh Muhammad Sharif 25, 201(fn)

'Attar, Farid al-Din 49, 100, 112, 115, 120, 196
Avicenna *see* Ibn Sina
Avini, Morteza 49, 50, 175
Ayari, Kianoush 184
Ayer, A. J. 177
Ayesheh (wife of the Prophet) 104
Azari-Qomi, Ayatollah 44, 45
al-Azhar 29, 201(fn)

bab(s) 19
Baduk 95, 102
Baghdad 19, 20, 22, 23, 28, 133
Bahonar, Mohammad Javad 27
Ballad of Tara (Cherike-ye Tara) 145
Bani-Sadr, Abolhassan 27, 201(fn)
Baran 39, 95, 112–119, *113*, *117*, *119*, 120
bazaari(s) 26, 31
Beautiful Mind, A 57
Behbahani, Aqa Muhammad Baqir 25
Ben-Hur 57
Benigni, Roberto 57
Bergman, Ingmar 59, 60, 181, 186
Berlin Conference 74, 86
Beyzaie, Bahram 139, 144–148, 149, 150, 153, 155, 156, 158, 159, 164, 173, 196
Biruni, Abu Rayhan 20
Blade Runner 171
Boroujerdi, Ayatollah 31, 46, 47
Boy and the Soldier, The (Kudak va sarbaz) 68
Boycott (Baycot) 95
Bresson, Robert 10, 60, 62
Buyid(s) 20, 21, 23, 133

Cairo 29
caliph(s), caliphate 17, 18, 19, 20, 22, 25, 29, 130, 133, 153, 212(fn)
Cannes International Film Festival 148, 159, 172, 173
Carrie 57

Carson, David 57
cartoon 37, 204(fn)
Centre for Islamic Art and Thought (*Howzeh andisheh va honar-e Islami*) 94
Centre for the Intellectual Development of Children and Young Adults (*Kanun parvaresh fekri kudakan va nojavanan*) 172
Chaplin, Charlie 81
Children of Heaven (Bacheha-ye aseman) 93, 95, 102, 107
Christian 7, 8, 9, 49, 60, 150, 153, 213
Christianity 9, 23, 54, 132, 152
cleric(s) *see* clergy
clergy (*see also* Akhbari, *faqih*, mullah, ulama *and* Usuli) 11, 12, 16, 24, 27, 31, 32, 40, 42, 43, 55, 68, 72, 73, 74, 76, 77, 79, 80, 82, 82, 83, 87, 89, 96, 125, 132, 163
 differences amongst 33, 72, 74, 79, 206(fn)
 growth of power 24–27, 31, 32, 72, 75
 income 26, 134
 responses to the introduction of cinema in Iran 40, 41, 42, 45, 55, 64
 role 11, 17, 25, 31, 67–92, 126, 196
 ties with *bazaari*s 26
Coen brothers 57
Colour of Paradise, The (Rang-e Khoda) 93, 95, 102–108, *103*, 110, 120, 14f6, 209(fn)
Constitutional Revolution 30, 32, 71
Crimes and Misdemeanors 170, 171

Damascus 131
Daneshmand, Hojjatol Islam Mehdi 125, 126, 127, 128, 129, 163
dar al-'ilm (dar al-hikma) 29

Day of Incident, The (Ruz-e vaqe'eh) 148–153, *149*, *151*, 155, 164
Daylam 20
de Bosio, Gianfranco 59
Death of Yazdgerd (Marg-e Yazdgerd) 145
DeMille, Cecil B. 57, 59
Diary of a Country Priest, The 10
Downpour (Ragbar) 144
Dragonfly 57

Esfandiyari, Abdollah 55, 56, 57, 58, 62, 99
Eshkevari, Hasan Yousefi 72, 74, 85, 86, 87
evil (*see also* good) 6, 25, 44, 87, 89, 102, 131, 171, 181, 182, 187, 192, 213(fn)
Exorcist, The 57

Faculty of Fine Arts, University of Tehran 203(fn)
faith 58, 59, 88, 91, 114, 152, 153, 169
Fajr celebrations 35, 202(fn)
Fajr International Film Festival (FIFF) 35, 36, 37, *38*, 40, 46, 53, 62, 63, 65, 68, 69, 81, 93, 94, 149, 155, 202(fn), 207(fn)
faqih (jurisprudent; see *also* clergy, ulama *and velayat-e faqih*) 44, 80, 88, 100
Farabi Cinema Foundation (Bonyad-e sinama-ye Farabi) 35, 36, 37, 40, 52, 53–55, 58, 63, 64, 65, 94, 99, 202(fn), 205(fn)
Fardid, Ahmad 46, 47, 52
Farrokhzad, Forugh 169, 176, 189
Fath 'Ali Shah Qajar 25, 136
Father (Pedar) 95
Fatimid(s) 21, 23, 29, 201(fn)
Ferdowsi 20, 77, 144
film farsi 42, 43, 57, 67

Final Destination 57
fiqh (jurisprudence) 25, 30, 40, 41, 43, 44, 45, 64, 74, 86, 90, 128, 195
Flatliners 57
Fleeing from Evil to God (Este'azeh) 94
Freeman, Walter 6
Friedkin, William 57

Gauguin, Paul 49
Ghadir Khumm 17
gharbzadegi see Westoxication
Ghost 57
ghost(s) 55, 56,
Gibson, Mel 4, 5, 10, 57
Gilbert, Brian 1
gnosis 55, 99, 114, 118
Godard, Jean-Luc 147
good (*see also* evil) 6, 21, 25, 79, 83, 87, 102, 117, 170, 182, 187, 192
Griffith, D. W. 6

hadith(s) 15, 25, 30, 31, 43, 44, 45, 57, 61, 62, 68, 96, 97, 104, 185
Hafez (Persian poet) 49, 95, 99, 112
Haji Aqa, the Cinema Actor (Haji Aqa, actor-e sinama) 58
al-Hakim bi-Amr Allah (Fatimid imam-caliph) 29
Hanafi 23, 25,
Haqani, Manouchehr 94
Hasan b. 'Ali b. Abi Talib (Shi'i imam) 126, 130, *134*, 138, *154*
Hasan al-Askari (Twelver imam) 19
Hasan-e Sabbah 21, 22
hawzeh see howzeh
Heidegger, Martin 46, 47, 48, 50, 51, 52, 53, 58, 172, 204(fn)
Hisham b. 'Abd al-Malik (Umayyad caliph) 20
Hitchcock, Alfred 7
Hortiz Passion Play, The 6
Howard, Ron 57
howzeh(s) (seminary) 73, 88

Hujwiri, 'Ali b. Uthman
    al-Jullabi 110, 111, 113
Hume, David 177
Husayn b. 'Ali b. Abi Talib (Shi'i
    imam) 12, 123, 124, 126, 127,
    128, 129–136, *134*, 138, 139,
    143, 147, 148, 150, 153, *154*,
    155, 156, 158, 159, 160, 164,
    211(fn)
Hussein, Saddam 132

Ibn Sa'd 130
Ibn Sina (Avicenna) 27, 30
ijtihad (*see also mojtahed*) 25, 30, 71
Ilkhanid(s) 23, 96
imam(s), imamate 4, 12, 17, 18, 19,
    21, 22, 24, 25, 26, 29, 43, 59,
    71, 83, 111, 123, 124, 125, 126,
    128, 129, 130, 138, *140*
Indigo 57
Institute of Dramatic Arts,
    Tehran 94
Intolerance 6
Iran-Iraq war (*see also* Sacred Defence
    Cinema) 1, 2, 3, 49, 69, 129,
    131, 175
Iranian Young Cinema Society 64
Iraq 22, 23, 24, 29
    war with Iran *see* Iran-Iraq war
'irfan see gnosis
Islamic Development (Propaganda)
    Organisation 47, 94
Islamic Republic of Iran Broadcasting
    (IRIB) 68, 128, 204(fn)
Islamic Republican Party (IRP) 27
Ismail Safavi (*see* Shah Ismail I)
Ismaili(s) 21, 22, 29, 201(fn)
    Nizari 21, 22, 23
    Musta'li 21
Ithna 'Ashari *see* Twelver Shi'i

Jabbaran, Mohammad Reza 43
Jalili, Abolfazl 148
Jami, Nur al-Din 100, 112, 120, 196

Jarman, Derek 171
Jashnvareh 37, *38*, *39*, 53
javanmard, javanmardi 77, 78, 150,
    153, 155
Jesus Christ 5, 6, 147, 150, 152
jihad 48
Judaeo-Christian 6, 10, 62
Judaism 5, 7, 54, 132, 204(fn)
jurisprudence *see fiqh*
jurisprudent *see faqih*
Justification (*Towjih*) 94

Kadivar, Mohsen 79, 85, 91
Kandinsky 49
Kant, Immanuel 170, 177
Karbala (*see also* martyr(s) *and*
    martyrdom) 12, 29, 30, 123,
    129, 130, 131, 132, 133, 134,
    136, 148–151, 155, 159,
    212(fn)
Karimi, Nosratollah 3
Kashan 29
Kashani, Ayatollah Abu'l-Qasim 31
Kerbala *see* Karbala
Khamenei, Ayatollah Sayyid Ali 193,
    206(fn), 211(fn)
Khatami, Mohammad 1, 75, 79
Khomeini, Ayatollah Ruhollah 26,
    27, 31, 32, 42, 64, 71, 72, 78,
    131, 132, 136, 193, 206(fn)
khums (*see also zakat*) 26
Khurasan 18
Kiarostami, Abbas 12, 39, 57, 129,
    144, 145, 147, 159–163, 164,
    165, 167–192, *179*, 194, 196,
    197, 212(fn)
Kitab usul min al-kafi 25
Kiyan 73
Kubrick, Stanley 61
Kulayni, Abu Ja'far Muhammad b.
    Ya'qub 25

Lebanon 24
Leyli and Majnun 112, 121

Leyli is with Me (Leyli ba man ast) 57, 68, 69
literature 65, 108, 125, 144, 156
  Persian 95, 99, 112, 119
  Sufi 105, 106, 119
Lizard, The (Marmulak) 42, 68, 69, 70, 75, 80–85, *80*, *81*, *82*, 86, 87, 88, 89, 90, 91, 196, 206(fn), 207(fn)
love 1, 15, *39*, 59, 78, 88, 90, 95, 97, 98, 100, 101, 102, 103, 104, 105, 106, 107, 108, 109, 110–119, 120, 121, 124, 127, 150, 151, 153, 181, 196
Lucas, George 7

Ma'nagara cinema 11, 36, 37, 39, *39*, 40, 46, 52, 53–64, 65, 68, 69, 94, 99, 150, 195, 202(fn), 205(fn)
maddah(s) 125, 126, 127, 128
madrasa(s) 16, 24, 27–32, 71, 125, 134
Mahdi *see* Muhammad b. Hasan al-Askari
Majidi, Majid 12, 39, 93–96, 101–102, *103*, 107–108, 112, *113*, *117*, 118, *119*, 119–121, 145, 146, 147, 148, 169, 196, 209(fn)
Makhmalbaf, Mohsen 1, 51, 94, 145, 147, 148, 204(fn)
Makhmalbaf, Samira 39
maktab(s) 31
Malek-e Ashtar *134*, *140*, *154*
al-Ma'mun (Abbasid caliph) 19
Manichaeism 132
maqam see Sufi stations
marja'-e taqlid 26, 31, 71, 72, 74, 128
marsiyeh 139
martyr(s) 130, 131, 133, 175
martyrdom 129, 130, 131, 199(fn)
  of Imam Husayn 132, *134*, 143, 148, 153, 155, 156, 159, 164
Marv 19
Mashhad 29

masjid see mosque
Mathnawi 88, 97, 121
Matrix, The (trilogy) 170
mawali 18
Maybe Another Time (Shayad vaqti digar) 146
mazlum-khan(s) (the reader(s) of the oppressed) 138, 139, *140*, *141*, *142*, 143, *154*, 158
Ministry of Culture and Islamic Guidance, Iran 3, 36, 42, 68, 126, 127, 202(fn)
Mirkarimi, Reza 68, 69, 85, 91, 94
Mohajerani, 'Ataollah 75
Mohallel (The Legaliser) 67
Mojahedin-e Khalq (MK, Islamic-Socialist party) 27
mojtahed see mujtahid
mokhalef-khan(s) (the reader(s) of the opposition) 138, *139*, 139, *140*, 158
Mongol(s) 22, 23, 25, 96
Montazeri, Ayatollah Hossein 'Ali 72, 79
Moravveji, Ayatollah 43, 44, 45, 64, 195
Mosaddeq, Mohammad 31
Moses the Lawgiver 59
Moses (the Prophet) 88, 117, 131, 182
mosque(s) 28, 29, 30, 41, 79, 83, 84, 85, 125, 134, 163, 211
Mu'awiya b. Abi Sufyan 130
Mu'izz al-Dawla 20, 133
Muhammad Shah Qajar 143,
Muhammad (the Prophet) 15, 16, 17, 104, 129, *134*
Muhammad b. Hasan al-Askari (Twelver imam and Mahdi) 19, 71
mujtahid(s) 4, 25, 26, 30, 32, 201(fn)
Mulla Sadra 56, 62
mullah (see also clergy) 40, 67
muqallid (emulator) 26

music 47, 101, 103, 123, 124, 126, 127, 136, *138*, 139, 151, 157, 174, 185, 189
mystic(s) 73, 88, 95, 97, 98, 100, 111, 118
mysticism (*see also* Sufism) 12, 49, 51, 93, 94, 95, 96, 97, 98, 100, 108, 109, 110, 121, 146, 148, 175

Najaf 29
naql (transmitted doctrine) 25
naqqal, naqqali (storytelling) 136, 137, *138*, 139, 143, 156, 157
Nasafi, Ahmad 20
Nasir al-Din Shah Qajar 143, 150
Nasir-e Khusraw 20
nativism 42, 47, 203(fn)
New Wave Movement 42
Nizam al-Mulk 28
Nizamiyya 28, 201(fn)
Not Without My Daughter 1, 2
nowheh (lyrics mourning the imams) 123–126

O Brother, Where Art Thou? 57
occultation 19, 22
Ohanian, Ovanes 49, 58
Oljeytu (Ilkhanid ruler) 23
Omar Khayyam 169, 176, 185, 186, 189
One Piece of Bread (*Yek tekkeh nan*) 61, 69
Original Oberammergau Passion Play, The 6
Others 61
Ozu, Yasujiro 146, 147, 148

Pahlavi (dynasty of Iran; *see also* Pahlavi, Mohammad Reza *and* Reza Shah Pahlavi) 32, 46, 49, 51, 136, 164, 172
Pahlavi, Mohammad Reza (Shah of Iran) 31, 32, 42, 67, 71, 131, 132

painting 9, 15, 16, 47, 101, 135, 144, 203(fn)
Paradise (or Garden) of Martyrs (*Rowzat al-shuhada'*) 133
pardeh-khani (story chanting) 132, *135*, 136, 156
Passage, The (*'Obur*) 68
Passion of Christ, The (*Léar Passion*) 6
Passion of the Christ, The 4, 5, 10, 57
philosophy 12, 20, 28, 46, 47, 48, 51, 52, 53, 56, 60, 97, 108, 109, 169, 176–180, 190
    and film 6, 170–172, 176, 180–183, 187, 191–192, 196–197
    and Sufism 101, 114, 115
Pilgrim, The 81
Pinocchio 57
pish-vaqe'eh 150, 151, 153
poetry (*see also naqqali*) 15, 39, 47, 50, 65, 168, 189
    and film 176, 185
    Persian 95, 99, 101, 112, 119, 185, 186
    and Sufism 99, 100, 101, 112, 120
    and *ta'ziyeh* 139, 143
Polytechnic College 30
prophecy 100
Psycho 7

Qajar (dynasty of Iran) 25, 143
Qom, Qumm 29, 32, 43, 79
Qur'an 15, 17, 18, 25, 27, 30, 31, 45, 57, 58, 61, 62, 88, 89, 96, 97, 98, 99, 117, 118, 131, 136, 181, 182, 185, 208(fn)

Rabid Killing (*Sagkoshi*) 146
Rafsanjani, Hashemi 'Ali Akbar 69
Raja'i, Mohammad Ali 27
Rapture, The 213(fn)
Rayy 29
religious cinema (*sinama-ye dini*) 53, 59–60, 63, 149, 150
Resnais, Alain 147

INDEX

Reward (*Padash*) 69
Reza Shah Pahlavi (Shah of Iran) 31, 41, 49, 64, 144
Rezadad, Alireza 37, 53, 205(fn)
Rostam 77, 107
rowzeh-khan, rowzeh-khani (narrating stories of the Prophet and imams) 41, 125, 126, 127, 131, 132, 133, 136, 163
Rumi, Jalal al-Din 49, 56, 62, 88, 95, 97, 99, 100, 101, 105, 106, 107, 109, 110, 111, 112, 114, 115, 116, 118, 120, 196

Sa'di 95, 112, 120
Sabzevar 29
Sacred Defence Cinema, (*Sinama-ye defa'-e moqaddas*) 3, 129, 149, 175, 199(fn)
Safavid(s) 16, 23, 24, 25, 29, 32, 71, 133
safir(s) 19
Saljuq(s) 21, 22, 28, 29
Samarra 19, 29
al-Samarri, 'Ali (Twelver imam) 19
Sasanid 21, 22
Sax, Geoffrey 57
Schumacher, Joel 57
Scott, Ridley 7, 171
self-annihilation 95, 96, 100, 101, 112, 115, 116, 120, 196
Seljuq *see* Saljuq
Sepanta, Abdolhossein 49
Sepehry, Sohrab 169, 176, 189, 190, 191
Seventh Seal, The 181, 186, 213(fn)
shabih (dramatisers) 138
Shadows and Fog 7
Shadyac, Tom 57
Shafi'i 23, 28
Shah 'Abbas (Safavid Shah) 128, 129
Shah Haydar 24
Shah Ismail I (Safavid Shah) 24
Shahnameh 20, 77, 107, 136, 137, 144

Shams al-Din Muhammad Tabrizi 100, 101, 109
Shamsolvaezin, Mashallah 73
sharia 30, 40, 68, 85
Shariat-Madari, Ayatollah Mohammad Kazem 72
Sherkat, Shahla 73,
Shi'at 'Ali 17, 21, 130, 131, 132
Shimr (Shamir) 130, 131, 139, 212(fn)
Shimr-khan (the reader of Shimr) 139, 147, 156
Shu'ubiya 133
Shyamalan, M. Night 57
Simon, Stephen 57
sinama-ye ma'nagara see ma'nagara cinema
sinama-ye rowhani 40, 55
Sixth Sense, The 57
Siyawush 135
So Far, So Close (*Kheyli dur, kheyli nazdik*) 68, 69, 94
Société Léar 6
Sohrab (character in the *Shahnameh*) 107
Sohravardi, Shihab al-Din Yahya 56, 62, 204
Song of Sparrows, The (*Avaz-e gonjeshkha*) 95
Soroush, Abdolkarim 70, 73, 76, 84, 85, 88, 91, 206(fn)
spiritual cinema *see ma'nagara* cinema
Spiritual Cinema Centre 53, 54, 55, 94, 99
Star Wars 7
suffering 77, 90, 95, 101–110, 120, 131, 132, 138, 182, 183, 184, 192, 196, 211(fn)
Sufi
  states 95, 96, 101, 110, 111, 112, 114, 117, 118, 119, 120
  stations 95, 96, 101, 110, 111, 112, 114, 117, 118, 119, 120
  *tariqa*s (paths or ways) 49, 96, 97, 110, 111, 114

Sufism 12, 23, 25, 93–121, 169, 208(fn)
poverty 101, 102, 116

ta'ziyeh 12, 41, 129, 132, 134, *134*, 135, 136–144, 147, 148–151, 153, *154*, 155–163, 164, 194, 196, 212(fn)
Tabrizi, Kamal 42, 57, 61, 68, *69*, 70, *80*, *81*, 82, *82*, 85, 91
Tales of Kish (*Qeseha-ye Kish*) 148
Taqavi, Naser 148
Taste of Cherry (*Ta'm-e gilas*) 159, 172, 176, 184–187, 188, 191
tawwabun (Penitents) 131, 132
techne 48, 50
technology 46, 47, 48, 50, 52, 170, 172, 175
Takiyeh-Dowlat 143, 144
tekiyeh(s) 134, 136
Ten Commandments, The 57, 59
The Cinema of Revolutionary Ideals (*Sinama-ye armanha-ye enqelab*) 149
theology 5, 6, 7, 8, 20, 25, 26, 48, 87, 171, 172, 175, 177, 178, 186
Through the Olive Trees (*Zir-e derakhtan-e zeytun*) 180, 181, 191
Time to Love, A (*Nowbat-e 'asheqi*) 1
Timurid(s) 23
Torabi, Morshed Valiollah Ostad *137*
Transoxania 23
Travellers, The (*Mosaferan*) 155–159, 164
Turan 135
Tusi, Nasir al-Din 20
Twelver Shi'i 16, 17, 19, 21, 22, 23, 24, 25, 29
Two Blind Eyes (*Do cheshm-e bisu*) 94

ulama (*see also* mullah, *faqih* and clergy) 11, 23, 24, 25, 26, 30, 31, 44, 71, 72, 87, 88, 125, 126, 127, 136, 164

'Umar 18
Umayyad(s) 18, 19, 20, 22, 130, 131, 133, 153
umma 131, 152
Uncle Moustache (*Amu Sibilu*) 144
Under the Moonlight (*Zir-e nur-e mah*) 68, 70, 75, 76–80, 82, 85, 89, 91, 196
Usuli (*see also* Akhbari) 25, 26, 32, 71, 74, 201(fn)

vali-ye faqih (Supreme Leader or Jurisprudent; *see also* velayat-e faqih) 71, 73, 79, 193, 206(fn)
Varamin 29
velayat-e faqih (guardianship of the jurist) 4, 26, 32, 71, 72, 73, 75, 79, 80
Vincent, Henry 6

Wachowski brothers 170
Wake Up Arezu (*Bidar sho Arezu*) 184
wakil(s) (trustees) 19
Ward, Vincent 57
Wenders, Wim 57
Westoxication 42, 49, 50, 146
What Dreams May Come 57
Where is the Friend's House? (*Khane-ye dust kojast?*) 172, 176, *179*, 180
White Noise 57
Willow Tree, The (*Bid-e majnun*) 93, 94, 95, 102, 108–110, 120, 209(fn)
Wind Will Carry Us, The (*Bad ma ra khahad bord*) 39, 176, 188–191
Wings of Desire (*Der Himmel über Berlin*) 57
Wittgenstein 171
Wittgenstein, Ludwig von 169, 176, 177, 178, 179, 180, 183, 184, 187, 189, 190, 191, 192, 213
Wong, James 57
Wyler, William 57

Yazid b. Mu'awiya b. Abi Sufyan 130, 131, 143, 160, 212(fn)

zakat (*see also khums*) 26
Zanan 73

Zayn al-'Abidin (Shi'i imam) 130
Zaynab (sister of Imam Husayn) 126, 128, 131, 153
Zoroastrian, Zoroastrianism 49, 132
Zucker, Jerry 57

www.ingramcontent.com/pod-product-compliance
Lightning Source LLC
Chambersburg PA
CBHW061439300426
44114CB00014B/1760